Management
and the Computer
in Information and
Control Systems

Management and the Computer in Information and Control Systems

Bartow Hodge, Ph.D.

Program Administrator,
Management Control Systems,
International Business Machines,
White Plains, N.Y.

Robert N. Hodgson

Vice President, Synergistic
Software Systems, Inc., Houston, Texas

McGraw-Hill Book Company

New York   Toronto   London   Sydney

To my wife, for just being herself

BARTOW HODGE

Preface

In the past decade, computers and data-processing methods have become an integral part of the business world. Most companies today use computers in some way or other—and successfully—in virtually every facet of corporate activity, from the control of physical operating units to the analysis of financial operations.

Early uses of computers tended to center on technical calculations or accounting procedures, such as payroll, inventories, or accounts receivable. With experience the range broadened into other areas, such as operations. Computers began to be used to aid in the scheduling of plants, the analysis of marketing data, and the evaluation of capital investments.

As use broadened and experience grew, a trend toward the design and installation of Management Information and Control Systems (MICS) developed. These systems, which are varied in nature, attempt to integrate large masses of information, often from quite different sources, into computer systems that serve many requirements and users. Presently, many systems are installed that serve the operational, financial, and management needs of a company. Systems of this type are designed to provide the sales manager, the controller, and the top executives with the information each requires and in a format each can understand.

The role of the manager in the design of such systems has become increasingly important. And herein lies a fundamental problem. Most managers are not skilled in data processing and yet they are necessarily becoming the major user of the new Management Systems. Because most managers are not familiar with computer technology, it has become more difficult for the manager (the user) and the computer expert (the designer and implementer) to communicate. They look at the problem area from different viewpoints. The manager sees his own operating environment and the decisions he constantly makes in that environment. The data-processing man sees the data files, input/output formats, computer-processing capability, and mathematical techniques. There is indeed a communications gap.

The problems of the data-processing man who meets with a manager to analyze a problem area are considerable. He must determine what data the manager needs for what decisions. He must know when the data are required and in what form. Experience has proved that the fundamental question "What kinds of data do you need for your decisions, Mr. Manager?" is virtually unanswerable. It is extremely difficult for any manager to quantify what decisions he makes and what data he uses for his decisions. Also, it is extremely difficult for the computer person to relate the answers he gets to this basic question to computer technology. And finally it becomes difficult to evaluate the economic incentive for designing MICS, because managers rarely think in terms of the tangible value of a decision. However, economic value must be determined and the manager, in the final analysis, must decide the value of a system.

It is because of the increasing trend toward MICS, the greater involvement of managers in data processing, and the communications problem that exists between the manager and the computer expert that this book has been written. We intend to satisfy some of the needs of the manager. The goal is to enlighten him in the behavior of information and decision-making integrating operational activity, economics, and present-day technology (hardware, programming systems, and mathematical tools and techniques). What the book provides is a framework that a manager can use to analyze his own problem area, and then relate this analysis to a computer-oriented frame of reference.

In other words, this book might be looked upon as a common meeting ground between the manager and the computer expert. The methods and procedures outlined should help the manager to begin to state, classify, and understand his problem in computer-oriented fundamentals without actually being a computer expert. This can be done because the concepts used in this book are computer-oriented, yet are explained and applied from the manager's viewpoint.

Control theory, decision models, information flow, and systems concepts are all computer-oriented procedures. We shall try to describe the fundamentals of these important tools and concepts and show how they apply to the management environment. Further we wish to show the manager how to begin to apply these tools to his own area of concern in order that he can state his requirements to the computer expert in meaningful terms, and thereby begin to bridge the difficult communications barrier that now exists.

The burgeoning amount of information now being thrust upon management demands a systems approach to assure that knowledge segments be focused on the total perspective of the corporation.

Managers at all levels of management must understand what computers can and cannot do and take responsibility for the use of these management-aiding tools. The corporation's short- and long-range aims must be made clear to all levels of management and systems people. Proposed methods of allocating resources and the control steps needed to keep the firm headed toward its goals must be defined. It is management's responsibility. The structure and the tools can be stated in a vocabulary close to that of business. The successful manager can understand, in fact must help originate, the relationship of the time-variant instructions. The required mathematics is within the reach of almost anyone who can successfully manage in today's modern corporation. The manager must assume the responsibility for the questions asked, for the assumptions asserted, and the interpretation of results.

We must dispel the air of mystery that has grown up around computer technicalities and techniques, exposing the computer for what it is—a handy and untiring servant allowing us to utilize the mathematics of yesterday and today in our quest for better decision-making formulas.

This book does not purport to be a comprehensive treatment of management science, computers, or the management process. We do hope to give the manager a new insight into how he may begin to apply control theory in his quest for MICS. In this spirit, no effort has been made to include an exhaustive bibliography. Selected references are included for those who may wish to pursue a given topic further.

We are deeply indebted to the large number of our coworkers who have aided and encouraged this undertaking with their many valuable suggestions. We are especially indebted to the editors of *Control Engineering, Automation, Chemical Engineering, ISA Journal, Journal of Marketing, Business Week,* and *Systems and Procedures Journal* for their permission to use their publications over the past few years for background material and references. Also we are indebted to the IBM company for their permission to use internal publications and case studies, some of which are at present not published for external use.

Bartow Hodge
Robert N. Hodgson

Contents

PART FOUR   Conclusions and a Look at the Future

Management
and the Computer
in Information and
Control Systems

Introduction

A new generation of computing power is finding its way into many firms. For some it will be another in a series of transitory steps which have taken the company through previous generations in computer hardware. But regardless of company size or the hardware horsepower involved, the move to a new generation of computing power should bring about a significant increase in management effectiveness.

The new generation of computers has no mysterious power to wipe away the sins of past systems, but it does pack a bigger punch than its predecessors and, properly applied, should pay off better.

The increase in hardware and capability is beginning to allow the application of management science to the activity of management—an activity whose components, unlike those of physics, are not notably quantifiable. Scientific methods are now being used to choose a product mix, select a portfolio, or determine a safe inventory level by giving a measure to such previously unmeasurable qualities as experience, intelligence, insight, intuition, or judgment. The application of new and old tools such as linear programming, statistics, simulation, and information flow is aiding the manager in digesting and interpreting data—to draw intelligence from the facts. The manager is asking and finding answers to such questions as:

What are the savings in the marketplace?

What is the strategy of competitors?

What are the costs of developing, producing, and marketing?

How will prices fluctuate?

How have they fluctuated?

A vacuum of the internal as well as the external world isolates the manager. The internal world wants intelligence about inventories of raw-material stocks (quantity and quality), product inventories, commodity flow, and on and on. The problem becomes one of collecting, digesting, and interpreting data. Management sciences are developing new tools to help the manager do all this better.

Computer control resembles a spectrum, parallel to a company's organization chart. Information from lower operational levels is communicated to higher levels, which summarize the information and send it still higher and also make control decisions to be sent back to lower levels.

Information is the essential factor within each organizational level. At the policy level higher management needs information to formulate strategic plans and to evaluate them. At the planning level, information is required to convert strategy into tactics (detailed plans and schedules and their evaluation). At the operational levels information is required to carry out production or refining or marketing plans. Finally, even the simplest loop controller in a process unit requires information from process sensors to produce their limited control action.

Each level requires a different category of information to achieve the types of decisions for which it is responsible. In general, this information will contain less detail as it rises through the levels of company organization.

The differences in control objectives from level to level within the company have important bearings on the computer hardware and software required to implement control at each management level.

We want to take a look at the "universe of control," at the applications and the diverse span. We want to define some of the terms in the semantic jungle of "process control," "industrial instrumentation," "information theory," and "management control."

We need to know where we stand today and see what people have done and what people are doing; then we shall take a glimpse into the future. We must talk about the mathematics of control, models, real time, etc.

We must inquire how the computer converses with the outside world—both physical process units and the human user. In effect, we must transform mathematics into real-life usefulness. This includes instruments, communications, displays, and more traditional data-processing input/output equipment.

FROM ART TO SCIENCE

Much as been said about real-time computer operations and on-line computer systems. Yet comparatively little has been done to integrate the system into instrumentation and people loops. This is very curious, since many computers are suitable for such applications, buffering and display equipment exist, and the techniques for implementation are known and understood. The principles are straightforward. The computer is a wonderfully flexible instrument, which can take over much of both complex systems control and trivial human tasks. Although experience in on-line systems is perhaps in some cases limited, the knowledge of software, like real-time executive control systems, is available to those who need it.

THE PERSPECTIVE OF THE COMPUTER AS A MANAGEMENT TOOL

Imagine yourself a member of the board of directors of a large corporation while a confident young man asks you to appropriate funds for a machine using Monte Carlo techniques, a machine that could:

1. Tell you which of your 3,000 employees is likely to have a heart attack tomorrow.

2. Predict which of 17 proposed capital investment plans is most likely to drive in the winning profit in your operations.

3. Tell an executive in a petroleum company whether he should buy a tanker of Iranian oil at today's price or step up production in the company's own oil fields in Venezuela; then tell him what percentage should be refined into gasoline, diesel fuel, and heating fuel; then actually operate the valves in the refinery to get the most economical production.

Today computer systems and mathematical techniques can do all these things; about 5,000 computers were in use at the beginning of 1961; 25,000 at the end of 1965; approximately 1,000 of IBM's new System/360s were delivered each month toward the end of 1966.

Computers are simple. Compare a computer to a mathematician seated before a desk calculator. You hand him a piece of paper with a problem and detailed instructions for working it out. This is the *program*. He calculates, writes the answer down, and uses the answer to make further calculations. The paper on which he writes is his *memory storage system*. He writes the final answer and hands it to you, types it out, or records it on a tape recorder. This is all a computer does, but it does it incredibly fast.

People are often mystified by computers when they should really be mystified by mathematics. If you drop a steel ball from the top of the Chrysler Building and you want to know how fast it is traveling when it passes the twenty-sixth floor, you cannot simply ask the computer. You must give the computer the formula for the velocity of falling bodies and then supply numbers for the formula. The computer retains the formula and the numbers in its memory storage system and calculates the results.

Computers really begin to shine when they handle extremely complex mathematical equations. One class of problems has thousands of solutions, and the computer can run through thousands of these calculations quickly and narrow in on the right one. This is the kind of problem that popular science writers refer to when they say the machine solved a problem in 4 hours that would take 400 mathematicians 400 years to do.

HARDWARE AND SOFTWARE

The actual computing machines are referred to irreverently as *hardware*. *Software* means the methods and techniques of conversing with the computer and instructing it in programming the tasks desired—the programs and instructions. The hardware of data-processing systems ordinarily consists of a combination of units including input; storage, or memory; processing, or calculating ability; and output (see Fig. A.1). They are designed to handle business or scientific data at lightning speeds with self-checking accuracy. The key element is the *processing unit,* a high-speed electronic computer capable of storing within its memory a list of instructions you wish it to perform. This instruction list is called a *program.* The science of automatic programming seeks to make conversing with the computer easier and more manageable. The goal is to build and program computers so that they accept instructions in everyday English, or French, or German. Even now systems read printed matter or instruments from a process unit or count the number and measure the velocity of automobiles on the expressway and respond in spoken words. A good example of a modern computing system is the telephone exchange. The input, your voice, is translated into a signal compatible with the transmission network. The program, the route over which the voice signal is transmitted, is determined by the sequence in which you dial the requested number. The output is then translated from the machine-recognizable pattern to the pattern recognizable to the human ear.

A data-processing system is designed to perform only a specific number and type of operations. It is directed to perform each operation by instruction. The instruction defines the basic operation and identifies the data, device, or mechanism needed to carry it out.

FIG. A.1   A modern data-processing system: the IBM System/360 model 40.

The entire series of instructions required to complete a given procedure is known as a program. These programs are stored in memory.

The possible variations of a stored program provide the data-processing system with almost unlimited flexibility. One computer can be applied to a great number of different procedures by simply reading in, or loading, the proper program into storage, or memory.

The stored program is accessible to the machine, providing it with the ability to alter its own program in response to conditions encountered during an operation. Consequently, the machine exercises a limited degree of judgment within the framework of the possible operations that can be performed.

Preparing a set of coded instructions, or program, for a computer is time-consuming. This, perhaps, more than anything else, held up the use of computers, much as the lack of written language would limit the advance of commerce.

But programming has developed rapidly. One of the most astonishing advances in the field is the creation of master programs, called *assemblers* or *compilers,* that turn the computer itself into a program-writing machine. (Future programs may allow a user merely to pose a problem.) The computer will then work the problem over, figure out how to solve it—if it is solvable with available data—and give an answer or tell what data are missing.

Programming has today developed to such an art that an Operating System (software) has been designed for the IBM System/360 that consists of language translators, service programs, and the user's problem programs. All these are supervised by a control program that executes the processing, controls the location, storage, and retrieval of data, and schedules the jobs to be performed—a real computer executive assigning priorities to work to be done and accomplishing this in microsecond intervals.

Today, computers are being used to design computers and supervise the production line. This is one reason why men write books about "thinking machines."

THE COMPUTER AND BUSINESS

In a way that has astonished even its inventors, the computer is altering the traditional limits of business management. It has opened new frontiers for science and education, changed military tactics, and created new conditions of life. Electronic data processing is a virtually unprecedented instrument of change that will continue to create changes as its use grows and its full potential as a business tool is developed.

Over a short two decades, the electronic computer has become one of mankind's most revolutionary tools. It has brought about a whole new set of solutions to some of man's most complicated questions and indicated attacks on others. Computers today control a potential for change that is probably greater than that already brought about.

Businesses around the world are realizing the potential offered by new management-science techniques possible with computers. More and more businesses recognize that not only does the computer provide a means for handling routine tasks like bookkeeping but that it can also change remarkably the whole way a company goes about its work.

Some of the changes wrought have been:

■ A new set of conditions for running business and government. New tools and techniques of data collection and reduction are shortening the information time span. The application of mathematical and scientific techniques is allowing management to achieve a far deeper insight into how its business organism performs.

■ An alteration of basic techniques in the areas of scientific research and engineering. Simulation and mathematical modeling are replacing empirical methods. The cut and try, the pilot plant, and the scale model are giving way to scientific methods.

■ New techniques of teaching and learning in education. For example, programmed instruction on an individual basis and gaming theory are broadening the educator's repertoire of educational tools.

■ Accelerated evolution of technology and development of products. The time span from concept of a product to its marketing is becoming shorter. New methods of determining the desires of the consumer are being applied to market forecasting.

■ New weapons and changed military strategy. Without the calculating ability of the modern-day computer, present military communication systems could not have been developed. Field commanders can now utilize computers in determining strategy and tactics.

■ Altered power structures within many businesses by placing the men who understand and control computers closer to policy-making and decision-making positions.

INFORMATION AND AUTOMATIC CONTROL

The availability of the electronic digital computer around 1946 marked the beginning of an information revolution. The next two decades have seen a development much like the industrial revolution that followed the advent of Watt's steam engine two centuries ago. In both instances, the advances of civilization had created a growing need for new ways of accomplishing vital tasks. The major technological breakthrough not only filled this need and opened new avenues in many areas but led to the discovery of new fields, where development would have been out of the question without the new tool. Rather than just advancing normal development, the electronic computer brought about a revolution in information processing.

In this information revolution the emphasis has shifted to the amplification of man's brain through computers and information-processing systems. The application of digital data processing (with its associated memory storage, communications, and displays) is limited only by the ingenuity of scientist, technologist, and management scientist.

The basic and fundamental difference between brawn and brain is exaggerated when they are extended and amplified by mechanical engines or electronic processors. A muscle or an engine consumes energy to accomplish work. This energy can never be recovered or reused. In contrast, information handling is nondestructive. Information may be used and applied without being consumed. It can be used over and over again, and many of the applications augment the original supply, but none can diminish it.* A computer manipulates information in a scientific or business computation and generates new information from it; the information can be retrieved and used repeatedly in many different ways. A brief look at the field where the engine and the computer work together will demonstrate, for example, the impact of the information revolution on automatic control. From this look we may begin to see the applicability of control theory to the management control problems.

Figure A.2 shows the basic structure of an automatic-control loop, in which the status of a physical system is detected through sensors or transducers and transmitted to a device labeled "computer." This device identifies any differences between the indicated status of the system and its desired status and activates controls to modify the physical system. The changes in status resulting from this modification are in turn sensed and transmitted to the computer, and so the operation of the loop goes on. The computer not only guides the system through a series of steps but can modify any future step on the basis of the results of previous steps.

This simplified diagram illustrates how the computer performs the function of a human operator. For example, consider the operation of a distillation unit. The conditions of the process unit are sensed by thermocouples (temperature-measuring devices), an analytical analyzer (which determines qualities of input raw materials and the output products), and pressure- and flow-measuring instruments. Transducers convert these readings into the language of the computer, and they are evaluated against desired operating conditions. The result is the control signal that gives the direction and extent of change in the controllable variable, e.g., flow of input

* This is not to say that all data should be kept forevermore. The data file should be used, obsoleted, and purged with regularity. Unlike energy, information is not consumed by use. For example, sales-order data may be used to determine a salesman's productivity, to tell the manufacturing department what to produce, to give information to marketing for forecasting, etc. The same information, in different forms, is used by many different groups to help solve many diverse problems.

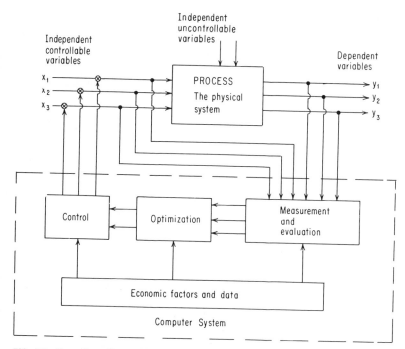

FIG. A.2   The automatic-control loop.

raw material, the crude oil. These signals in turn physically open or close the control valves regulating flow. The computer, through a mathematical model representing the interrelations of the variables of the physical process, performs the logical decision functions of a human operator. With a fantastic speed of reaction and calculation, resistance to fatigue or distraction, and great variety of inputs and outputs, the computer can replace a human operator in many physical systems. More important, it can assume tasks too taxing for human beings and thus make new physical systems feasible. The launching of a satellite, for example, could not be handled by anything short of an automatic computer system.

But man's place in automatic control is still a vital one. The loop shown in Fig. A.2 is usually part of the more complex loop shown in Fig. A.3. The desired status mentioned in the discussion of Fig. A.2 is determined by man. He observes the physical system and applies his intelligence, his ability to judge situations rather than respond to them deterministically, and his set of values. He establishes the criteria and the end goals to be achieved by the system and communicates his conclusions to the computer via programming. This is a critical input to the computer. It cannot be absent, as might be inferred from Fig. A.2, although it may precede in time the actual operation of the system.

This powerful combination of man, computer, and physical system multiplies the resources of all three. Automatic control com-

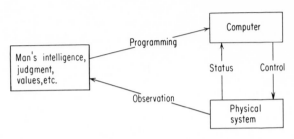

FIG. A.3   The man loop.

bines the benefits of the industrial revolution and the information revolution, giving man an extension of his brain and his brawn, both applied to the same task. The digital computer makes this system quite distinct from the man-engine combination alone. It handles great quantities of data at tremendous speeds, extending the realm of operations that can be performed. Programming techniques also combine decision making with mathematical calculations, and this permits discontinuous or discrete control to be intermixed with the various kinds of continuous or smooth control afforded by analog devices.

It can be seen in Fig. A.3 that man's portion of the loop, proceeding from physical system to the computer, parallels the direct sensing of system status by the computer. Both connections are necessary, as each exploits the individual characteristics of its medium: man or machine. Some outstanding computer developments were directed toward man's turning over as many as possible of his own functions to the computer. Much of the programming process is continually being made more automatic.

The computer may be *multiprogrammed,* i.e., may time-share or interweave a number of independent or interrelated programs run at the same time. It is now feasible to have one computer run a program that controls the physical system based on the results of an independent program being run at the same time to derive economic and business criteria. For example, if the inventory and order control for a business are maintained by the same computer, the output of the physical system will be based on the current requirements and permit very rapid response times. In addition, multicomputer systems are commonplace and with appropriate communication links further broaden the variety of tasks that can be handled by computers in the automatic-control loop.

The programming of the computer in the automatic-control loop is far more complex than most people anticipate. The program is actually interposed between the computer and the process or physical system it is to control. It is a necessary link in the computer-controlled system. Automatic programming techniques, compilers, and multicomputer systems add to the complexity and impose the need for far more sophisticated interrupt features and techniques for their application. The skill required to formulate the computer program is major, and the task is far more difficult in complex interconnected computer systems. It should be clear that greater training for many more people capable of doing this work is essential.

It must be recognized that more and more is being done by computers that it was once thought only human beings could do. Pattern recognition is one extension of computer capabilities. There exist today devices for recognizing printed symbols in a number of different type fonts without human assistance. This makes possible the introduction of text from a printed page into a computer, where formerly translation into a digital form such as holes in paper was necessary. Similarly, it is possible for computers to read maps and match them with the areas they represent.

Rather than belittling the activities of man's brain, these imitations of thought by computers show man's superior intelligence more clearly. The programming of artificial perception calls not only for the same perception on man's part but also a transcendent awareness of how that perception works. By reflecting on the way his own mind operates, man has been able to reduce many of its functions to the sort of simple instructions a computer can follow.

Artificial learning is a field that has come into being as a result of mechanizing thought processes. The computer in the three-way loop can modify its own program according to occurrences in the physical system. A man can program a computer to play a game and then be beaten by the computer. Investigations in this area are shedding new light on the problems of educational psychology.

The area in which computer technology has made the most significant contribution to automatic control is in the optimization*

* Optimization is the process of determining the adjustments that should be made to the controllable variables to bring the plant or unit to optimum operating performance.

of continuous processes. This optimization is achieved in two ways. By taking advantage of the computer's computational capabilities use of data on the internal variables of the process can be more effective. The computer also has the unique ability to help man to optimize a process on the basis of variables external to the process but related to it.

Process optimization on the basis of internal variables is taking place through the development of computer programs that continually modify process parameters in the light of empirical experience. These are really automatic learning programs, in which the computer uses a model of the process to predict the response of a change in an operating variable. The computer then makes the change in the variable, observes the response (through sensory instrumentation), and modifies predictive methodology in the list of its empirical experience. For example, consider a refining process that consists of a catalytic reaction upon naphtha feed stock for upgrading into higher-grade gasoline. Flows, pressures, temperatures, and feed- and product-stock composition are measured and recorded. In addition to these variables, which can be measured directly, are others which are significant to control for better performance of the unit in terms of yield of desirable product and/or increased throughput, but which cannot be measured directly, e.g., boiler efficiency, catalyst activity, or vapor-liquid loading in the separation towers. Values for these immeasurable variables can be calculated from known relationships. In many cases these relations (the model) can be derived empirically from past data using statistical techniques. As more and better data are gathered from the unit during operation, the model's predictive performance is continually improved. Second- and higher-order relationships may be included in the model as more knowledge is gained about the physical process itself. Quantities like boiler efficiency, catalyst activity, and others summarize a considerable amount of information about the state of the unit or plant. By providing rapidly computed operating guides, process performance can be considerably improved.

Process optimization on the basis of external variables is a concept that depends entirely upon the computer's unique capabilities. Going beyond the concept of integrating the various loops in an individual process, work in this area is directed at integrating several individual but related processes, plus such business variables as product orders, delivery, and inventory.

The benefits that can result from these two approaches to process optimization are obvious. However, the problems of realizing these benefits are formidable. Success hingers upon how well we can integrate man, machine, and process into an effective closed loop. To do this requires an interdisciplinary effort on the part of the control, operating, and computer engineers.

Much work must be done on control theory and on formalizing the operating methods that are still largely intuitive. Before we can program computers to perform the control functions effectively, we must deepen our understanding of the basics of continuous processes, and we must be able to establish explicit criteria for defining an *optimum condition*. We must also learn how to translate the "feel" human operators have for the process into computer programs.

Effective application of the digital computer to control is not only an analytical problem; it is also a software problem of major proportions. After the analysis, it is the computer systems engineers who must accept the final responsibility for developing and applying the proper software and programming skills, such as multiprogramming and multicomputer programming, that will effectively relate the computer, the processes, and the man to each other. It is the user, the manager, who must define the problem and the objectives to be achieved.

In a limited way, computers are reciprocating the effort to make them behave like men. They seem to be showing men how to behave like computers. The quantities of information handled in modern data-processing systems have necessitated new approaches to the problems of indexing, storing, and retrieving information. The newly developed methods can be applied to situations not involving electronic computation at all. Even if all the electronic computers in the world ceased to exist, the effects of the information revolution would be felt and would exercise their influence on the future of civilization.

INFORMATION-FEEDBACK CONTROL THEORY

The concept of servomechanisms (information-feedback systems) serves as the foundation for total Management Information and Control Systems (MICS) * This concept evolved during the 1940s and 1950s as an aftermath of the necessary work to develop fire control systems for weapons. Until the middle of the 1960s we were

---

* In the preceding discussion we have been dealing with the computer in its process-control role. Now we are proceeding to a more advanced concept that is already realized, or almost so, in a few cases. Total MICS means intercommunicating computers at various levels of the overall company organization. This concept is developed and further defined in Chap. 1.

insufficiently aware of the effect of information time delays, amplification, and structure on the dynamic behavior of an industrial system (a subject to be expanded later). We then began to realize that interactions between system components can be more important than the components of the system themselves.

We may define an *information-feedback system* as a system in which the environment leads to a decision that results in action which affects the environment and thereby influences future decisions.

This definition contains every conscious and subconscious decision made by people. It also includes mechanical decisions made by devices called servomechanisms. Information-feedback controls are fundamental to all life and human endeavor. To illustrate:

1. Room temperature drops. A thermostat receives this information and starts the furnace. This raises the temperature, and the furnace is stopped.

2. On an icy walk, you sense that you may fall; you correct your balance and thus are able to stand erect.

3. New manufacturing decisions result from a rise or a fall in orders and inventory levels to correct inventories or to fill orders.

4. The competitive need for a new product leads to research and development expenditures that produce technological change.

In these information-feedback control loops, the regenerative process is continuous, and new results lead to new decisions, keeping the system in continuous motion. Such systems are not necessarily well behaved. In fact, a complex information-feedback system designed in accordance with what may be intuitively obvious will usually be unstable or ineffective.

A study of feedback systems is useful in helping understand how the amplitude of corrective action and time delays in interconnected components can lead to instability of control. A familiar example of driving an automobile will illustrate.

The information and control loop extends from the eye, to the road, to the hands or feet, to the steering wheel, brake or gear pedal, and back to the eye. This complex system is accepted as second nature by a driver. Now let's introduce a small change in the information source (the eye) and a time delay. We can do this by blindfolding the driver and letting his front-seat companion give him information and instructions. The resulting few seconds of increased information delay and disturbances caused by inserting voice and ear between the observing eye and the driver's brain would cause most erratic driving. Now let the driver's companion see only where he has been. The situation would be chaotic. This is the environment in which many industrial systems presently operate. The only thing executives can tell, and that with only partial certainty, is what happened in the past.

In an information-feedback system it is always the presently available information about the past which is used as a basis for decisions on future actions. Information-feedback systems, whether they are mechanical, biological, or social, owe their behavior to their characteristics: *structure, delays,* and *amplification.* The *structure* of a system gives the relation of the parts or components to one another. *Delays* exist in the availability of information, in decision-time to make decisions, and in taking action once decisions are made. *Amplification* usually exists throughout such systems in the decision policies of an organization. An action or reaction may be more forceful than first implied by the information inputs to the system. For example, an influx of orders may call for increased production facilities on a crash basis. This indicates increased hiring, and Personnel, to be sure they are not the laggards, hires the people before they can efficiently be used.

Military exigencies exerted the necessary pressure for the development of the engineering and mathematical approaches to make information-feedback control systems feasible for business. The appearance of the digital computer provided a tool for using these management-science techniques in industrial system controls. In 1966, there were essentially no restrictions in applying information-feedback control to the vast area of important managerial and economic questions.

THE COMPUTER CHANGE

Just how far computers have come in cutting time and effort in fields as diverse as atomic research and common bookkeeping is the secret of their success. The University of Chicago (in 1966) had an IBM 7094 data-processing system installed. It took about an hour of computer time to do the equivalent of 1 million man-hours of desk-calculator work. Since the university charged $575 an hour rental for contract work, and $50 an hour for unsupported work, just about 1 cent, at the higher rate, bought the equivalence of 3 man-days of desk-calculator effort; $1 bought a man-year of calculating effort. With the IBM System/360, the cost per calculation is even less.

The implications of that speed differential have great importance. Most major industrial revolutions were initiated by changes that were merely on the order of 10. (Mathematicians call this amount an *order of magnitude*.) The first steam engines were just about 10 times as effective as animal power. Steam locomotives and automobiles were 10 times faster than animal-drawn vehicles. Aircraft outsped land vehicles by an order of magnitude. Rockets, an order of magnitude faster than airplanes, replaced aircraft as military weapons. All these single-magnitude developments clearly brought about profound changes.

Computers, however, bring about a change of six or seven magnitudes. They are up to 10 million times as fast as the mechanical calculators they replace. This means, in one specific instance, that a scientist with a computer can easily do things that he never would have considered 15 years ago—even given an unlimited budget.

The faster and larger computers become, the finer and more accurate mathematical models relating to business and the managing of business can become. Simulation techniques, linear programming, and critical-path methods, along with higher-order differential-equation models, have become everyday tools, which allow the manager to have better and more timely information, reduced from the data available, for better decisions.

Subtly the computer is changing the management structure and corporate strategy. As management science develops, the machines tend to melt into an altered company framework.

THE TOTAL SYSTEM

Progress has been so great that only those totally involved with computers are capable of keeping track of these subtle changes in management. Most companies seriously concerned with putting computers to work already have a "total system" plan in their files. First goals were to shorten the intervals between receipt of an order and delivery of a product. The total-system goal is to reduce inventory, eliminate rush orders and duplication of effort, improve customer service, improve purchasing through better vendor records, end double-record keeping, and schedule production—up to and including the actual running of the plant. Other goals of the total systems are to standardize nomenclature, reduce employment fluctuations, keep personnel records, provide engineering information services, and give management a frequent but simple picture of what is actually going on in the company, compared to schedules and forecasts.

When talking about the total system, we mean *one computing system* for the company but *not necessarily one computer*. It may be a whole network or hierarchy of computers linked together by a spider web of communication lines. All the separate bits and pieces of hardware are in existence today to perform the total-system complex.

More and more human abilities are transferred to the computer through total-system programming and thereby become part of a new kind of library of skills. The jobs that people do are beoming very different. The computer program accumulates and preserves skills.

In point of fact, a company going over to computer operation does not experience a great day-to-day change. The changes occur in a number of gradual steps, taken department by department.

Computer programs, not computers, are really what is new. Since they are the first nonmechanical means that mankind has found to preserve skills, they consist, in essence, of the accumulation of the special expertise formerly possessed only by a highly trained people. It is entirely possible that the job of future management will not be as it was in the past, to learn to duplicate in detail the skills and techniques of its predecessors. Rather, it will be to improve the skills collected in the computer program.

Computers are being organized to serve many people at once and to be capable of drawing on huge libraries of programs for their skills and on even larger libraries of historical data. They collect information at or near its source—the scientific library, the production floor, the product designer's office, the point of sale.

Automation of the design process makes it possible to produce special products to order at a cost not much higher than standard products, possibly even lower than some of today's standard short-run products.

As a result, business operates more on a continuous basis. Managements are reexamining how business operates and the accuracy of the data it uses. Better understanding of process plants is the result of simulation and detailed mathematical models.

The art of "seat-of-the-pants" direction now has the capability of developing into a management science.

Present-day computers give the manager four assets: (1) a person can get accurate, detailed information quickly; (2) he can turn an idea into action as soon as he has formulated the idea; (3) he can obtain quick answers to questions asked in the language of mathematics and logic; (4) he can share in, and profit from, the constructive effort of an intellectual community in ways never before possible. Those are four very important assets for anyone who would solve a problem, make a decision, or contribute creatively to the fund of knowledge.

The computer and man's ability to use it enable the executive to clear away some of the uncertainty that surrounds him, to subtract some of the variables from the circumstances that fret him, to convert many ill-structured and inherently insoluble problems into well-structured and partly soluble ones, to rely less on hunches and intuition and more on analysis, to behave less like an artist and more like a scientist in disposing of routine matters, and to save his creativity and imagination for more important work.

VALUE OF INFORMATION

Information is the substance from which managerial decisions are made. As with other products, the quality of the raw material partially determines the quality of the output. The manager is well aware that information sources are important. But does he know with any assurance the measures of information quality?

Information sources, like other flows in the industrial system, are subject to distortion, which depends on the time-varying character of the information.

The manager is interested in more useful information on which to base decisions. Greater utility can be obtained both by improving existing information sources and by basing decisions on new and different sources that have not been used in the past. The cost of obtaining improved information can usually be estimated with fair accuracy. But what is better information worth? This is not so easily answered. Better information is worth the value that we attach to the improved industrial performance which results when the better information is available. Unless we can determine the change in system performance that will result from a changed information flow, we cannot determine its value.

The value of information has usually been determined by highly subjective means that necessarily include an estimate of what the information will do to the dynamic behavior of the system. It is to be expected that one of the weakest areas of managerial judgment is in placing a dollar value on an information source.

Machine processing of business data is usually justified on the basis of machine-processing costs relative to costs in the previously existing system. For lack of any real measure of the value of information, this justification is almost never made on the basis of the relationships between information cost and information value.

Experience with industrial organizations shows that some of the most important and useful information is going unused and untouched. At the same time, great efforts are devoted to attempting to acquire information that even if available would do little for the success of the organization. As an example, some organizations have succeeded in speeding up the flow of sales information and production scheduling to the point where the random-noise* variations in the market can now be directly imposed on the production process. This tends to ignore the proper use of inventories for absorbing such variations. Carried to an extreme, the result of more timely information can be harmful. The effect can be to cause the manager to put more and more stress on short-range decisions. *System improvements may not result nearly so much from changing the type of information available or its quality as from changing the sources of information and the nature of the decision based on the information.* This does not mean that the kind, type, and quality of information are unimportant. But a thorough systems analysis on information needs based on decisions for given objectives may indicate a much more valuable source of information than that presently being tapped.

A system model can be used to see how changed information flows will affect the system. Doing this requires a firm hypothesis about how the information affects decisions. Herein should be the first test of much of the information generated in industrial organizations. For much of the information selected, it would be nearly impossible to suggest a hypothesis about the way such information affects the flow of business activity. Inability to suggest a use for an information source raises the possibility that it is not useful.

A detailed study of a system might lead to the conclusion that the solution to better system behavior lies not in more information but rather in a change in the operating policies of the information-distribution system.

SUMMARY

The knowledge of existing control theory, mathematical techniques, and the computer, now being applied at the lowest levels of control of physical processes, if applied to higher levels of control in

---

* Noise is the unwanted data that confuse the true data or signal interpretation—the discordant data. Random noise means these unwanted data are measured with the true sample at unpredictable time intervals. Average noise levels may be measured over a given sampling period. As in sound, noise makes the true value of the data hard to measure.

the management hierarchy, can lead to vastly improved information for better decisions.

The role of the manager in designing his control system and information sources for decision making is becoming increasingly important.

The ever increasing amount of information now being thrust upon management demands a systems approach to assure that knowledge segments be focused on the total perspective of the corporation. Managers at all levels of management must understand what computers can and cannot do and take responsibility for the use of these management-aiding tools. The computer can become an efficient problem-solving tool for the manager.

PART ONE

The "What"

CHAPTER ONE

The "What"
of Management Control

*Management is guiding human and physical resources into
dynamic organization units which obtain their
objectives to the satisfaction of those served and with a
high degree of morale and sense of attainment on the part
of those rendering the service. This definition in the
business world implies continuity, specialization
among employees, coordinated, interacting parts, and
satisfaction.*

This chapter is concerned with what might be called the *automatic
company,* an advanced concept that is already here, or almost so, in
a few cases. It is a concept of intercommunicating computers at
various levels of the overall company organization. Although these
computers still leave room for management decisions, they are programmed to mechanize such decisions as far as possible, thus taking
care of most of the routine decision making and leaving management largely free to concentrate on decisions that cannot be anticipated. This is the concept that is sometimes called the hierarchy
of computer control. Starting with computerized process control at
the lowest level, it proceeds through higher levels of information
gathering, communication, and decision making. These involve
such functions as production planning and scheduling, correlation
of the efforts of various plants, inventory and shipping control, and
the supply of condensed economic information for management,
bearing on such matters as costs, profits, market and other trends,
and whether and when to expand.

COMPUTERS IN DECISION MAKING

Management control is a subject so big and so specialized that it is like the elephant that baffled the blind men. Each man described the elephant in terms of the particular part he happened to be touching, but no one opinion or composite of them all bore much resemblance to the animal as a whole.

Instead of approaching operational control systems in the traditional application-by-application way, let us embrace the entire business complex and consider the hierarchy of management levels —an information and control system which will provide all management levels with the information required to best perform their respective functions in meeting the objectives of the total business operation.

Some companies today are modeling their corporate planning activity and daily using Operation Research (OR) tools and techniques for policy decisions and directives. In a particular petroleum company, for example, at this top level the decisions made include crude selection and rate, market commitments, plant improvements, and the like. A paper company is structuring a corporate-wide information-gathering system; the results will be a daily market inventory and schedule for individual plants. The central computer complex monitors results of several plant-control computers, optimizing production for the entire company and, accordingly, controlling the operation of the individual plant-computer systems. In effect, the central computer monitors such systems and sets the targets for daily and monthly operations. In the chemical and petroleum industry at the refining or plant level several installations are completed or being installed. One such is that of the American Oil Company's Texas City refinery. There the operating-management information system determines the guidelines for running the various refinery units the best way for meeting product demands at minimum product cost.

At the unit level, applications span the universe of industry—from quality control of auto assembly lines, ammonia and ethylene in chemicals, catalytic crackers and crude distillation units for petroleum, to kilns for cement.

Technology in hardware, programming systems, and mathematical techniques are supporting the imagination and creativeness of today's manager by giving him the tools to push forward into new frontiers of business control.

It is the idea of applying computers to decision making at all levels of the corporate structure that concerns us. In such a hierarchy of computer control the word control takes on a much broader meaning than simply the control of process variables. Making decisions, which results in control, is inherent in every level of the structure. Control implies such top-level decisions as what to make, how to distribute it, what to charge for it. It implies the determination of costs and profits (or losses) that would result from each decision.

Similarly, lower organization levels call for many other necessary decisions on such matters as raw-material selection, production scheduling, inventory control, transportation options, maintenance problems, not to mention the control of production processes.

Plant operations, maintenance, and finance can be represented by the three sides of a triangular pyramid. On-site data-gathering and computing facilities can provide answers in all three areas. Moreover, these areas are directly and closely related, and computers can provide the communication among them. One cannot discuss the financing and financial reporting of a plant without discussing its ability to produce the product, and at what maintenance cost. Neither is it possible to discuss maintenance without discussing the plant's operating condition and the finances available to provide maintenance.

As an example of the interdependence of the many facets of the company, the operator of one of the production units turns in a report indicating lower than anticipated yield. A process engineer tracks the trouble down to heat transfer in one of the heat exchangers. Maintenance is alerted; it inspects the exchanger and recommends retubing. Since Inventory finds that suitable tube bundles are not in stock, Purchasing is brought into the picture. It checks with Finance to make sure the budget can support the purchase this month, and finally places the order.

How the several levels of computer control tie together can be illustrated schematically by Fig. 1.1. Here, information orginating in the operations at lower levels is communicated to higher levels, which, in turn, produce command decisions that are transmitted down to the lower, production levels. A diagram of this type illustrates the flow of information and decisions necessary to the operation of any manufacturing concern, whether or not it incorporates computers. When computers are introduced, decisions at all levels can be greatly expedited, routine decisions can be automated, operations can be optimized, and management information can be transmitted in real time, while it is still current and useful rather than after it has become history. (Chapters 8 to 10 discuss some tools useful in automating decisions and optimization. Chapters 6 and 7 deal with the application of these tools.)

THE MANAGEMENT CONTROL HIERARCHY

Let us look at a large, international, integrated oil company. (A description of any manufacturing company would form a similar organizational pattern.)

The corporate management of a parent company forms the apex of the organizational pyramid of subsidiaries wherever they are operative. It acts as the top echelon, and its functions comprise the development and determination of the long-term goals and strategy

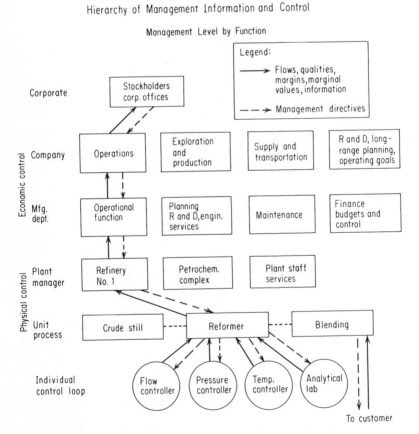

FIG. 1.1 Overall computer control may operate on five different levels of the company organization.

for the group as a whole.

One of the companies in this group has the following table of organization:

1. *Corporate Level.* Supervises and coordinates the plans of each division for final decision by the top corporate management.

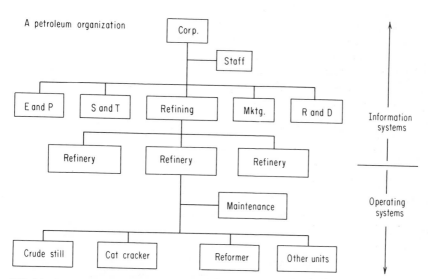

FIG. 1.2 Schematic of an integrated oil company.

2. *Divisional Level.* Each division—domestic, international, and petrochemical—has a planning organization of its own.

3. *Regional Level.* Provides coordination for the local level through limited economic and planning units cooperating with the divisional levels at headquarters.

4. *Local Level.* Represents actions only.

In the competitive world of today the widespread operations of an internationally integrated company are subjected to rapidly changing conditions. Extreme flexibility and swift adjustments are essential to achieve optimum utilization of all physical, financial, and human resources of the company. The drive for highest efficiency in the planning operations is the more important, the larger and more inclusive the operations of the groups grow.

For this company, the total Management Information and Control System (MICS) performs three overlapping functions:

1. Provides optimizing process control for the lower levels in the hierarchy.

2. Supplies management information based on the principles of management by exception.*

3. Furnishes information to all levels of management as shown in Fig. 1.2A.

In performing these functions, exceptions are noted for management decisions, routine decisions are made, control is exercised, various parts of the system are reoptimized, and appropriate levels of management are informed. These functions are carried out at the lowest possible logical levels so that the hierarchy of computations can be clearly understood and easily manipulated to fulfill management needs. This particular real-time control system gives awareness to operating problems and their solution at proper operating-management levels.

There are various ways of looking at the several levels of control. One way (see again Fig. 1.2A) is to consider that the MICS has four levels that can be considered economic and a fifth level of process control (physical control).

The highest control level might be termed *company* or *policy*. In this petroleum company, for example, at this level the decisions made include crude selection and ratio, market commitments, exploration expenditures, plant improvements, and the like. The next lower level might be called *department* or *anticipated operations*. The computer programs here take the form of mathematical statements, e.g., a linear-programming matrix that represents anticipated operations for the next day, the next 30 days, and so on.

Imputs at this level include anticipated crude properties and refinery change rates, gaining inventory levels and qualities, predicted market demands, as well as operating properties of the refinery. This linear-programming matrix runs on a daily basis. Its purpose is to generate an environment that represents anticipated optimal operations for the next day and the next month. As in Fig. 1.2A, it also generates information, e.g., shadow prices, concerning the values and economic effects associated with the various streams, capacities, and qualities of the system. Here the term optimization refers to the

---

* Management by exception is a management philosophy very similar to the idea involved in automatic process control (see Chap. 2), wherein a process controller makes corrections only when a difference exists between a desired operating condition (the set point) and the controlled variable. The comparable management idea exerts management only when exceptional conditions are detected, thus relieving management of the need to become bogged down in routine decisions.

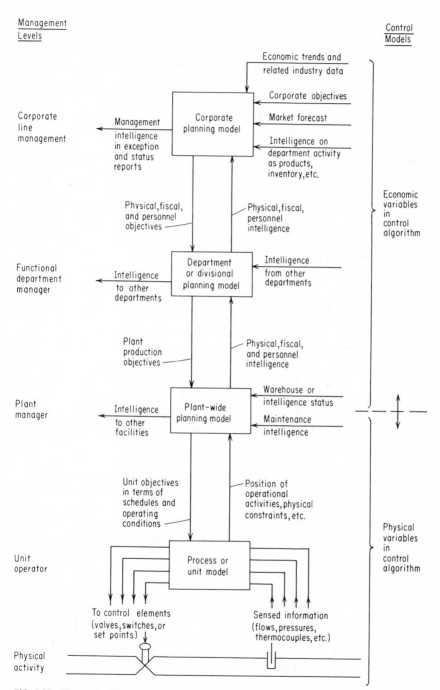

FIG. 1.2A The control hierarchy, a process-industry example.

whole operation, and sub-optimization to the optimization of a part, such as an individual refinery or plant.

This last statement defines the next lower, or *plant-complex,* control level also. At this level (again see Fig. 1.2A) it consists of a number of independently functioning sub-optimizing computers, each monitoring the operation of an individual plant unit, using economic information derived from the linear program, together with plant data pertaining to the properties of materials currently being processed. This information is reworked on an hourly basis to determine optimal operational targets of the individual plant units.

Outputs of this level, in terms of such information and commands as desired reformate octane, cut points, operating temperatures, and the like, then serves as input to the next lower *process-unit* level. Here the refinery computer has responsibility for controlling the refinery at the conditions specified by the department level. It is supplied with data on market forecasts and available crudes, so that overall manufacturing strategy can be planned and the various crudes and their shipping schedules (crude slate) selected.

The process-unit computer system then supervises the control of the individual processing units at the lowest level, directly or through satellite controllers of either the analog or the digital type. The process-unit system keeps complete and concise records of yields, production summaries, and labor, material, and operating costs, thus integrating both the information and the control function. The information so produced, in this reduced and readily comprehended form, now flows up the management ladder, enabling command decisions to flow down.

Below the process-unit level, at the *function* level of control, we find the process controllers that monitor and regulate the individual control loops of the process, either singly or in groups. In the past, this has been the function of analog controllers of conventional type. Digital controllers, direct digital control, or DDC, are now replacing the analog controllers in situations that involve a considerable number of control loops.

The lower control levels require mathematical models of the subsystem under their control in order to generate the necessary physical control decisions and commands. The higher levels of management activity are found to have entirely different information requirements than those for control of physical operations. These are not necessarily more complex, but they do involve a hierarchy of command that must be based on economic considerations, as distinguished from the physical operational-control models of the lower levels.

At the lower levels, data inputs are physical, i.e., pressures, flows, and material analysis that determine the necessary physical variables of the unit or plant. At the upper levels, inputs are economic, i.e., commands from management, engineering, market research and product development that specify what to make, when, and how much.

Use of electronic data-processing systems on the corporate level started in the late 1950s and early 1960s. For long-term physical and financial planning, a number of oil companies are now on the threshold of replacing the archaic tabulation or traditional methods with complete corporate computerization. The oil industry was destined to benefit on all levels of its organizational structure from a dynamic MICS. Such a system was spawned by the development of a new generation of computer hardware.

The concept of total MICS has to be achieved to make the move from the application of the digital computer for a specific field action or a limited business segment toward corporate-wide use. This concept is the ability, provided by the data-processing system, (the computer and associated input/output devices) to make available to top-level management timely information recorded on a dynamic basis, expedited as it occurs and continually assessed and reassessed by the management as an aid to the decision-making process.

Management has at its disposal in the total-information concept (TIC) a practically unlimited wealth of facts and figures of economic, technological, and environmental information, which are kept in storage (sometimes called the *data bank*) for ready use.

To crown this concept, simulation techniques have been extended to cover corporate facts and actions. *Corporate simulation* is a technique whereby the many functions of a corporation are described in the form of mathematical models and where the interrelationship of the various functions is studied and utilized in the decision-making process with the aid of a computer. Variables such as crude-oil production, refinery runs, prices, manpower, tanker availability, etc., are examined by the machine in units and/or money. Optimum solutions are indicated to corporate management for decision making.

The total-information concept (TIC), as illustrated in its basic structure in the flow chart in Fig. 1.3, keeps the data input flowing into the data-processing system from all levels: from the action level, the operational or local level, the regional or division level, and from the top.

Information and results might go from the storage center to all levels, except that programming can prevent indiscriminate access to the data bank. Thus, information for the exclusive use of the corporate management or other levels could be made inaccessible by the data-processing system to lower levels, which are not authorized to deal with this information.

The TIC utilizes a kind of pilot plant representing the management of the entire corporation, which permits management of this company to analyze the effects of various alternative decisions. It provides a means of accomplishing the following end product:

1. Establishment of general plans, goals, and strategy.

2. Establishment and control of physical and financial budgets.

3. Optimum allocation of capital to various segments of operations.

4. Capital investment analysis for each project or acquisition in their long-range effect on the overall operations—determination of discounted cash flow rate of return, etc.

5. Establishment of a total product-movement system and world-wide supply and demand reporting.

6. Forecasts, including those of self-cash generation.

7. Effects of outside financing.

8. Dynamic budget reporting and continuous control to maintain flexibility; postmortem evaluation of planning results.

9. Permanent control of physical, financial, and human resources.

Traditionally, the means of communicating with a computer had been punched cards or paper tape. However, with today's computers, a large variety of Teleprocessing terminals can be located all over the world and include typewriter terminals, teletypes, visual displays, card and badge readers, and even voice answer. This facility of man-to-computer communications has greatly aided the TIC.

Decision making by corporate management is speeded up by TIC's utilization of present-day computers as communication devices to assist management in its drive for efficiency and adaptability. TIC serves as an effective tool in long-term financial planning on a worldwide scale, but as efficient as this tool might be, the human factor is not replaceable by the machine.

The general business philosophy of the top management, permeating to all other levels of management and operation, its business acumen, personal experience, and judgment weighs heavily in the applications of TIC. It is man who feeds into the machine the correct and essential nutrition. Lacking the right diet, no data-processing system is able to deliver the correct results to the problems submitted by man, and it might be pushed into the regrettable position, for instance, of a trial lawyer who is misinformed by his client.

MANAGEMENT CONTROL CYCLE

Management is the process of converting information into action. The conversion process we call *decision making*. Decision making is in turn controlled by various explicit and implicit policies of behavior.

A *policy* is a rule that states how the day-by-day operating

Management

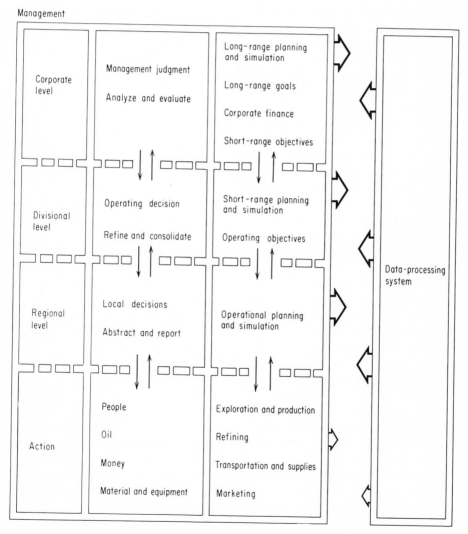

FIG. 1.3 Objectives of management information systems for international oil operations.

decisions are made. *Decisions* are the actions taken at any particular time and are the results of applying policy rules to the particular conditions that prevail at the moment.

If management is the process of converting information into action, then it is clear that management success depends primarily on what information is chosen and how the conversion is executed. Every person has available to him a large source of information. He selects and uses only a small fraction of this available information. Only incomplete and erratic use of that small fraction is made. The manager's accomplishments are dictated by his choice and priority assignment to certain classes of information and sources of information. Relative weights assigned to different information sources, the speed or slowness with which information is converted into action, and the creation of desired objectives from the available information define the adequacy of information and its use.

Viewing the manager as an information converter at his own particular control point in the organization shows why we are interested in decision making and information flow. An industrial organization is an interlocking complex network of information channels. These channels emerge at different points to control physical processes such as running a process unit, building a plant, recruiting new employees of the desired skills and experience, or maintaining an inventory level of raw material. Every activity point in the system is backed up by a local decision point whose information sources reach out into other parts of the organization both horizontally and vertically in the management hierarchy and into the surrounding environment.

For example, if this manager controls one plant in a corporation which has ten plants, the activity of the other nine plants affects his objectives, just as his actions affect the objectives of the other nine managers. His actions set the objectives for process units under his control. The results of his activity affect the status of the manufacturing department and thus become information for use in decision making by the department vice-president.

Figure 1.4 shows a decision stream in the simplest framework of an information-feedback system. Information is the input to a decision-making point that controls action yielding new information. In each of the structural boxes there are delays. Decisions do not respond immediately to available information. Information about actions is not instantaneously available. The execution of activity called for by a decision requires time. Information may amplify or decrease the decision output. Action may amplify or alter information or decision. Distortion and disturbances create noise in the information-decision-action cycle. The management control cycle at any particular level in the management hierarchy may be depicted as in Fig. 1.5.

The manager assesses his present position. What is the physical plant doing? How close is it to desired objectives? What is the trend? Then he evaluates his objectives on the basis of available resources

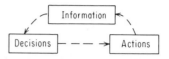

FIG. 1.4 Decisions and information feedback.

and present information on performance. External factors from surroundings must now be taken into account. Has upper-management policy changed in regard to objectives? What changes in the outside environment must be compensated for? For example, a supply of raw materials has been delayed by a storm; our recruitment has resulted in overhiring a certain number of people; the company directors set a policy of more factory automation.

The result of evaluating information is a plan for utilizing available resources best to meet objectives. The allocation of resources results in activity. This action changes present status, which calls

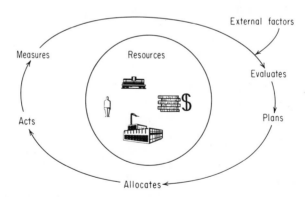

FIG. 1.5 Management control cycle.

for new measurement, etc. And around and around the never-ending cycle goes.

The information-feedback loop is not simple. It is a very complex, multiple-loop, interconnected system.

Decisions are made at many points throughout the system. Each resulting action generates information that may be used at several decision points but not all. This structure of cascaded, complex, interconnected information-feedback loops, when taken as a whole, describes an industrial system. Within a company, these decision points extend from the process-unit supervisor, the stock clerk in the shipping room, and the instrument foreman to the very top of the top echelon—even to the board of directors.

The decision-making process consists of three parts, the formation of a set of concepts indicating desired conditions, the observation of what appear to be the actual conditions, and the generation of corrective action to achieve the desired conditions. Information about actual conditions is distorted and delayed but this information forms the basis for creating the desired values from the apparent conditions. Corrective actions are delayed and distorted by the system. The distorted and noisy corrective actions influence actual and apparent conditions.

In determining the desired state of affairs we ask the questions: What should we like to have the condition of the system be? What are we striving for? What are the goals and objectives of this particular decision point? In determining the apparent state of actual conditions, our available information leads us to certain observations that we believe represent the present state of the system. These apparent conditions may be close to, or far removed from, the actual present state, depending on the information flows being used and the amount of time lag and distortion. The action taken for corrective purposes will be in accordance with any discrepancy which can be detected between the apparent and the desired conditions. In general, the greater the discrepancy, the greater the resulting action, although this entire process of forming a concept of desired conditions, detecting actual conditions, and creating from these a course of action is highly nonlinear and noisy. Very small discrepancies between observed and desired conditions may seem of no consequence and create little action. A mounting discrepancy may lead to more and more decisive attempts to change actual conditions into desired conditions.

Decision making is a continuous process. It is a conversion mechanism for continuously changing varying flows of information into control signals that determine the rate of action in a system. The decision point is continually yielding to the pressures of the environment. It is taking advantage of new developments as they occur. It is always adjusting to the state of affairs. It is always attempting to adjust toward the desired goals. The amount of action is some function of the discrepancy between goals and observed system status.

An important cornerstone for applying management control systems is the better understanding of decision making. The automatizing of military tactical operations in the 1950s led to the pioneering of automatic decision making. It was necessary to translate the tactical judgment and experience of military decision making into formal rules and procedures. The human organization's ability to cope with the increased pace of modern military operations was exceeded, but the military demonstrated that operational policies could be automatized and aptly demonstrated that carefully selected formal rules can lead to short-term tactical decisions that excel those made by human judgment under pressures of time and organizational rigidity. The resulting body of practical experience in determining the basis for decisions and the content of judgment is now becoming available for business use.

As in military decisions, we see that there is an orderly basis that prescribes much of our present managerial decision making. Decisions are not entirely free but are strongly conditioned by the environment. We can set down the policies governing such decisions and determine how policies affect industrial and economic behavior.

POLICY

The word *policy* was defined before as a rule that states how day-by-day operating decisions are made. *Decisions* are the actions taken at any particular time and are the results of applying policy. We may redefine policy as a description of how the decision process converts information into action. What action will result from given information imputs? What conversion relationships hold between information sources and resulting decisions? Or in other words, policy is the formal statement giving the relationship between information sources and resulting decision flows. In physical systems, particularly in the field of servomechanisms, the corresponding term is *transfer function*. The transfer function tells how the output of a particular box depends on the stream of inputs. The transfer function does not necessarily deal with the particular physical way whereby the conversion is accomplished. We are satisfied if the transfer function tells us adequately well, for a particular purpose, the present resulting action as a function of present and past inputs to the box.

In industrial organizations, some policy is very formal. It has been reduced to writing for the guidance of the decision makers in the organization. Most of the guiding policy is informal but every bit as influential. It depends on habit, conformity, social pressures, concept of goals, power centers within an organization, and personal interests.

We have progressed through three different levels of decision-making abstraction. At the lower level is random, unreasoned action which does not depend on inputs and which has no basis. At the second level are unrationalized intuitive reactions which in fact result from the available information but where the participant has no comprehension of the structure and the basis of his actions. At the third level of abstraction, there is an awareness of the formal reasons for decision, and we are able to anticipate with some reliability the kinds of reactions that others will exhibit in response to changes in the state of their environment.

A further explanation of the analogy between a servomechanism and business may be enlightening. A manager must plan, organize, and control. *Planning* means describing and exploring the surrounding environment. *Organizing* means exploring the internal operation. *Control* is making sure that the internal operation fits the external system. A servomechanism consists of an input going into a system yielding some sort of output. In addition, some information about the output is fed back into the system. This is called *feedback.* An example is the home thermostat, the furnace being the system. The input is fuel going to the furnace. The output is heat energy. The feedback is the temperature indication of too high or too low.

The characteristics of a servomechanism are (see Fig. 1.6):

1. *Response Time.* How long it takes to achieve command (input).

2. *Dynamic Range.* The range over which the device will faithfully reproduce output.

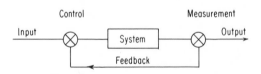

FIG. 1.6 The feedback loop.

3. *Distortion.* The deviation from faithful reproduction.

4. *Dynamic Stability.* A measure of the oscillation and damping factor of the device before it settles down.

Linearity is assumed for servomechanisms; i.e., when two commands are given simultaneously, it is assumed that the output is the sum of the individual inputs. We know that business operation is not linear, so that the usefulness of the analogy of business with a servomechanism is therefore limited. The input is the environment of the business. The system consists of capital, administrative and analytical skills, resources, and organization. The output is eco-

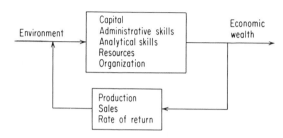

FIG. 1.7   The business feedback loop.

nomic wealth. Feedback is some measure of effectiveness: sales, production, etc. In diagram form it looks like Fig. 1.7.

Just as a servomechanism cannot operate without power, business cannot operate (for long) without profit. But the purpose of the servomechanism is not power but the signal, and the purpose of the business is not short-term profit but economic wealth.

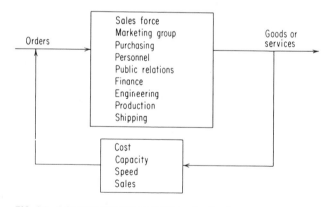

FIG. 1.8   A further example of business feedback.

There are loops within loops in the business organism, and this makes analysis very difficult. For example, consider the following loop, as shown in Fig. 1.8. Going one step down to the operations of a worker and machine, we have the situation shown in Fig. 1.9.

We pay for control in the form of the time of the inspector. Comparison of the cost of inspection versus the cost of scrap leads to an optimization problem.

Now expand this feedback loop to the hierarchy of management and we have the situation shown in Fig. 1.10.

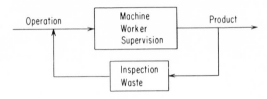

FIG. 1.9   A simple feedback loop.

In some cases, the "individuals" controlled, being inanimate, e.g., a machine tool, are predictable, as in a chemical process control such as a catalytic reactor or distillation unit. In some cases the individuals controlled, being people, are not predictable except en

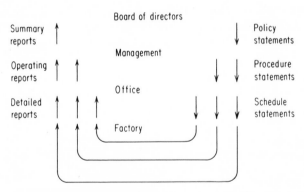

FIG. 1.10   Performance feedback.

masse, in the sense of such statistics as average performance, standard production, etc.

DETECTING THE GUIDING POLICY

We must now consider whether we can detect the guiding policy with sufficient accuracy so that we can use it to understand the behavior of the industrial system. There are several opinions on this question. The literature on decision making implies great difficulty and subtlety in the subject. The social scientist makes tentative simple experiments with groups of three or four people, in an effort to determine how their decisions are arrived at in reacting to one another. The *New York Herald-Tribune* in the 1965 New York mayoralty election used less than one-half of 1 percent of the voters to predict very accurately the results of a three-candidate race. When we raise the question of understanding the human decision-making process, the frequent answer from scientists is that not even a good beginning has been made yet. Yet you and I, together with the historian, the novelist, the manager, every day discuss why "so-and-so" acted in a particular way. By so doing, we are discussing his guiding policy. We are discussing how he responded or should have responded to information sent to him.

Let us illustrate by an example. In developing a long-range plan (5 to 10 years) for expenditures of funds for expanding production in a major aluminum company, it is clearly impossible to introduce the actions of the federal government into a formal model of national economic behavior that will affect our decisions. We do not know the process by which governmental decisions are reached, e.g., the federal action in 1965 of selling on the open market the government stockpile to counteract the proposed rise in sales price of aluminum by $\frac{1}{2}$ cent per pound.

But as a routine matter, when developing long-range plans for expenditures such as above, we are expected to know the factors that would lead to particular governmental actions. In other words, we are expected to know the essential nature of the policy that guides the stream of federal decisions. To be sure, there is a high noise content that can cause timing variations and uncertainty in the extent of a response. However, the broad underlying outlines of guiding policy such as inflationary actions, the great society, and political thinking are expected to be within our understanding and comprehension.

There is an excellent analogy to the above in our thinking about inventions. There is great argument and little agreement in any discussion of how new ideas are generated and how invention and research results are achieved. Yet we are essentially in total agreement in acknowledging that more intelligent and more experienced people and greater research-budget expenditure and greater motivation and greater need for the results will enhance the probability of a successful outcome. This agreement on the nature of the conversion function that couples financial and manpower inputs to scientific output is the basis for congressional action and defense appropriations.

As seen in Fig. 1.11, at the lower levels of the management hierarchy, the guiding rules (or policies) are more firmly established and grasped than the policy that guides the manager's decisions at higher levels. On the lowest level, we see that many of the operational control rules are firmly established. When the rules can be

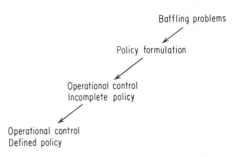

FIG. 1.11   The evolution of decision making.

explicitly described, they lend themselves to automatic decision making. Some familiar examples are payroll preparation, order entry, product blending in the output of a refinery, and the automatic closed-loop control of a chemical process unit or electrical generating station. Just a few generations ago the automatic reordering of goods sold or calculating payroll would have been classed as a managerial prerogative.

In the next area up the scale, we have semiautomatic decisions made by middle management but closely circumscribed by corporate policy, i.e., inventories, production schedules, and employment levels. At this level also fall such decisions as the strategy for plant operations. Most of the rules can be set down in either a decision-tree fashion or described in terms of a set of mathematical equations. But all the rules cannot be so described completely, e.g., new plant start-up.

In the third level, we progress more toward top-level decisions, i.e., capital investment, advertising budgets, sales forecasting, profit motivation strategy. We here continually try to define the relationship and variables in the company environment and outside it that affect our operations. As the quality and quantity of information that bears on the particular operational strategy increase, we use the new management-science techniques, such as linear programming, statistics, critical-path methods, etc., to define the rules for making decisions. As the policy-guided decisions become automatic, and today's judgments are prescribed by policy, the creative manager will be faced by new baffling problems and opportunities. He must then devote himself more to the major decisions of strategy and less to the routine decisions and short-term tactics. He must rid himself of the minor repetitive decisions by putting them under control of well-defined policy so that he is free to push back the management frontiers. After all, it is for this that a manager draws his pay.

The management control structure discussed later is helping to expand the areas of automatic decision in lower levels of management. It is extending the region of operational control by helping design policies capable of machine inplementation to cover more of today's vexing management decisions. It is providing a tool for building a background against which to make intuitive judgment decisions in policy formulation. This gives management the time and opportunity to push out into the frontiers of unexplored areas in industrial management and economic development.

To reemphasize the points above, let us take another example. Many people seem to believe that a sharp break exists between automatic decisions that are completely formal and other regions of management decisions. Such persons are unwilling to accept the possibility of even the existence of formal policies that could describe the major aspects of management in the other decision-making regions. Any manager must of necessity admit the existence of the region of automatic decisions, since these are common practice. The majority of managers will argue that the region of the intuitive-judgment decision is so subtle that no reasonable approximation can be made to it through formal decision rules. Yet these same managers, when faced with a decision that they recognize as lying beyond the capabilities of their intuitive judgment, will once more fall back on formal decision-making procedures. The fields of sales and market forecasting and penetration rates and economic forecasting, when done on the basis of statistical analysis of past data or by routine procedures of collecting information, fall into this area. Forecasting is essentially a decision-making process. It consists of taking past-available and presently available information and converting it into results that indicate a course of action. For lack of anything better, managers rely on certain formal statistical decision procedures with respect to some of the more subtle and difficult decisions, even using such tools as Bayesian* statistics without a qualm. But they reserve the middle ground as a region for

* A statistical technique developed in England in the early 1700s which allows weighting factors based on intuition, judgment, or experience to be included with factual data and treated mathematically.

judgment, which they assert is untouchable for formal decision rules.

This middle region is not the obscure and subtle desert that it has so often been pictured. Men are not good calculators of the dynamic behavior of complicated systems. The number of variables that they can in fact properly relate to each other is limited. The intuitive judgment of even a skilled investigator is quite unreliable in anticipating the dynamic behavior of a simple information-feedback system of perhaps a half dozen variables. This is true even when the complete structure and all the parameters of the system are fully known to him. The verbal and mental model we have to explain the dynamics of industrial and economic system behavior probably does not rank in effective dynamic complexity beyond a third- or fourth-order differential equation. We think we give consideration to a much larger number of variables, but in reality we probably consider at one time five or six at most. In dealing with the dynamics of information-feedback systems, the manager is not a subtle and powerful problem solver. He must use the management-science techniques to help formulate policy and make decisions.

When we try to understand the corporate information-feedback system, we must not become lost or isolated in a particular small segment of the system or on the other hand try too gross an approach to the solution of the entire problem. It is from an intermediate viewpoint that we can best know the working environment and best capture the true character of the operation. An example may be in order. If we are formulating the rules for operation of a refinery, the best position is at the next higher management level. As the refinery manager, we become too engrossed in the particular operational problems and fail to feel the effect of the outside environment on best policy. Likewise, if we see this refinery from the point of view of the board of directors, the true operating problems escape us and too gross a view is presented. It brings to mind the old saw "when lost in the woods, you can't see the forest for the trees." But you don't want to be so far away from the trees that you cannot see their silhouettes.

In a dynamic information-feedback system, the human decision maker is generally using a great deal less than the total amount of information available to him and the information is less than commonly presumed. In general, a manager's actions with respect to any given decision stream will be almost entirely conditioned by fewer than 10 information inputs. His use of these few information sources is apt to be rather stereotyped. Some will be used to create a concept of desired objectives; others will serve to form his impression of the true state of affairs. The differences will result in reasonably obvious actions. But the obvious may not be best. Some of the biggest improvements that can be made, and are being made at lower levels of operations, in the dynamics of our industrial systems will come from the following procedures that tradition and folklore have led us to believe are precisely in the wrong direction. For example, we know of one case where jet fuel is supplied to a major airport not from the next-door refinery but from the same company's refinery a thousand miles away. When all the information is used, it is more profitable to change the objective of the local refinery to maximize gasoline and heater oil and transport by pipeline from the distant plant the jet kerosene directly to the airport. Our understanding of the dynamics of complicated systems is so inadequate that our intuitive judgment often cannot be trusted to tell us whether an improvement or degradation will result from a given direction or policy change.

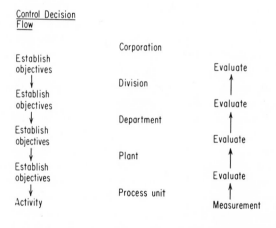

FIG. 1.12 Planning and resource allocation. (The function of planning is to establish specific targets and objectives for lower echelons in relation to the best allocation of available resources in respect to overall company objectives.)

Let us attempt to understand decision-making policy by defining the evolutionary steps in the hierarchy leading to computer-directed automatic decision making. At the upper level (see Fig. 1.11) decision making would be that where actions were random and irrational. This leads to a level where actions are reasonable and rational but with no awareness of what the governing policies might be (see, for example, the aluminum company mentioned above).

Next in the hierarchy of the evolution of decision making we have a verbal or mental descriptive model of a rational policy that creates the stream of individual decisions. This is a major fraction of the step toward the ability to formulate explicit, quantitative, policy-governing decisions. The next step is one in which art and intuitive judgment are applied to the development of a better understanding of policy.

At the last-mentioned step, art, judgment, and intuition are no longer applied to the individual separate decisions but to the definition of a policy that governs the stream of individual decisions.

Many economists, information theorists, and control engineers have been attempting to develop statistical methods that can be routinely applied to extract from quantitative data the governing decision policies. But first we must understand how to use art, intuition, and judgment in the extraction of the decision policies themselves. After this process is understood, we may be able to reduce this method of analysis of an organization to a rigid and orderly procedure. At each point in time, art and judgment must be devoted to establishing the rules whereby the lower levels of management decision making can be automatized.

An example of orderly rules relating to decision making is computer programming. A short time ago, the only way to use a computer was to write a specific machine code for the solution to a problem. Next it became possible to write a program of logical instructions to tell the machine how to create its own running program for a specific problem formulation, e.g., assemblers and compilers. Now new concepts are developing that allow the computer to formulate the specific statement of the problem, which another computer will turn into daily operational use.

To approximate the controlling policy at each significant decision point in the system, we must be able to represent at least the central essential skeleton of the decision-making structure. An understanding of policy can be accomplished if:

1. We have the proper concept of what a decision is and of the significance of the policy that describes the decision process.

2. We have the proper structure relating system status to policy, to decisions, and to action.

3. We realize that the process is noisy and we shall not get and do not need high accuracy of decision-making representation.

4. We use to best advantage the extensive body of experience and descriptive information on decision making.

5. We realize that a formal quantitative statement of policy carries with it no implications one way or the other regarding absolute accuracy.

We can make a formal quantitative statement corresponding to any statement that can be made in descriptive English. Lack of descriptive accuracy does not prevent quantifying our ideas about decision policy. Assigning a number does not enhance the accuracy of the original statement. The common belief that we cannot quantify a decision rule because we do not know it with high accuracy is mixing two quite separate considerations. We can quantify regardless of accuracy. After that, we deal with the question of what is sufficient accuracy.

It has been demonstrated that these things can be done. Actual effective decision functions in a company or in an economy go much further than the formal policy that is set down in executive memoranda and in laws. The "effective policy" is the framework for reaching decisions and is established by the environment, the sources of information that are in fact available, the measures and rewards that affect people at each decision point, the priority order of food and shelter and luxuries, the mores of society, and the prejudices and habits impressed by past experiences. When decisions are examined in the light of this circumscribing framework, we find that they are far from the unpredictable actions they are sometimes supposed. Even for a particular individual we can assume a certain degree of consistency and can meaningfully discuss probable effect of various pressures on him. For a class of persons in similar environments, the likely average response to changes in specific environment forces can be estimated with even higher confidence.

In formulating a model to study the influences of policies on system behavior, we must extend the concept of policy beyond its usual meaning. All decisions in the model come under the complete control of policy. The policy represents the basis for controlling flows at all points in the actual system. The concept of policies governing decisions goes well beyond that of the human managerial decision. A model must also make "decisions" that are of a physical nature, e.g., how many unfilled orders can be filled depending on the state of inventories?

We may classify decision as an *overt* decision to want or to attempt and as an *implicit* decision which creates the action, recognizing the existing true state of the system as well as desires. An example of an implicit decision would be the present ability to deliver an order, depending on the present status of inventories, or taxes due as a result of profit, or the production rate as a consequence of available production equipment and material. An overt decision may be the decision to increase employment, to increase production, or to raise product quality.

When considering a model of the information flow and decision-making stream, both implicit and overt decisions may be included. These respectively deal with the actuality and the desire. Conditions lead to a desire for change (increased profits) ; the wish interacts with the state of the resources of the system to determine what, if anything, is to occur.

These two concepts are one factor that eliminates the necessity of simultaneous equations that arise in some models, such as making production decisions continuously equal to consumption decisions. Such decisions are actually made separately and independently, and eventually coupled through inventories, prices, and various information flows.

In formulating decision functions, we must take care that the decisions are generated from the variables that would actually be available at the decision point. Generally the information available for overt decision making is not identical to the primary variables that it represents. The information may be biased, noisy, or delayed. Overt decisions are usually based on information about the primary variables. Implicit decisions are more mechanistic in that they control routine flows and are dependent on the actual state of the system and therefore on the true values of the variables involved in a model. Let us illustrate the difference between the true value and information about a variable by using an inventory. The present true state of the inventory decides the ability to deliver an item to service an order. The overt decision function that controls reordering may depend on information about the inventory, which may be inaccurate and delayed. From this information about the inventory, we decide what the desired inventory should be. A model, like the real world, often represents both true values of variables and also associated variables that represent the values that are measured or conceived for decision-making use.

Are estimated decision functions good enough to be useful? Perceptive observations, searching discussions, study of existing data, and examination of specific examples of decisions and actions illuminate the principal factors that influence decisions. In considering a factor influencing a decision, we progress through four stages:

1. What factors are significant enough to include?
2. What is the direction of effect of each factor?
3. What is the magnitude of effect of each factor?
4. What nonlinearities should be recognized of each factor?

In deciding how to formulate a particular decision function (policy) in a model, the first step is to list those factors which are important influences on the decision. The answer is often obscure. What at first may appear to be a most significant factor will sometimes be found to have little influence on the model behavior or on the actual system. A factor that is ordinarily overlooked in everyday management practice may turn out to hold the key to important characteristics of the total system.

The extent of the direct influence of the factor on the decision is not the only consideration. We must also consider the degree of feedback or repercussion of the decision on the factor entering into the decision and the timing of such feedback. Relatively slight influences on decisions can be important in positive-feedback conditions, where the variable factor influences a decision and the decision affects the input factor to create still more change in the decision.

There will usually be little doubt about the direction in which a decision will be influenced by changes in a particular factor affecting the decision. However, we must be alert to represent properly the worse-before-better sequences that often arise. The short-term and long-term influences on a decision by a particular factor are often in opposite directions, and the dynamic behavior of a model can be seriously affected if only the long-range effects are included.

The dynamic behavior of information-feedback systems is determined by the way in which *changes* in one variable cause *changes* in another. This might lead one to expect a high system sensitivity to the exact values of parameters in the decision functions, but such will usually not be true.

If the model is properly constructed to represent the actual information-feedback structure of our industrial systems, it will have the same self-correcting adaptability that exists in real-life situations. In the preferred model formulation all parameters that must be estimated for decision functions are acted on by the values of levels to obtain the rates of flow that are controlled by the decisions. An inaccurate decision-function parameter can then lead to compensating readjustments of levels in the model until rates of flow are properly related to each other.

We should be more concerned with what the model tells us about the factors that will cause *changes* in the rates and levels than about the accuracy in determining the average magnitudes of the rates and levels.

A properly constructed model is often surprisingly unaffected by plausible changes in most parameter values—even sometimes severalfold changes. In a model, the sensitivity to selected values of parameters should be no greater than the sensitivity of the real system to the corresponding factors. It seems obvious that our actual industrial and economic activities must not be highly sensitive to their fundamental parameters and that these parameters do not change rapidly. This must be true because the significant *characteristics* of our organizations persist for long times. The successful company tends to remain so for extended periods—a success that is founded in basic organization and policies (including the essential aspects of its leadership). Our national economy has exhibited surprisingly similar economic cycles throughout its history, in spite of vast changes in technology, monetary structure, transportation and communication speed, relative importance of industry and agriculture, and magnitude of government activity.

The decision functions of a model will necessarily incorporate only the more important factors that influence decisions. A host of minor influences will unavoidably be omitted. The omissions can represent two quite different categories.

In the first category are the slight influences from those variables which are a part of the system and of the model under consideration. These omissions are actually the elimination of some of the feedback paths between the model variables. This will often happen because of the necessity for simplification. Omitting a variable within the model from a decision function is the omission of an input that may be correlated in time with the decisions created by the decision function. We cannot substitute for this type of omission by a random variable incorporated into the decision process of the model.

A second class of omission from the decision functions has a very different character. These omitted factors are the ones that are not themselves affected by each other or by the other variables of the model. Their source is outside the real system being represented and independent of it. This flood of noise of a random and unpredictable form adds its contribution to all decision points in our actual social systems. We can approximate these by including noise variation in the decision functions in the model.

The practical question of what noise characteristics should be included in a model will, like many other inputs, be decided primarily by such knowledge as we have of the system being represented.

Noise inputs to decision functions can be used to represent the influence of the above-mentioned second class of omissions from the decision functions in a model, where the omitted factors are unrelated to the system being modeled. Noise cannot substitute for the first class of omissions, which constitute a simplification and omission of parts of the information-feedback structure of the system.

We sometimes fail to realize the importance of an initial hypothesis about the dynamic behavior of a system. Often we feel that to propose modes of behavior before a model is constructed is to prejudge the answers. But in a sense this is precisely what is needed. We build a model to see whether the modes of behavior can exist and whether the model can result from initial assumptions. Then experimental work proves or disproves our initial hypothesis.

The initial hypothesis is part of the establishment of the initial questions and goals. Without an initial mental and verbal model we have no basis for deciding what factors are important and what factors may be neglected. It is not likely that a decision model would result from aimless wandering through an organization. Thinking about a problem in terms of a solution focuses the mind on that area. Overlooked are other possibilities. We must initially identify the problem, "What am I really trying to do?"; then apply the solution.

SUMMARY

In this chapter we were concerned with the concept of the automatic company. Starting with computerized process control of process units, this concept of hierarchy of computer control proceeds through higher levels of information gathering, communication, and decision making; it embraces the entire business complex and considers the hierarchy of management levels, providing all levels with the information required to best perform their respective functions in meeting the objectives of the total business operation.

MICS system has three overlapping functions: providing optimized process control for the lower levels in the hierarchy, supplying management with information based on the principles of management by exception, and furnishing information to all levels of management for planning. The computer and associated input/output devices and displays (the data-processing systems) provide management with timely information recorded on a dynamic basis as it occurs, with continual assessment and reassessment to aid the manager in his decision-making process. With an almost unlimited wealth of facts and figures and the ability to use them intelligently through present-day management-science tools such as simulation, statistical analysis, mathematical programming, and the calculating and data-processing ability of the computer, the manager has better and more timely information at his disposal for better decision making. The decision-making process can be speeded up.

Process-control theory, with feedback and feedforward, offers new approaches for looking at all areas of the business environment.

The enlarged and more timely information can aid the manager in the formation of a set of desired conditions, in the observation of what appears to be actual conditions, and the generation of corrective action to achieve the desired conditions.

Tactical and strategic judgment and experience may be stated in formal rules and procedures. At the lower levels, the guiding rules or policies are more firmly established and grasped than the policy that guides the manager's decisions at higher levels. When the rules may be explicitly stated, they lend themselves to automatic decision making. In the next area up the management scale, we may have semiautomatic decisions made by management but closely circumscribed by corporate policy, e.g., inventories or production schedules. Strategy for plant operations also fall into this class. As we progress toward top-level decisions, e.g., profit-motivation strategy, the information system can help define and clarify the relationship and variables, both in the company environment and outside it, that affect the kind and nature of decision to be made. Here the quality and quantity of information bears on the particular operational strategy. Management-science techniques, when applied correctly, help the manager gain a closer insight into the variables and their interaction affecting the particular strategy for solving his problem. These techniques aid in the application of intuitive judgment.

When considering a model of the information flow and decision-making stream in an organization, both implicit and overt decisions may be included. In formulating decision functions, we must take care that the decisions are generated from the variables that would actually be available at the decision point. Generally the information available for overt decision making is not identical to the primary variables that it represents but is based on information about the primary variables. A model, like the real world, often represents both true values of variables and associated variables that represent the values that are measured or conceived for decision-making use.

CHAPTER TWO

Control Functions

Information is the basis for management action and decisions in the performance of its function. ANON.

INFORMATION

A few decades ago, the New England industrialist had a total management information system. It was tucked under the inside band of his stovepipe hat. The essential documents and records kept there were adequate to his needs since he knew the inside of his business as well as he knew the inside of his hat.

With the growth of enterprise, management was forced to functionalize and decentralize. This in turn created problems of communication and decision lag and difficulties in maintaining a unified overall policy for the company.

Management's answer, in part, has been to continue to refine accounting and budgetary control techniques. In recent years, there has been an eagerness to mobilize hardware technology for the handling of industry's most important commodity—information.

The basic job of the business office is to gather, interpret, and transmit information; to provide and sift the flow of facts and opinions that form the basis for decisions; and then to relay the instructions and effect the transactions by which the decisions are carried out. The physical plant of today's modern office is totally different from what it was a few years ago or from what it may be a few years hence. The tools of information handling are making fantastic advances. Computer systems, new methods of voice and data communications, display and control devices, and such management-science techniques as linear programming are offering new approaches to information storage and retrieval.

Integrated data processing is no new concept, but the data-processing, storage, and communications capabilities available now are taking on new dimensions. It is possible now to create a mechanized master file of all the information needed for a company's operation. In one master corporate memory can be assembled all the company's operations—information about products, customers, sales trends, competitors' operations, economic environment, and the like. Geographically remote points now may have immediate, direct access to such information, with the possibility of continuous updating in the central file, and with the dissemination of the new information and instructions acquired to all concerned.

Most large corporations in this country are now to some degree planning new corporate-wide information systems, and a number already have such systems in operation. The following technological developments are making corporate information systems feasible:

1. Progress in programming software, such as IBM's Generalized Information System (GIS) and Operating System/360, which makes it easier for people who are not computer technicians to communicate with the central processor; the development of a machine-independent language.

2. Computer memory systems of practically unlimited capacity and random accessibility.

3. Improved means of capturing information at the source and entering it into the computer system.

4. New terminal devices making possible direct input and inquiry into the computer with output in the form of visual displays, audio response, or nearly instantaneous hard copy. These terminals may read a room thermostat or process meter, a counting register or paper check and enter the information into the system. The output can control a pump at a remote generating station or open a valve on an oil well many miles away.

5. Advanced communications switching and data transmission coupled with today's computers, distinguished by time-sharing capabilities, can handle many terminals simultaneously.

Any corporation, no matter how far-flung its operations, can have completely centralized files, with the desired degree of on-line access and real-time information. Depending on the investment in hardware, any level of management can be in as close touch as it wishes with any phase of operations in real time,* by means of video-tube displays or even through computer-generated voice re-

---

* By real time we mean that a condition requiring corrective control action can be sensed in time for the action to be taken. On a process unit, this may mean seconds; in upper-level management this may mean months.

sponse. Through such displays, the computer can be brought to the board room or to special management information rooms. These ideas take their lead from the military command control centers.

From an economics viewpoint, an information system can be considered as a way of buying the perishable commodity information and adding operational control as a function of management in reducing costs and in increasing the value of production, giving an ace in the hole against keen competition.

A management information and control system (MICS) weds operational activity of physical equipment to economics (the profit motive) making full use of present-day technology (hardware, programming systems, and management service tools and techniques).

In the previous discussion, we have looked at information and control as covering the complete hierarchy of company organization. The flow of information and putting decisions into action have been discussed as a total company MICS. We shall now isolate a particular part of the organization, the plant, for a more detailed insight. By understanding something about the application of mathematics and control theory in operating physical processes, e.g., a cement kiln or chemical plant, we may see how these same principles apply and offer solutions to other management control problems in other areas. Chapter 12 shows the application of these concepts and principles to an inventory control problem.

WHAT DO COMPUTERS DO IN PLANTS?

Automatic controls range all the way from the infinite complexity of the computer to the familiar simplicity of the thermostat on a home heating system.

In a continuous-process plant, many "thermostats" control parts of the process; some regulate temperature, others pressures and flows. Finding the best setting for each of these controls is complicated. One solution is to have an operator feed data into a computer that calculates the best combination of settings; then operators regulate the instruments accordingly. *This is off-line computation and control.*

It takes time for people to collect instrument readings, and errors can creep in. When the instrument readings are fed directly into the computer, it is called *on-line, open-loop computer control,* because people still play a part in resetting the thermostats in accordance with the computer's suggestions.

In *closed-loop computer control,* both the instruments and the control settings of the controllers (the instruments that control physical variables, e.g., furnace gas flow) are connected directly to the computer.

Where systems do the same job as human supervisors, we have *supervisory closed-loop control.*

A more sophisticated system is called *dynamic closed-loop control.* Here the computer reads the instruments, analyzes them, works the data against a model (a set of mathematical statements describing the interrelations and relationships among the process variables), and sends its order directly to valves and motor controls. It has no need for many of the old thermostat types of instrument. Dynamic control can handle more precise jobs than other systems.

Operational control systems involve computer programs that pertain to the control exercised by management over the flow of work through the plant or facility, the setting of inventory levels, balancing assembly lines, and allocating fuel and utilities economically to the processing facilities.

To integrate these computer programs, simulation techniques are used today. Methodology and survey techniques are in common use. Programming libraries are crammed with programs available for the use of both executive and engineer.

COMPUTER CONTROL FUNCTIONS

The functions of the computer control system for the plant or process unit are the following (see Fig. A.2). Through the *estimation function* the operating state of the process is determined by reading instruments attached to the required process variables and performing any required additional calculations. Based partly on information developed by the estimation function, and partly on information about the technology and economics of the process stored in the form of a mathematical model, the *optimization function* determines the most profitable operating state of the process and the values of the controllable independent variables that correspond to this desired state. This set of values is constantly changing because the disturbance variables are constantly changing. The *control function* then determines the changes to be applied to the controllable variables in order to bring the plant safely and swiftly to the new desired state. When the disturbances are relatively slow compared to the response time of the process, and if no problems of instability exist, this function reduces to merely changing the settings of the controllable variables from their present positions to the new, desired optimum conditions. When it is necessary to take into account the dynamics of the process, the control function becomes considerably more sophisticated.

THE MATHEMATICAL MODEL

To achieve control of the plant outputs, we clearly need to know the effect on each output of manipulating each input. In order to permit the computer to operate on the problem, it is necessary that the required relationships be expressed in mathematical form. Developing these relationships, the model,* if it is not already available, is a crucial step in applying computer control to a given process. Depending, of course, on how much of the required information is available at the start, building the model will require not only time but also expert knowledge in the technology of the process.

Ideally, the user provides the model, as it is entirely an expression of the workings of his process, but in practice there seldom is sufficient information in usable form initially, and further study of the process, both theoretical and experimental, is ordinarily called for.

In all cases, a *steady-state* or *static model* will be required in order to perform the optimization. A static model ignores transient effects and gives the relationships that hold after equilibrium is reached and transients have died out. In some cases, depending on considerations discussed under the control functions, a dynamic model is required. A dynamic model contains the static model but gives, in addition, the relationships that hold during the transient state.

OPTIMIZATION

The principal use of the mathematical model of the process stored in the computer is to determine the adjustments to be made on the controllable variables to bring the plant to its optimum performance. Some variables must be kept within upper and lower limits, called *constraints,* during normal operation. These constraints may represent physical limitations imposed by the equipment used or limits set by product specifications.

The region inside the constraints is called the *feasible* region.

Optimization consists of finding the point within the feasible region which maximizes the *objective function* † either through linear- or nonlinear-programming techniques, the latter being more complicated.

* A model is never more than a partial representation of the system. It is a good model if, despite its incompleteness, it can accurately predict the effect of changes in the system on the overall effectiveness of the system.

† The *objective function* is the mathematical statement of the objectives of the unit, the plant, the marketing force, etc. For example, the objective of a process unit may be to maximize throughput. The objective function would be the expression of variables affecting throughput.

It is important to stress the fact that the optimization calculations, by whatever method they may be performed, are made entirely on the model and in no way affect the operation of the plant except through the final result of the calculation, which is the location of the desired optimum point.

In the concept of *automatic optimization,* the computer is linked directly to the process-controller set points, e.g., the desired temperature you set on your home thermostat, and repositions these set points to maintain optimum operation automatically. Although the operator is still required to handle unusual situations which are outside the scope of the computer program, the computer operates in a closed-loop supervisory capacity most of the time.

The computer accepts inputs concerning the process operation and also receives information on factors such as desired production rates. It continuously monitors the process to ensure that all variables are held at the values which will result in optimum unit performance, in accordance with predetermined criteria. The computer, through the mathematical model, takes into account the required production rates, the operating characteristics of the unit, the cost data for the unit, and the time variations in operating characteristics.

The output of the computer is linked to the set points of conventional analog or digital controllers.* These controllers then function in the normal manner, controlling individual loops at fixed values. The computer, however, has taken the place of the operator during normal plant operation, resetting control points as required. Many installations of on-line computers were first installed to yield data concerning the process relationships on which to base optimizing control in the future.

The problems inherent in closed-loop operation must be considered. One difficulty stems from the fact that many processes exhibit large time lags. Automatic optimization under these circumstances is difficult if instability is to be avoided. In addition, fast, accurate analytical instruments are required to provide data on product quality and end-point conditions. Primary elements have to be accurate enough to permit the model to recognize and evaluate small changes.

The links between the controllers and the computer can be de-

* An example of an analog controller is the flow control valve regulating gas flow to a furnace. The control loop would consist of the sensing element (a temperature-measuring device, a logic circuit that determines whether the sensed temperature is too high or too low, and an error signal that tells the flow valve to close or open).

signed to "fail safe," so that computer shutdown will merely leave the process at the last set of operational conditions, not necessarily the optimum condition.

OPTIMIZATION BY MATHEMATICAL MODEL

One approach to automatic optimization is to use the computer to solve the equations relating the measured variables to the secondary characteristics. This type of optimization is also known as *predictive control*. From the measured primary variables, the computer calculates the secondary characteristics or other control criteria. Then it relates these factors in accordance with fixed mathematical expressions to determine the corrections for the controller settings.

Either an analog or a digital computer can be used. Since the process is controlled dynamically by the instruments, the optimization routine of the computer remains in the supervisory control loop and places no heavy time burden on the computer operation. This permits time sharing the computer between several off-line problems such as trim calculations, engineering calculations, and indeed payroll computations.

A control system which changes its mathematical model or its control parameters based on changes in the system being controlled is known as *adaptive control*. Adaptive-control techniques are being adopted for military and industrial applications.

To control an entire process unit, and to account for all the interactions between the various elements of the process unit, the nature of the tasks is such that the digital computer, with its stored-program, logic, and general-purpose computational capabilities, lends itself much more readily to changes, even of major nature, which may occur in the operation of a process or in the requirements placed upon the control function. By merely changing the program and adding, if required, necessary inputs and outputs with no replacement of existing equipment, changing requirements can be continuously met with a digital computer.

PROBLEM AREAS

We sometimes encounter areas of difficulty in applying digital-computer control techniques. They must be examined critically each time we study a process and typically include:

1. *The Lack of Analytical Instruments Necessary to Furnish the Computer with Required Process Information.* Although it is true that many of the quantities important in the operation of a process cannot be directly measured, rapid advances in the state of

the art in instrumentation are overcoming this deficiency. With the computational capability of the computer, a quantity of importance may frequently be found by making direct measurements on other quantities and then, by using either theoretical or empirically established relationships, computing the desired quantity. As an elementary example, a gas density may be determined by measuring the temperature and pressure of the gas and by computing the density through the use of either appropriate gas-law equations or empirically determined gas tables stored in the computer's memory.

2. *The Lack of Understanding of the Process Itself.* This situation exists and will continue to exist as long as new processes are being developed. One must, however, face up to the fact that new processes are being operated and will continue to be. Sufficient information is now available for acceptable, if not the best possible, effectiveness. New processes can be operated more efficiently by applying control techniques based on the present state of understanding and on the operating data available, or possible to make available, by studying the process carefully. The control computer can perform an additional function of logging and analyzing the data continuously as they become available. Correlation techniques can be used on operating data to formulate acceptable and usable models. On the basis of these models, the proper control functions can be performed in the absence of a complete theoretical understanding of the process.

3. *The Necessity of Reliability.* Using digital computers for process control demands an exceedingly high degree of reliability before it can be considered. This is in contrast to using digital computers for scientific and business computation, where breakdown of equipment, although distressing and inconvenient, can be tolerated. When failures do occur, maintenance and repair must be accomplished simply, rapidly, with readily available equipment, and in the field. Even so, the process unit must continue operating during the relatively short repair time, since process shutdown and start-up are expensive and time-consuming. Continuous operation of the process itself can be assured by having the computer adjust the set points of conventional controllers and by having the set points remain at their last established value or return automatically to a predetermined value in the event of computer failure.

The objection to computer application most frequently mentioned is the lack of sensing devices. It is conceded that additional and more sophisticated sensing devices will be needed by industry in the years to come. However, sensing devices presently installed and operating are not being used, to any great extent, for process analysis. Instead, so many data are being generated and recorded that it is difficult, if not impossible, to manually select proper data for thorough correlation. The control computer, on the other hand, can take the same data, add more, digest them rapidly for immediate analysis, and allow better decisions to be made by both operating and management personnel.

THE TREND TO COMPUTER CONTROL

The computer control market developed rapidly in the sixties. The users of control computers demanded and obtained the on-line measuring instruments they desired. For instance, of the approximately 3,000 gas chromatographs (an analytical analyzer) installed in 1966, about 10 percent were on line. By 1970 probably 90 percent will be used in on-line control installed directly on the measured variable in the plant and reporting directly to, and controlled by, an on-line digital control system.

Demand for higher purity requires closer control of many processes. Rising plant investment costs make it necessary to eliminate overdesign and excess surge capacity, thus reinforcing the need for tighter control. As new processes are developed that require faster reaction time, they require physical equipment which borders on the limit of instability and which must be controlled more closely.

The main frame of the computer represents only a part of the total system cost. The larger part consists of the input/output gear, process instrumentation, programming, and systems engineering costs.

The trend to tighter control and reduced inventory expands the influence of control-engineering theory. As normal plant operation becomes less steady-state and more dynamic, not only must the control engineer learn more of the process dynamics, but the design engineer must learn more of the control dynamics. The goal is true integration of the plant and the control system. The trend is toward the type of plant that simply cannot be started up, continued, run, or shut down without automatic control.

The development of computer technology has broadened and deepened the concept of data and data analysis, revealing the previously unappreciated usefulness of masses of highly detailed data.

Users generally agree that measurement is the bottleneck in the development of control technology and that transducer engineering is a major activity. The trend to tighter control of faster, low-inventory processes brings about new demands for higher accuracy, reliable, fast, environment-engineered, and stable sensors. All industries demand sensors to measure product quality directly.

Fluid amplifiers, solid-state effects, lasers, ultrasonics, and magnetic resonance provide a basis for measuring sensors. In digital control the great need is for compatible sensors, i.e., sensors whose outputs are compatible with the language of the computer. Analog-to-digital conversion is difficult and expensive. The wedding of semiconductor phenomena and microelectronic circuitry produces an answer to the digital transducer and is beginning to solve the problem of lack of analytical instruments. This technique is even now being applied in medical electronics. Displays are recognized as a key factor in providing efficient man-to-machine communications. Displays are the major elements in closing the loop between man and machine as the human processes become increasingly tied into automatic systems. These displays include small cathode-ray tubes, plotters, and other graphic elements along with the familiar IBM typewriter.

CONTROL SYSTEMS

Some fundamental descriptions of control systems and their place in the management control hierarchy may help clarify where each level fits.

Digital process-control systems may be divided into two types: supervisory control systems and direct digital control (DDC) systems. In the first case, the digital computer is used to supervise and reset the control points of conventional analog controllers. In the second case the computer bypasses the analog controller, and its outputs are used to control the process directly. A DDC machine may perform some supervisory functions as well.

The ultimate value of the digital control system lies in the power of the computer to perform calculations and logical decisions which are far more complex than those possible with analog techniques. It is generally agreed that the efficiency of a given control loop can be improved by elaborating on its control function—by introducing gain changes, compensation for nonlinearities, adaptive tuning, time-varying factors, and inputs from elsewhere in the process. For a better idea of what constitutes a control loop, refer to Figs. 1.6 to 1.9. Gain changes and the compensation for nonlinearities allow the control model to represent the actual condition more accurately. By adding the time factor, the dynamics of a process or business can be improved in the model. Adaptive tuning of the coefficients of the control variables actually allows the coefficients themselves to change as the process or business environment changes. These changes can be better tracked and more closely controlled, whether we are concerned with an inventory status or flow of material achieved. An example of the application of the principle of adaptive control is given in the inventory control problem of Chap. 12.

It is well to remember that the hardware is only a tool of the program. It is the program which contains the real "why" and "wherefore" of any particular application. Nearly all the factors relating to digital-control hardware are influenced to some degree by the program. Speed, reliability, degree of control, and maintainability are influenced by the program.

Unlike programming for scientific, military, and business applications, there are few independent control software organizations. This is because the required analysis can be made only by those persons who are thoroughly familiar with the process. This is the user; and he often finds that without detailed process analysis and process simulation, the reactions and interloop disturbances cannot be determined or programmed. Likewise for all other elements of the business system, the man with the problem must define his problem. The trend toward specialized languages continues making it easier for the person who knows the process to program the hardware. An example is PROSPRO,* an interpretative system developed by Humble Oil Co. and announced by IBM as an available library program in September, 1967.

On the lowest level of the management control structure (see Fig. 2.1), the direct digital computer control system (DDC) can be used to perform the functions of conventional controllers by making the comparison of set point and process variable, computing the

* Too often computer control programs must be written by process engineers who have had little or no computer programming experience. PROSPRO is an interpretative language conceived and developed for use by process engineers, not computer programmers. It requires detailed understanding of the industrial process and its control characteristics but not of computer programming. This particular programming system incorporates six types of data-information forms. With a fill-in-the-blanks technique, the user describes the process and develops the control scheme. Through the use of the appropriate form the engineer identifies a process variable with its target, with a general action, or equation, and the control adjustment with pertinent reference lists or coefficients in the control equation. PROSPRO then generates the operational program. Both measured and calculated variables may be included in feedback and feedforward modes of operation.

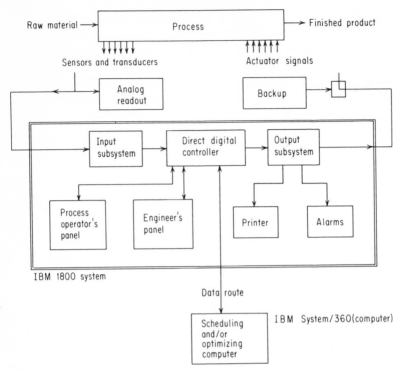

FIG. 2.1   Direct digital control.

proportional, reset, and rate corrections, and transmitting the result to the final control element. This is done on a time-shared* basis under program control; thus many loops can be handled rapidly.

A DDC program allows the use of control techniques not possible with conventional controllers, e.g., advanced ratio and cascade and feedforward control. Process loops with dominant lag times or transport delays, which provide severe problems for conventional controllers, can be handled easily and with greater stability. Logical and sequence control can be introduced to provide for automatic cut-in of auxiliary process units. Often, the DDC system can perform additional tasks such as report preparation and supervisory control.

* Time sharing means the use of the computer's calculating ability by several different programs essentially simultaneously. In, say, 1 second several different programs may be run concurrently with the computer working on one program for a few milliseconds then switching to another and so on, keeping track of the activity on each program automatically.

On the next level, we see the process supervisory control system, as in Fig. 2.2. Frequently, the most effective way to realize an increase in process efficiency is through a computer-directed supervisory control system, once information on process functions is evaluated. Signals from instruments are fed to the computer, which performs heat- and material-balance calculations to determine the state of the process. The computer then calculates adjustments to controlled variables and sends them out in the form of set-point signals to conventional controllers. This technique compensates for changes in raw materials and other uncontrolled variables, keeps the process stable, and produces the desired product at optimum rates.

Through communication adapters, the supervisory control system can be tied to higher- and lower-level computers, providing a link in an advanced MICS. Then, if this is a manufacturing operation, we can progress to a third level, as shown by Fig. 2.3.

The piecemeal approach to process control is no longer valid. It is now necessary to recognize that "control" embraces the whole

Integrated Plant Information and Control System

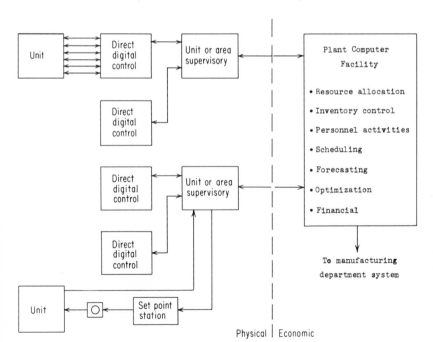

FIG. 2.2 A process supervisory control system.

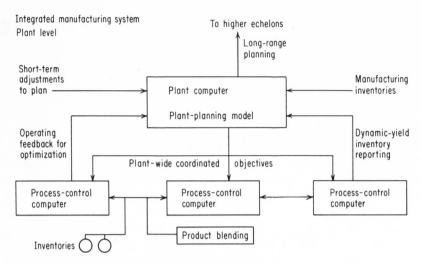

FIG. 2.3 An integrated manufacturing system.

operation of a business and must be planned accordingly. Thus, future planning dictates that the system designer start with business goals and work within economic boundaries to evolve a dynamically stable control system which embraces both business and operational control. We must produce a truly integrated system of control encompassing all levels of the management hierarchy.

CHAPTER THREE

Management Control Systems

*The philosophy of a real-time MICS envisions neither
centralization nor complete decentralization of data
processing but rather a balance of data processing between
home office and the plants themselves.
Management-oriented reporting serves the needs of
management at the manager's own level; e.g., the plant
manager and his staff are provided management-oriented
information to enable them to select the best control
operational strategy for the plant, encompassing
financial, operations, and maintenance activities. The
stored-program computer allows each level to have
information, not just data, that makes use of such
mathematical tools as statistics, simulation, and
linear programming.*

"Management control systems" is a popular phrase. Researchers in computer sciences, engineering, and management claim that MICS is a proper subject for their interest. Management reaction varies from wild enthusiasm to utter antipathy, often colored by a fear of managerial unemployment. The cost makes skeptics of the optimist, and the problems of building a useful system staggers the well-read scientist. But we cannot dismiss the MICS for another decade or so! The aims of some companies are to put every number in the company except the address on the letterheads in their data files, and recent advances in generalized information systems make even this possible. Some of the objectives of MICS are inventory savings, customer service improvement, stabilization of the size of clerical force, lower costs and higher profits, and the time and tools to examine prospective improvements. If only a few of these objectives can be met, that company's competitors had better keep their eye on the improving technology.

But what exactly is MICS?

SOME DEFINITIONS

We may define control as the functions and activities which are designed to compel events to conform to plans. It is thus the function whereby every manager, from the president to the foreman, makes sure that what is done will be that which is intended. For the scientist, control may be defined as "a system or device which exerts a restraining, governing, or directing influence." Control is a process. As such, control can take on many forms, and it means different things to the foreman on the assembly line, to the electronics engineer designing machine controls, and to the manager.

Our attention is directed to those systems which aid a manager in the decision process, particularly at the higher levels of business activity. Physical control systems for the industrial plant were discussed in the previous chapter.

By system we mean here that which controls more than one part when parts are related in some way to each other.

AN IMPLICIT DESCRIPTION

A MICS, in a physical sense, is hardware, computers, communications, physical files, the computer program, and input/output devices. We can examine the objective of a MICS and the criteria for measuring its performance. This environment, the input and output, describes the system. But we are more concerned with what the management control system will do.

TYPES OF CONTROL

Control may be divided into several categories related to the classes of resources available to the firm. It may help to classify some of these.

1. *Personnel-management Control.* Its function is to apply the firm's personnel resources in the best manner to meet the firm's objectives. The very fact that the controlled element is people makes this area subjective and difficult to control, particularly when the output is a product of men's minds rather than their hands.

2. *Financial Control.* Its function is to assure that money, as a

resource, is best applied to meet the firm's objectives. The control is dollar control; the firm's objective, the profit motive, is measured in terms of dollars. Financial control receives special emphasis since the contribution of all resources may be measured, in part at least, in terms of a money increment. But financial control is easier to exercise than other types of control because of the ease of measurement.

3. *Inventory Control.* Inventory represents a potential contribution to both the firm's profit and costs. The size, distribution, turnover rate, and other variables of inventory control are important. Advances in operations-analysis techniques and computer technology make inventory amenable to control and represent a significant extension of the control process.

4. *Production Control.* Control of the production process varies from an occasional "How are things going?" to a computer model of the entire production process, with constant comparisons between the predicted and actual performance. In the previous chapters, we have shown examples of plant control. Production control includes automated oil refineries, electrical generating and distribution systems, and automobile assembly lines. (PERT* is primarily a production control technique.) The firm's objectives are stated in terms of desired outputs and constraints, and the production control system attempts to match that output within the constraints. Production control includes quality control, since the output can be specified not only by amount but also by a range of acceptable quality.

5. *Technical Control.* A firm's technology is becoming an increasingly important resource. Control of technology is very difficult. It consists of both the written resources and the information which the scientific and technical personnel have for their use.

Most companies generally concentrate on financial control and are satisfied to have little or no explicit control over their other resources. Business history has shown that an initial amount of financial control quickly produces decided results in reducing the costs of running an organization. Progressive increases in the amount of financial control do not produce comparable increases in efficiency, and a point is soon reached beyond which further financial controls do not pay off.

---

* PERT (performance evaluation and research technique) developed by the Defense Department to measure and guide the production of the Polaris missile system. Extensions are CPM (critical-path methods), arrow-diagramming, etc., applied to the commercial world.

An increase in technical control has a somewhat similar effect. It will produce increasing results until some maximum is reached, beyond which creativity begins to be stymied.

Because of the ease and simplicity of financial control, and preoccupation with it, many management control systems are automated accounting systems. *This is not management control.*

Control may be classified also in terms of the techniques employed. These become:

1. *Continuous Control.* The output is continuously measured, and this information is fed back to the control elements. Most of the plant controls discussed earlier fall into this category. Real-time inventory control may be also classified as continuous.

2. *Sampled-data Control.* The output is measured at intervals, either periodic or random, and the information is used for control.

3. *Aggregative Control.* The output is measured and the results accumulated, and this aggregated information is fed back to the control elements. Most accounting systems provide aggregative control.

We may also classify control by the time-variable delays (positive, zero, or negative) in the feedback loop. These include:

1. *Delayed Control.* The information feedback is delayed in time from the output. This delay may either be stabilizing or destabilizing to the system. Accounting is delayed control.

2. *Real-time Control.* The measurement of output and comparison with the reference level (desired output) are made simultaneously. Control systems used in generating and distributing electric power and oil refineries or other continuous-process plants are usually real-time control systems.

3. *Predictive Control.* Because of the dynamic characteristics of the external environment, it is often desirable to compensate for internal delays by comparing the predicted output at some future time to the reference level. This type of control is perhaps most effective where the production process is well defined and takes a relatively long time. An example may be control at the plant level.

TYPES OF DECISION

The purpose of a MICS is to assist in the decision-making process. Thus it is important to recognize the spectrum of decision types. Decisions do not fall uniquely into a single class, but for ease of explanation it may be helpful to distinguish between two types, programmed and nonprogrammed, i.e., routine and nonroutine.

Programmed decisions may be described as those which are repetitive and routine. To an extent, a definite procedure has been worked out for handling them, so that they do not have to be treated as new decisions each time they occur. Obviously if a particular problem recurs often enough, a routine procedure will usually be worked out for solving it. An appropriate algorithm* will yield programmed decisions, and when people say that "computers make decisions," they usually mean programmed decisions. The models which operations analysts use to select inventory levels, staging levels, distribution patterns, production allocations, and so forth, are algorithms which yield programmed decisions. (The decision to override such a solution is a *nonprogrammed decision.*) When the factors affecting the decision can be quantified and the procedure for the decision made explicit, these decisions can be made by a computer.

Heuristic programming or artificial intelligence offers an approach to the problem of nonprogrammed decisions. In heuristic programming, the results of experience are used to modify the algorithms or program, and the computer can, in some sense, be said to "learn." The Defense Department has had some success in applying this approach to management decisions. Probably much more research needs to be done before it can be applied wholeheartedly to business decision making.

THE DECISION-MAKING PROCESS

A mathematician likes to consider a decision as a simple choice between courses of action; but business decisions cannot be accurately characterized by this simple choice. The environment must be searched for conditions calling for decisions. This is intelligence activity. Then possible courses of action must be invented, developed, and analyzed—the *design activity.* Finally, a particular course of action must be selected. This is the *choice activity.*

Choice activity may result in a terminal decision which is a selection of the course of action and terminates the sequential activity. For various reasons, the decision may be to continue to search the environment to obtain more information. Time delay and cost are associated with the latter alternative, which is often accompanied by a reluctance to make a decision, rather than a conscious wish to increase the accuracy of the decision by using additional time and accepting the cost of additional information. Obviously timing of decisions is important, and difficult to define. This consideration

---

* A mathematical method of computation usually stated as a set of arithmetic expressions.

alone precludes computer solution to a large class of decisions: the factors affecting timing are more subjective than the decision itself. Most of the decisions in business are programmed decisions and as such could conceivably be automated. However, the most important decisions are nonprogrammed, and most are not now amenable to automation. *Automation of programmed decisions can give the manager at all levels in the hierarchy the additional time he needs for more important nonprogrammed decisions and that important factor of communicating with the firm's staff.*

THE DECISION-MAKING ENVIRONMENT

The decision maker needs three types of information:

1. *Intelligence Information about the External Environment.* This includes knowledge of the competitors' activities, the general economy, government activity, and the like. Intelligence does not include "status information" of the organization. A business information system is not a business intelligence system.

2. *Status.* The knowledge of the firm's activities and the available resources—personnel, equipment, raw material, and financial plans and objectives.

3. *Policy Constraints.* The decision maker does not have complete freedom of choice but only a limited set of choices. These limitations are policy constraints.

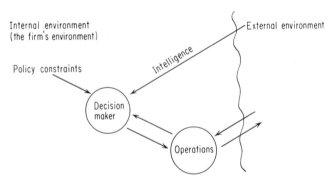

FIG. 3.1 The decision maker's environment.

Figure 3.1 illustrates the decision maker's environment and the information flow.

Decision takes the form of direction, which can be the result of control on this level or reference (desired) level for the next lower level of the hierarchy. Operations interact with external environment.

Control requires that a performance measurement (a measurement of output or results) be made and compared with some reference level. This requires planning in a specific sense before the decision can be classed as a control decision. When plans are vague and undefined, control becomes meaningless and nonexistent.

THE OBJECTIVE

Now, after these definitions, the objectives of a MICS can be stated. *The MICS should make those control decisions which can be programmed and provide the information (or data) to assist the manager in making nonprogrammed decisions.* Although this objective is stated simply, fulfilling it is a difficult task. Management scientists have little insight into the management process. Great strides have been made into evaluating various alternatives by such techniques as cost effectiveness, but many decisions are still made on the basis of feelings, impressions, and "other factors." Exactly what decision-making process managers use is still an open question. The selection of what information is important and the decision whether it should be presented are difficult tasks. A look at past decisions may give an apparent answer, but future decisions may require completely different information or presentation methods.

An objective is to the manager what a drawing of the finished building is to the architect. It is a visual concept of the change to be brought about. A real manager must be a planner—long and short range. There has to be an objective if there is to be a sense of attainment, a real value in the expenditure of effort.

Responsible people cannot be free of responsibility. There has to be an objective in order that the nature of the responsibility can be clear to all. The objective must be stated in such a manner that the degree of attainment may be measured.

For example, when output from a particular information system was not matched to the manager's needs, the system failed because the manager did not use the system. It is the manager's responsibility to make sure the system fits his needs.

FUNCTIONS OF A MANAGEMENT
CONTROL SYSTEM

Some basic functions are found, in varying degrees, in every management control system. We shall discuss some of these as a basis for better understanding of the next section.

In any control system there must be a model of the firm. This model may be so simple and unsophisticated that it is difficult to recognize as a "firm" model. It may emphasize only one phase of the firm's activities, e.g., the accounting of money as a resource. Alone it can be used in financial control, but it is only part of an integrated control system. A fully integrated control system is illustrated by that of Pittsburgh Steel Company.*

Models have both external and internal variables. One of the first problems is to choose which the variable should be. Current demand may clearly be an internal variable: it is the orders a firm is receiving for its products. Predicted demand may be internal to the management and control system, and hence obtainable as an output, or it may be treated as an external variable and be a required input. Generally, as the model becomes more sophisticated, fewer external variables will be required. Since a computer, as such, has "no feel" for the data, many managers prefer key variables to remain external or in some cases to review the computer's predicted values.

A management control system contains a management information system. The information necessary for making either programmed decisions or nonprogrammed decisions must be available to the management control system. A management information system does some communications and data processing, but the most important function is data storage and retrieval. Even to prepare reports there must be some form of storage and retrieval. An information system must be designed for all levels of management. Many times, it omits top management. The system must match the organization. More information is necessary than just dollars. The system must be capable of giving concise, pointed reports and not massive encyclopedias. Both internal and external operations must be covered. There are different information needs for the different levels of management; the output must be designed to support the particular organization by giving the right information to the right people. One of the latent benefits of any MICS is that these questions must be considered and specific answers are required for system design. Although many a MICS, if we consider only the hardware, does not satisfy all these requirements, they must be met by some source of information, or by guess and by golly.

The MICS must have sufficient flexibility and capability not only to produce reports but to retrieve specific information. Data storage and retrieval is one of the most difficult technical problems in designing a MICS. Advances in separating application programming

* A Steel Company's Date with a Data Machine, *Business Week*, May 4, 1963, pp. 142ff.

in the computer from a corporate data bank, i.e., independency of data and problem, offer solution to this problem.

The heart of any MICS is data processing. The comparison for control, summarization and selection of information, computation for models, and communication all require data processing. Most MICS formerly were sold on the basis of the data processing they would do, often only the accounting data processing. This is the simplest function to perform, and often the only one understood. (There is no question of the high state of development of hardware technology.)

Communication is an important function that is often taken for granted by everyone. It should not be. A large part of any firm's communication is written communication. Much of the communication in a firm is direct conversation and informal telephone calls. The traditional way of handling written communications often places a severe limitation on quick-reaction capability. Communication is one of the important functions of any large MICS. Information should flow from one part of the organization to another without extensive delay for routine processing and transmittal. The design of the MICS input/output should place emphasis on communication as a function. Delay, noise, or misrouting of information can seriously degrade the management effort. A MICS can reduce the misrouting problem, i.e., send the right information to the right people, and radically decrease delay time due to transmission. Communication as a function must be most carefully considered in system design.

PERFORMANCE MEASUREMENT

In order to control performance it is necessary to measure it. If a management control system is used, performance measurement becomes an even more difficult problem since these measurements must be numerable, rather than a subjective feeling. Experience in personnel management demonstrates how difficult this can be. With assembly lines the performance can be measured in number of items produced in a given time period. Service at the local utility is more difficult. Operations researchers have developed many quantitative performance measurements that can be used for control, and further research is extending this ability. Every manager should be acutely aware of exactly what performance measurement is being used—often a substitute is used which does not measure the fulfillment of a firm's goal.

Even when some performance measurement can be prescribed,

like measuring the rate of return on investment for managers, emphasis may be placed on the factors which directly affect the measure, sometimes to the detriment of other objectives which are equally important but less amenable to measurement. Suboptimization is an ever-present danger. For example, we may optimize sales travel expense and even reduce it to zero, but we affect sales, which is the firm's objective.

THE LANGUAGE BARRIER

Although much effort has gone into enabling men to communicate with computers, man-machine communication still is a serious problem. Computers, at best, can speak only faltering English. But there are solutions. The new programming language PL/1,* introduced with IBM's System/360 line, offered hope of a common language. Machines and people now speak COBOL and FORTRAN.† PL/1 replaces both of these. The concept of a vector or a matrix is quite broad and business in the future will probably talk about the "cash accounts vector" or the "customer accounts matrix." Selecting delinquent accounts for a department store may be translated into "all customer vectors with a negative component."

The language barrier and handling natural language with a computer have been the greatest technical barriers to rapid advances in MICS. Advances in language translation, data-retrieval techniques, indexing, and programming are all making rapid strides toward better solutions.

MANAGEMENT CONSIDERATIONS

By documenting individual applications one may proceed to interrelate the controlling functions into MICS just as a building is constructed of blocks. The path along which the integration of the individual applications into the whole should take place must be decided. In most cases this decision will be based on economics and policy.

In a large system each organizational level will interpret policies and regulations differently. Hence, in an integrated system, strong management control is essential. Management must have sufficient

---

* See *Science*, vol. 148 (June 4, 1965), pp. 1270ff., for a description of PL/1 programs.

† COBOL (common business-oriented language) for accounting applications and FORTRAN (formula translation) for engineering and scientific applications.

insight into local differences to intelligently compromise them and still allow for those unreconcilables which will always exist. Serious consideration must be given to handling regulatory changes, especially when they emanate from two or more independent organizational elements whose data-processing functions have been interrelated.

A basic question of whether to aim at "total" integration or concentrate on an interim solution must be considered. What are the company aims? The long-range concept furnishes a logical goal. An overall framework within which to move in the interim is essential. The incremental approach makes it possible to achieve early benefit, to gain immediate experience, and to pave the way toward the ultimate goal, which may change with experience and requirements. If one works only at the long-range "total" integration concept, one's efforts are likely to be somewhat theoretical. If, on the other hand, one concentrates solely on the short-range interim improvements, one probably will not come close to the level of integration and profit represented by the long-range approach.

In talking about management information and control systems, it becomes very easy to generalize the concepts to such an extent that although everyone may be inclined to favor such systems, none will have a precise understanding of what is meant by the terminology. We have seen, for example, such terms as total-systems approach, integrated-systems approach, management operating systems, etc. In order to minimize ambiguity, we shall concern ourselves in future discussions with what is a reasonably specific MICS and in particular with discussing the problems in planning and implementing such a system. The treatment of the dynamic behavior of management as a feedback control system with the mathematical functions of planning, staffing, organizing, directing, and controlling an organization is further defined and amplified in Chapter 9.

CHAPTER FOUR

Managers and Management Information Systems

Company success depends on the interactions between flows of information, orders, materials, money, personnel, and capital equipment. The way these six flow systems interlock to amplify one another and to cause change and fluctuations forms a basis for anticipating the effects of decisions, policies, organizational forms, and investment choice.

Science is emerging with the power and scope to deal with today's practical management problems. Science is developing more rapidly than it is accepted by managers. Science becomes a basis for further development of the art of management.

The result is that the task of the manager is becoming more challenging and his training more rigorous. When the new tools and techniques of management science are used correctly, they become new competitive advantages toward business success.

In the classical concept, management is declared to be "an act that is performed by man, and that involves the functions of planning, organizing, directing, and controlling." The functions have been debated, but there has never been any question that managing is an act that is performed by men.

The characteristics of management have changed fundamentally regarding man's role. Advanced formalized systems have helped alter man's role. Consider the following illustrations:

1. The "manager" of a large warehouse may have nothing to say

about the selection or placement of items to be stored in, or filled from, his inventory.

2. The plant "manager" may have no control over scheduling his workload or his machine load.

3. The "manager" of purchasing may have nothing to say about inventory levels, economical order quantity, or replenishment timing.

4. The sales "manager" may have nothing to say about shipping schedules or pricing.

5. The credit "manager" may have no control or approval authority over a large portion of the acceptable orders.

Integrated data systems have made these things so. Automatic order entry systems provide for an automatic series of interrelated activities to be performed the instant an order is received by the company. From that point on, all succeeding events are formalized and programmed.

The union of man, methods, and machines into an integrated program for accomplishing those things which it has been determined must be done produces a formalized system for operations. That system is in a very real sense management. The system exists as a thing apart from people and is the means by which the operations accomplish the requirements in a consistent and orderly manner. Systems manage or are capable of managing many aspects of the business operations.

Many of the benefits of advanced systems will be blocked until the role of decision making of management is better understood. As an operating MICS is defined more precisely, the role of the manager will be to select that system which will yield the greatest assurance of achieving the defined objectives.

ELEMENTS OF THE BUSINESS SYSTEM

Management information systems are only a part of the total business and operational system. Others are decision, environment, and process. *Decision* is making a selection from two or more controversial possibilities. Since the possibilities are controversial, logic alone cannot be used, and a decision is an intuitive thing. There are also many specal decisions made within a business organization, because the event is so rare that it is uneconomical to procedurize the function. Man is still the most versatile mechanism available for such a variety of jobs. In addition, men make those real-time decisions for all other business operations that are not covered by management systems.

Decisions are made to create, implement, and perfect systems that will manage the operations better. Decisions are made about the opportunities for doing new things, or to assess and weigh the relative desirability of available alternate courses of action. Since the area of decision is so intimately related to the management information system, a suitable interface must be developed with this exclusive domain of man.

Environment, as it affects the management information system, can be considered in two parts—that which is legal and that which is demographic or competitive. The most obvious legal involvement is in the area of contracts, ranging from those with customers and vendors to those with societies (trade unions, etc.) and investors. Innumerable statutes and precedents impinge upon any particular management information system, and many government agencies issue orders, directives, or guidelines with which any business must deal.

In the demographic and competitive environment, gross national product and its correlation with national markets, share of the market, preference statistics, and population trends are appropriate areas to be considered. The competitor's modus operandi is to be taken into account, along with sensitive indexes to sense demand. These and other items are environmental factors.

Process is the related system of production and, for most companies of any size, is a system primarily of logic rather than art. In some areas, such as chemical production, the entire production process has been reduced to a system. The gross steps have been from process definition, to process monitoring, to process control, where the process algorithms have been mechanically modeled either digitally or by analog. The interface between the process and management information systems is in the area of resource allocation, asset and cost control, and the sales and financial functions of order processing.

DYNAMIC FUNCTION

Management information systems serve a dynamic function within the business enterprise, which is itself a dynamic institution. Unfortunately, preoccupation with carving an enterprise up into functional areas for inspection and analysis has tended to obscure the whole point of its complete and dynamic structure. Men have analyzed and reported on the business enterprise much as the blind men "saw" the elephant.

The interests to be dealt with by management information systems embrace areas ranging from the abstract (philosophy, a function of decision) to the concrete (areas of performance or process involving technology and logic). Systems input is rigid and structured, but the output is limited only by the ingenuity of the system designers. The input to a management information system must be logical and structured data since the management information system is a system of logic; i.e., each input must be discretely defined, and subject to AND, OR, and NOT relationships.*

The statement of objectives as usually given is too abstract for inclusion in an information system. Objectives must be reduced to simple Boolean † relationships by statements of prognostication and statements of policy. The ideas are then in such a form that they can logically be stored, manipulated, and retrieved. The dynamic process of the MICS is continuous, with action the result of decision, and objectives or other parameters sometimes being altered as a result of action or environment. The cycle starts with the board of directors or principals who arbitrarily establish some objective for the enterprise. These objectives are reduced to logical statements of policy, statements of plans, and budgets that can be manipulated by machine processes. Predictions are a matter of judgment and decision, derived by intuition or probabilistic algorithms once the management information model has been established. Even though management-science techniques are used to make a projection, the results must still be evaluated by intuition and a decision made as to its reasonableness and utility.

ORGANIZATION AND PROCEDURES

Having decided upon the kind and amount of business anticipated, the next step becomes the job of establishing the organization and policy by which to accomplish the stated ends. The policies are arbitrary but are designed to accomplish the objectives and to serve as a base upon which to build the procedures, i.e., a particular course of action. Use of the word policy here means only authority,

---

* An *and* in mathematics means that a resultant action appears only when several variables are present as inputs or stimuli. All the variables must be present for action to result. An *or* relationship means any one variable of the set if present results in an action. *Not* relationships are similar to the negative of *and*.

† Boolean algebra is an algebraic discipline analogous to the ordinary algebra with which we are familiar but which follows different rules. Boolean algebra was originally developed as the symbolic interpretation of some forms of logical reasoning and as a method for describing the relationship between mathematical classes and sets. It develops "yes-no" logic. (George Boole 1815–1864.)

responsibility, and criteria. Once policy has been reduced to a series of logical statements, i.e., a determinate method prescribed for performing the operation, and made a part of the management information system, the input supplied by the area of decision and judgment is almost completed.

After objectives and overall policies are established, a set of procedures must be developed. Presumably all business enterprises function within the intent of the statutory constraints placed upon them. Therefore, any procedures developed will take cognizance of this legal impingement. A business procedure is a rule, i.e., a prescribed guide, systematic method or practice, or a series of rules, for the collection, storage, manipulation, and retrieval of data and any associated physical function. Thus it is a series of logical, conditional statements which can be manipulated by man or machine.

The analysis of the dynamics of the information flow starts with the decision system, establishing a satisfactory interface through logic. The analysis continues with the management information system and then interfaces with the process system (see Fig. 1.2A).

This interface produces the final item of input into the business intelligence system, the history of events and transactions. A well-designed system accepts into corporate memory explicit and logical statements of plans, rules, legal constraints, and the record of transactions. Since all these statements are logical and structured, the system is capable of manipulating and retrieving the data or extracting the essence of information.

Information is confined to data that can be used, and aside from the necessity of fulfilling requirements of law or curiosity, is the only valuable part of the data. Information has two parts: one is the definition of the problem, from which values are established; the other part is the data appropriate to the problem. The latter part of the data creates the costs, such as collecting, assessing, storing, and reporting. Both parts must be present in order to generate information. Study of data systems will disclose that very little information is retrieved and that some systems were designed for the scorekeepers and not for the players.

The first output from the management information system is the consideration of internal control and validation of prior transactions. There is no value to erroneous data, and their proliferation in the data bank tends to render the system useless. The data bank should be purged of useless data periodically and systematically.

Errors fall generally into three classes: (1) errors of logic, which are mathematical in nature and rather easy to detect; (2) errors of probability, or trend, which are statistical in nature and require an analysis of prior transactions to determine that incoming data are not deviating too greatly from the prevailing records; and (3) errors representing a philosophic breach or violation of corporate parameters, which are the most difficult to define and isolate by system. Just to test transactions for authority according to the company policy definition is no small task, and this is only the beginning. All data must be tested by all applicable criteria to see that the philosophy of the company has not been violated.

MANAGEMENT DATA OUTPUT

By manipulation of the rules established by policy statements and procedures, by the transaction history, and by time, the system can generate a variety of action notices. Indicated actions develop for one of two reasons; some are a function of time, and some are a function of previous activity. Such things as employee review notices or payment of taxes are a function of time, while reorder points for inventory, or creation of a debit memo to a vendor, are a function of activity. All are initiated and carried out by virtue of company policy, procedure, statute, and time, or a combination of several such factors. These outputs will trigger a servo effect at the performance level and act as correction stimuli to operating personnel much as a thermostat starts corrective temperature action. In some cases the system itself can take appropriate action, while in other circumstances a decision must be made by an individual.

A characteristic of data is that some are static and some are dynamic. *Static data* are like taking a picture at a point in time. *Dynamic data* are developed in conjunction with a continuum of time. Accountants have attempted to deal with these two aspects in the balance sheet (static data) as compared to the profit and loss statement (which is a dynamic of sorts). Accounting systems fall far short of the requirements for a management information system. In the first place, accounting has a preoccupation with dollars. Not all—not even most—management information is expressed in dollars. It has to be quantified, but not in terms of money. The stuff management information is made of may be in pieces, tons, hours, or any other unit of measure which will describe the process activity. For instance, labor transaction data not expressed in dollars include labor realization, departmental loading, machine loading, scrap analysis, etc., all of which are items of management information.

The second shortcoming of accounting systems, as management information systems, is that accounting transaction data are given only two considerations, debt and credit. There may be subsidiary ledgers where greater detail is kept, but in only a few cases are the data considered in more than two basic associations. Important as accounting is in balancing, controlling, and reporting such statistics, it has contributed little information germane to the operation of a business.

This brings us to the next level of output in the form of operating results, i.e., the current period in contrast to the past period above. These reports are reasonably detailed and to be useful must be associated with the forecasts. This is true of formal or informal, manual or automatic systems. In poorly designed systems the greatest amount of money is wasted on operating reports because of the outpouring of volumes of paper containing data with low information content and with no associated goal such as a budget. If the transaction data are not compared to forecasts and other parameters, the system will not produce information but merely data. In order to compensate for inadequate planning and forecasting, a manager is required to construct parameters intuitively each time he pores through a massive pile of data in order to draw judgments about the condition of affairs.

The data of the future are forecasts, plans, and goals. These can be just guesses, or they can be developed systematically by management-science techniques from demographic data and corporate intelligence, i.e., the ability to comprehend the interrelationships of the presented facts in such a way as to provide action toward the desired goals. The predictable factors that effect the company's growth and prosperity can usually be isolated and studied by present-day mathematical tools.

The relative nature of the "success factors" of the industry can be identified in order to project more accurately. More effective use can be made of economics, decision rules, probability theory, and statistical analysis. The last formal system effort is to develop logic to provide the most useful information possible by management-science techniques to assist management with decisions. The development of models, regression analysis, linear programming, and a host of other existing techniques have provided a valuable set of tools for management information systems.

The statistical and competitive data alone remain to be considered. Management is provided with management-science projections and other information based upon past actions and with a picture of the customers' and competitors' attitudes and operations, which is the environment interface. Management must then decide whether the previous course established is still desirable or should be altered. The management information system's cycle is a continuous action of stimuli upon the business and reaction by modification and change of the system's criteria.

Modern-day businesses are dynamic, or active. Thus, in the analysis and manipulation of the data, an added dimension, time, must be included. New tools have been given us to aid in the analysis. One of these is *industrial dynamics,* a way of studying the behavior of industrial systems to show how policies, decisions, structure, and delays are interrelated to influence growth and stability. It integrates the separate functional areas of management—marketing, investment, research, personnel, production, and accounting. Each of these functions is reduced to a common basis by recognizing that any economic or corporate activity consists of flows of money, orders, material, personnel, and capital equipment. These five flows are integrated by an information network. Industrial dynamics recognizes the critical importance of this information network in giving the system its own dynamic characteristics.

Most managers and professional men are accustomed to dealing with a structured world. They have the responsibility for making things happen, for getting things done, and for keeping problems from becoming explosive and threatening to their organization, their work group, and themselves.

PROCESS CONTROL

In the early sections, we discussed management hierarchy levels, the organizational elements in the company, decision making, and guiding policy. Then we discussed information systems and their relation to management control. Let us regress now to the lowest level of control, process control, and look at it as an information system.

There is a fundamental difference in the continuous-process industries, such as petroleum and chemical, between control of business or commercial operations and control of physical operations. The former is subject to economic and policy considerations, while the latter is subject to unchangeable natural laws. Physical operations involved in the manufacture of products are generally referred to as processes, hence the term *process control.*

There is no clear-cut line separating business control from process control, but a line can be drawn through the hierarchy of control and decision-making levels in a typical process company which will approximate the interface between the two types of control (see Fig. 4.1).

Above the line drawn through the plant box, it is common practice to arbitrarily arrange the operations of manipulating data to fit a machine or computer. Consider, for example, the accounts payable operation of a typical petroleum company. The means by which data are manipulated is irrelevant as long as it meets accounting objectives and is economical. A complete rearrangement of the procedure is permissible because the final product, the vendor's check, does not react to the precedence. In a general sense, the money disbursed is in no way influenced by the manner in which the check is presented.

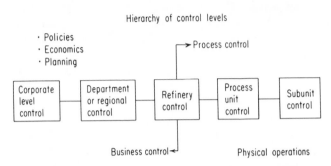

FIG. 4.1   Hierarchy of control levels in a typical process company.

This is not so in the control on continuous processes. Process control, which is subordinated to the primary economic and policy objectives of a company, is nevertheless determined by reactions, separations, conversions, all dictated by nature's unchanging physical laws. In the past, process control was performed with individually instrumented control loops, usually employing pneumatic transmission and actuation. It was the practice to automate only the regulation of the process, and instrument engineers designed controllers to regulate pressure, temperature, flow, and level to the dictates of the process designer. Someone else was concerned with relating the unit process to overall economic objectives. Thus, all control systems were, in fact, only regulatory in nature and were composed of independent loops normally designed for steady-state conditions without consideration of interactions with other process variables or process unit.

In just a few years, a continuing evolution in process control has taken place—from single, individually mounted controllers to large central control systems using pneumatic and then electronic transmission devices. In the 1950s, data loggers, which came into being under the forced stimulus of the atomic-energy and aircraft industries, were superimposed upon some industrial processes. These quickly fell into disrepute. A massive flood of data, without the hardware and management-science tools to convert them into intelligence, was economically useless.

Since 1958 considerable attention has been devoted to the place of the computer in the scheme of process control. In spite of difficulties, automation of process units gained momentum, and computer control became a logical extension of the conventional control principles. By the end of 1965, about 1,000 systems were on order or installed in the area of process control. The number in the petroleum and chemical industries alone exceeded 250 at that time. A large process user was the power industry, with primary metals and mining a not too distant second. Every major chemical and petroleum company either had or was planning installations of digital computers for process-control purposes. This is a logical trend, for the chemical and petroleum users have been pioneers in process-instrumentation developments, including their early acceptance and use of electronic controlling instrument devices. Several prognosticators estimate that there will be over 1,000 process computers in these two industries (petroleum and industrial chemicals) by 1970. Individual processes under control now include ethylene, hydrocarbon oxidation, ammonia, synthetic rubber, polymerization, acid plants, distillation, catalytic cracking, catalytic reforming, gasoline blending, tank terminal systems, isomerization, alkylation, and others.

We would be remiss in not mentioning again a significant development in application of computers to process units. This development is direct digital control (DDC), the time sharing of a single digital control device for many control loops. The significance is not that it replaces conventional types of equipment, but rather that it has permitted the control designer to solve the problems of dynamic control without an economic penalty. A DDC system makes it possible to use advanced control algorithms in a practical manner. Such techniques as nonlinear, feedforward, and adaptive control, plus entirely new control laws, can be developed and successfully applied to the process. An important consideration is the fact that a DDC system uses a small digital computer which makes it genuinely compatible for communications with supervisory and operations control computer systems. In fact, DDC opened a new era of process control for the process engineer, the control systems engineer-designer, and the management systems engineer.

SUMMARY

Many decisions formerly made by man have been formalized and programmed into automated decisions for action by the computer system.

As automated management control systems develop, we see that the management information system serves a dynamic function within the business enterprise, which itself is a dynamic institution. Unfortunately the complete and dynamic structure of the concern has tended to be obscured by our preoccupation with dividing the enterprise into functional areas for inspection and analysis. Inputs to a management information system must be logical and structural data and each input must be discretely defined. Objectives must be stated in such a form that they can logically be stored, manipulated, and retrieved. The dynamic process of the MICS is a continuous process with action the result of decision. Action sometimes results in objectives being altered. The manager must evaluate the results of the information system projection for reasonableness and utility.

Organization and policy must be established to accomplish the stated ends. Procedures then must be devised marking the way or method of proceeding toward the stated ends.

Analysis of the data bank is the interface to the information system. This interface produces the definition of the problem, from which values are established, and generates data appropriate to the problem. This data generation creates the cost of the information system such as collecting, assessing, storing, and reporting.

Outputs from the management information system are for internal control and validation of prior transactions, current operating results, and future forecasts, plans, and goals.

There is no clear-cut line separating the levels of control in the management hierarchy. Business control cannot usually be separated from process control, but an interface can be approximated. Process control is determined by reactions, separations, conversions, all dictated by natures' unchanging physical laws. In contrast the means by which data are manipulated in business control are irrelevant as long as they meet the objectives and are subjected to economic and policy considerations.

The ability for us to make programmable decisions is moving up the hierarchy of management. The growth of DDC, the control of process units, and new plants indicate the changing characteristics of management in the lower levels of control. Analysis of the business system and the physical systems indicates that the application of the tools and concepts used in the latter may be applied in the former.

PART TWO

The "How"

CHAPTER FIVE

Basic Definitions
and Stages of
System Design

In the first section of this book the reader was introduced to the basic philosophy of a MICS. Control theory, decision models, computers, feedback; all these terms and many others were discussed as being important elements of a MICS. Many of the current trends in computer technology and their future implications were discussed. The need for management participation in the somewhat alien world of computers was stressed. At this point the manager may be somewhat confused about how this material relates. He may further be curious about just what a MICS looks like.

In this section many of the ideas touched on in the first section will be tied together and the manager provided with a set of guidelines that will enable him to become an active participant in the world of computers. The method used is not intended to make a computer expert of the manager, for that is not his responsibility. Rather, the manager will be provided with a set of guidelines that he can use to analyze his own requirements, as far as computers are concerned, and communicate these needs to the computer specialist. We are trying to bridge the communications gap that exists between the manager's world and the world of computer technology.

Regarding the question raised earlier about "what a MICS looks like," we shall stress that there is no set description of such a system. Each system that the authors have examined has been different in size, complexity, scope, etc. Even though this is true, and no prototype exists, we have identified a set of common characteristics that most management systems contain. It is this set of characteristics that will aid the manager to identify his requirements. This then will lay a foundation upon which a system can be designed. Further the manager, by understanding certain basic principles, will be able to effectively participate in the design of "his" system, at the stages where his participation is imperative to successful implementation. This point cannot be overemphasized. Every successful MICS that we have examined had one overriding trait. The management group that was responsible for implementation and use of the system participated in the design and implementation. Conversely, most systems that failed to meet system objectives failed primarily because management did not participate. This point has been brought out time and again by independent surveys of computer installations.

In this section the close correlation between basic control theory and management control will be described. The basic principles of system design will be discussed from the manager's viewpoint. The use of decision models and their relation to the management process will be stressed. And finally all these tools and methods will be presented in the form of a set of basic principles that the manager can use as a participant in the design of an MICS. For, in the final analysis, this is the intent of this book: to help managers and executives become active participants and guiding forces in the design of management information and control systems.

BASIC DEFINITION—MANAGEMENT
INFORMATION AND CONTROL SYSTEMS

Before proceeding into a discussion of management's part in the design of management information and control systems, it would be wise to define the characteristics of such a *system*. Such a definition is necessary because there are many descriptions, and no standard definition exists. To illustrate, let us review briefly some of the descriptions of management information systems.

At one end of the spectrum we have the concept of the total system. This approach has been undertaken by many companies with varying degrees of success. Basically, this concept implies that all information, data, and related computer processing are handled by a *single all-encompassing system*. This implies that all data in the corporation and all reports required anywhere in the corporation, by any user, are generated by the *system*. This approach obviously represents the ultimate goal in data processing. Most companies active in data processing head toward this goal.

At the other end of the spectrum, we have a large number of rather routine off-line batch-processing applications that are performed; these also are called *management information systems.* Such applications as payroll, accounts receivable, purchasing, budget forecasting, etc., have all been designated at one time or another as management information systems.

Between the two ends of the spectrum, we have seen *systems* of all sizes and shapes develop. It should be pointed out that a large percentage of the work done has been quite significant and contributed greatly to the current state of the art.

For our own purposes, so that we are building on a common base, let us define a MICS conceptually with the following characteristics:

1. A computer-based system.

2. A system that interfaces directly with management and provides management with the information required to operate the facility the manager controls.

3. A system that incorporates the manager's needs into the system in the form of budget, target, limits, goals, etc.

4. A system that the manager can communicate with to obtain information as required.

5. A system that as a minimum provides the current status of the facility the manager controls, in a realistic time frame.

6. A system that maintains the historical results of the facility.

7. A system that can project, even if in simple terms, the future behavior of the facility.

8. A system that operates in a decision-making environment and not merely in a reporting environment.

9. A system that provides the manager with "control" information.

The above characteristics are very broad and at first glance may seem to include every computer system built. In our opinion this is not so. For example, most accounting systems, by themselves, do not meet these characteristics. Nor do most management-science applications fit, since these are for the most part discrete solutions to discrete problems. As we proceed, systems that do fit these characteristics will be mentioned. Further the reader should be able to visualize where systems with these characteristics apply.

REVIEW OF BASIC METHODS AND CONCEPTS

In the opening chapters we covered many of the basic concepts that apply to the use of computers by management. Of these many concepts, there are several on which we wish to concentrate from the standpoint of designing a MICS. The major elements with which we are concerned are:

- Control theory and feedback (information)
- Decision models
- Information systems
- Management control principles

Later in this section we shall weave these concepts into a single cohesive approach that will enable the manager to participate in the design of systems that involve management control. We deal only with those factors that concern the manager since other texts deal adequately with the pure computer aspects of system design.

Even though the final implementation and detailed design of a computer system must be carried out by highly trained specialists, the manager must play an important role in all design phases. In fact, in the past this has been one of the more conspicuous weaknesses in system design, in that too often management has delegated the entire project to personnel who did not have a clear picture of management objectives. If the type of system toward which we are pointing is to be successful, management must play more than a passive role in system development. To do this, management must have a clear concept of what it wants to do and how to go about doing it. It must participate in each phase of design. Let us look at the stages of designing a system.

STAGES OF SYSTEM DESIGN

Any information system, regardless of size or complexity, must go through several stages of development. The manager should know and understand what these stages are and what his role must be at each stage. Basically there are five major stages as follows:

1. Problem recognition
2. Problem definition
3. System design
4. System implementation
5. System modification

Although it is difficult to identify in quantitative terms the manager's participation at each of these stages, we can identify in qualitative terms his degree of participation. This is depicted in the chart in Fig. 5.1.

From our involvement and experience in the past, the following conclusions are drawn.

1. *Problem recognition* is the prime responsibility of the manager. The problem is his and he should be able to recognize it. In some cases, because of exposure to similar situations, the computer expert may be able to point out a problem area. However, in general, it is the manager who must identify the problem.

2. *Problem definition* is also the prime responsibility of the manager. It is usually desirable for the manager to call in a computer specialist at this stage to help with the definition. It is now that we begin to think of a management problem area in terms of a computer solution. This usually will be a team effort, but with the manager taking the lead in problem definition.

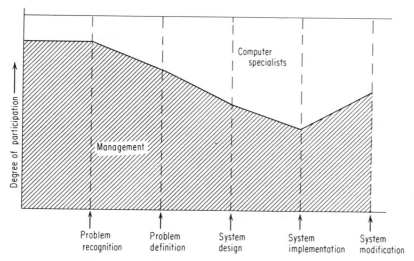

FIG. 5.1   Management participation.

3. *System design* is where the computer expert takes over the majority of the effort since most of the work in this phase tends to be computer-oriented. But the manager cannot abdicate his responsibility. He must be available for consultation during design, and he must "sign off" on the final system design.

4. *System implementation,* which includes programming, testing, and conversion, is almost totally a computer expert's job. The manager may wish to have a general understanding of what is being done, but in most cases he will not be concerned with this detailed phase.

5. *System modification* is a stage that always occurs and seems to surprise many managers. The general feeling seems to be that once a system is designed and implemented, "Why does it need to be changed?" The reason is quite simple. First, a system has probably never been designed that performed exactly as it was intended. It is always necessary, even after a system is in and operating, to tune it up. Second, and more important, once a manager uses a system and learns its operation, he wants to make improvements. Third, a

system may have to be modified because the manager's needs change with time. Regardless of the reason, the manager should understand and accept the fact that his system will change with time and require modification. This point should not be looked upon negatively but as a positive factor, since it is at this stage that the manager can really make the system meet his true needs.

Now we shall analyze some of the basic activities that must take place in each of these phases as far as the manager is concerned.

PROBLEM RECOGNITION

This phase of system design is perhaps so obvious that one might wonder why it is included as a part of the design phase. The reasons are many.

Too often management, when initiating a management system, charters the design team to recognize and state the problem that will be solved with the system, when in fact the managers themselves are the only ones who can truly define the problem area. Problem recognition has been a major consideration for system designers, and it simply is not feasible to leave problem recognition to the specialist when talking of true management systems, such as we are describing. These are systems "of" and "by" the manager.

An important reason for stressing this point is that many management problems are difficult to recognize. This may be caused by either an unawareness of a problem area or by misdirection of attention. It has been stated many times that in general 10 to 20 percent of a series of events account for 90 percent of the results. A handful of customers will normally produce the bulk of the orders; a handful of products, out of hundreds in the product line, produce the bulk of the volume, etc. This principle seems to apply to sales effort, inventory, research, etc. A small percentage of the items always accounts for a large percentage of the results. Hence, if management can control the problems in the selected number of events, it will normally be controlling the bulk of its company's operations in approximately 20 percent of the time allotment. We encountered a classical example of this in a major application area: that of plant maintenance. In discussions with many plant managers, most of whom were spending up to 50 percent of their expense budgets for maintenance, we found that they generally were unaware of the efficiency of their labor force. Plant managers assumed it was about 60 or 70 percent. But when this area was pointed out as a source of trouble, labor effectiveness was measured, and it was found that the labor force was working at an average level of 40 percent efficiency.

Another difficulty in problem recognition is solution of the wrong problem. There is nothing quite so useless as doing with great efficiency what should not be done at all. We hope to help the manager avoid this problem by focusing on the real problem, namely, the management control problem. Criteria for doing this will be covered shortly.

The major point is that management, with perhaps assistance from systems personnel, must properly recognize the problem area. In the context of this text this means that the manager must identify the resources he is trying to manage. Those resources associated with his problem must be isolated. This statement regarding resources is important in that most problems of the type with which we are dealing involve the control of some physical resource. By making this statement we are, of course, eliminating many categories of management problems, such as organization, industrial relations, personnel, salary administration, etc.

PROBLEM DEFINITION

Once management has recognized a problem or class of problems that lend themselves to the type of solution under discussion, the next stage is problem definition. Here again the manager must be an active participant. He cannot or should not shirk this responsibility. This is not to say that he cannot call on specialists, such as mathematicians, operations research people, etc., to aid him. In fact, this is highly desirable, since most managers will not be familiar with many of the methods used to define a problem in the computer sense. However, the manager must be the final judge of the problem definition, since it is his responsibility to make final decisions. One point should be stressed here (and this was mentioned before): we must not be solving the wrong problem. This mistake is often made.

From the manager's point of view, there are several factors to consider in this phase. Among these are:

Problem statement
Management objectives
Control elements
Alternate solutions

We shall now discuss each of these in turn.

Problem Statement. "A well-stated problem is half solved." The problem statement must be management's responsibility. Further, this statement must have meaning and direction. To illustrate the importance of this point, let us look at two examples or problem statements.

CASE I: A marketing manager is making only 75 percent of his sales quota. His problem is to make 100 percent of sales quota. His statement of the problem: "We have to raise sales, and our sales force needs better training."

CASE II: A plant manager is having trouble reaching full production. His company needs to have this plant at full capacity. His statement of the problem: "We need to design a system that will monitor plant performance, by unit, every 24 hours and then develop figures that will tell the performance of each unit, on a daily and month-to-date basis, compared to the specified target for each unit."

Although these examples are oversimplified, they illustrate the need for a good problem statement from management. In Case I, the real problem is ill-defined; the Case II problem statement has meaning and direction.

The problem statement as a minimum should include:

1. Type, quality, location, frequency, and reliability of source data.

2. Type, frequency, and content of reports required.

3. Who the users of the system will be and the categories of decisions made by these people.

4. A definition of the facility in which the system will be functioning, i.e., a refinery, an oil field, a paper mill, a marketing area, etc. This definition should identify the bounds of the facility.

5. A description of the external environment in which the system will function, together with an analysis of whether the external environment will affect the system. For example, if we were dealing with the design of a marketing system, the consumer and the competitive environment would both tend to affect the system.

Management Objectives. Referring back to the characteristics defining a MICS, we see a strong interplay implied between the manager and the system. For this interplay to be effective it becomes obvious that the basic objectives of management as they pertain to the system must be defined. Putting these objectives down on a piece of paper in order for a systems analyst to consider them is not an easy task. In fact it is probably the most difficult aspect of the problem definition.

This description is really a description of how the manager views his job. And in many cases, until a manager has come in contact with the specifications required for a computer system he probably has never had to be so definitive. It is important that the manager attempt to define his objectives because they have a tremendous impact on system implementation. Without management objectives the analyst must guess, an undesirable alternative. The manager should also understand that this description is not one that can be provided in a short interview (say 1 hour) with the systems man. It may take several months (of several interviews) to develop a meaningful set of objectives to guide the design of the computer system.

Among many objectives these might include such points as:

1. The desire and degree of budgetary control
2. The need to know current operation status
3. The need to know when targets are not being met
4. The need to know competitive behavior.

Control Elements. Later we shall be discussing techniques for identifying the management control elements. For now, though, let us say that the manager must be aware of the areas or variables which he can and must control. This identification of control elements is an important part of the basic problem statement in that it focuses attention on the areas of main concern.

Here too, it is often difficult to define control elements, and we are stressing control, because management usually has not formally tried to identify itself with these elements.

Alternate Solutions. Alternate solutions are perhaps the most difficult phase of problem definition. The manager must basically attempt to identify how he reaches his decisions. He must try to assign a relative value to alternate decisions. Alternate solutions is a area in later stages of system design where decision models will begin to be used. However, before any such model can be built and incorporated into a MICS, the manager must think in terms of his decision process and decide what types of decisions the system might help him with.

SYSTEM DESIGN

Once the problem area has been recognized, and the manager has developed a realistic *problem definition,* the actual *systems design* phase begins. It is performed primarily by computer experts, with the manager functioning as an advisor as questions arise. At the completion of this phase the manager should give his approval, since the output will basically be a description of how the system will function and his use of the system.

Depending on the computer organization in a given company, the system designer's area of responsibility will vary. However, for our purposes we shall identify the following functions as systems design:

1. System flow charting to lay out the basic flow of information through the system, major program segments, and data formats.

2. Design of computer requirements, including memory, input/output units, machine operations, and machine configurations.

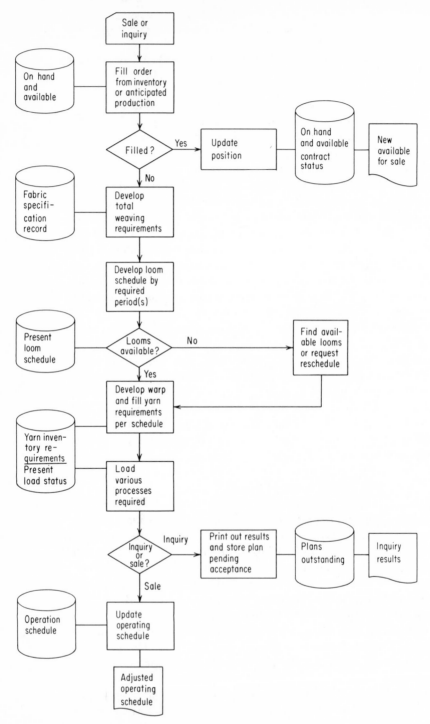

FIG. 5.2 A typical flow chart.

3. Design of data source requirements, source documents, and report formats.

4. Error procedures required for data control and program recovery.

5. Documentation required for use of the system by the computer operating group, the operating instructions.

All these items comprise the system design and are necessary before actual programs can be written. The manager must understand how the system will operate as designed. He should give approval at this point before programming starts.

The system-design phase is particularly important to the manager. It is in this phase that a problem originally stated in management terms is transformed so that it is computer-oriented; i.e., it is in this phase that the major communication problem, mentioned earlier, exists between the manager and the computer expert.

With no intention of making the reader a computer expert, it is desirable to include some examples of the material the computer specialist develops and uses in this stage of analysis. It would be difficult to exaggerate the crucial importance of the system's study phase in the development of a computer-based management information system. It is at this point that the real challenge is first met. A systems study provides an opportunity for a comprehensive examination of an organization's information-handling procedures. At the present time the only real limit to the information-handling work that computers can do is the limit which may exist in ability to investigate a problem and reduce its elements to a design which such a system can handle.

By the time work toward installation has begun, initial studies have usually determined what applications are to be prepared for the data-processing system. In making these studies, systems analysts have documented a general description of the application. This has included a description of source data, of their format and of how they should be processed to develop reports and other necessary output information. Exhibits, volumes, and time-cycle requirements of data and reports should also have been recorded.

SYSTEM IMPLEMENTATION

Once the design phase is complete and the manager has approved the design, implementation begins. In this phase the detailed programming necessary to implement the design is done. This work is carried on by professional programmers, who have been specially trained. Included, in addition to the actual programming, is the detailed layout of the information flow. The manager must understand the complexity of implementing systems of this type, even though he may not be familiar with the minute details or understand all that the programmer is doing.

Once the system is installed, the manager must become active in the final phase of system acceptance. The manager is the final judge of system operation. It is he who must determine whether the system meets his needs. If it does not, he must precisely define where the system fails to meet his requirements.

Block Diagrams. A block diagram has been defined as a graphic representation of the procedure by which data are processed. It provides a programmer with a means of visualizing the sequence in which logical and arithmetic operations should occur. It also makes clear the relationship between one portion of a program and another.

The amount of detail in a block diagram varies. Three levels of detail are sometimes employed. The first level may be called the *general block diagram.* This merely represents a general statement of the procedure in its major elements. This *semidetailed block diagram* is used to expand the general blocks into smaller component blocks. Any serious error or omission should become apparent as this more detailed procedure is charted. The *detailed block diagram* expands each of the semidetailed blocks into a series of small operations. It is from this diagram that the programmer prepares the data-processing system programs.

Programming. Programming should not begin until the problem is defined and the record and input-output formats are complete. The reason for this is to minimize the number of alterations in the program caused by changes in the format of data and in problem definition.

Documentation. During the development of a data-processing system a great many specific decisions will be made, and many details will be considered. Most of this will occur many months before the system is actually in operation.

It is an impossible task for one or a few individuals to remember all the details concerning each program in an installation. Moreover, there is an obvious danger in relying entirely on the presence of particular individuals to run or maintain an application. To avoid this problem it is desirable to document all activities as explicitly as possible.

SYSTEM MODIFICATION

Once a system has been installed, the manager must remain an active participant. As time proceeds, his need will change. Also, items that he originally considered important will diminish, and elements that were overlooked originally in the system design will need to be incorporated. The only sure thing that can be said is that any good system will change with time. In a physical sense it is the hardware, communication, physical files, computer programs, and input/output devices that enable every manager, from president to foreman, to make sure that what is done is what was intended.

CHAPTER SIX

Applied
Control Theory

In the last chapter the point was made that it is difficult to describe a MICS since every system in existence today is essentially unique. We did list some general characteristics that help identify the type of system with which we are concerned and pointed out that regardless of the type, any system must go through certain major phases of development.

In this chapter another set of basic characteristics will be described. These characteristics are to be found in any true MICS and relate to the basic concepts of control theory that were touched on earlier. The relationship of control theory to a wide range of management problems actually represents the nucleus of the approach.

We may state this in another way: while every MICS has a different *content,* it has a single basic *form.* And, further, it is our contention that the approach which we advocate will enable the manager to identify the best *content* for his system by building on the single *form* or framework which we now discuss.

A good illustration of the idea of content versus form is shown by Ackoff and Rivet in their book, "A Manager's Guide to Operations Research" (published by John Wiley & Sons, Inc., New York, 1963). They point out that while dozens and dozens of problems have been solved using operations research (OR) methods, all problems fall into one of eight recognized *forms* in OR, and these eight forms are made to solve a wide range of problems by varying the *content.*

We are trying to make this same important point, except that instead of eight basic forms we shall cover one basic form. This at first glance may seem a gross oversimplification, but our experience has shown that a class of systems is in existence (and can be built) that has one basic form. Our objective is to identify this form, and show the manager how to use it to state his requirements, classify his problems, and implement a system that meets his needs.

The underlying concept of this *form* is control theory. At first it may seem strange, particularly to a marketing manager, to talk about control theory in areas where the terminology is virtually unknown. However, we intend to show how these principles can be applied in many management situations that at first glance seem to have no relationship to the technology of control theory.

Control-theory methods have been implemented and tested in many successful systems. What has not been done is to bridge the technological language barrier that exists between the method and the user, in this case the manager.

BASIC CONTROL PRINCIPLES

In the Introduction a thermostat was used as an example of control. For clarity let us get even more fundamental. There are three basic terms to consider: independent variables, dependent variables, and the model. To illustrate the meaning of these terms, consider the following example.

The equation

$$Y = AX + B$$

is the standard form of the equation for a straight line. Or, in terms we have used before, it is the standard *form* for a straight line. In this equation it is normal practice to classify Y as the *dependent variable* and X as the *independent variable*. The coefficients A and B are constants that describe a particular straight line. They are the *content*. In this equation the usual practice is to say that for any value of X the value Y can be computed. That is, Y is dependent on X. Hence X is considered independent and Y is dependent. In the table below we see this shown numerically for the equation

$$Y = 3X + 2$$

X	Y
1	5
2	8
4	14
10	32

So given the constants A and B and any value of X we can compute Y. The relationship between X and Y is described by the form of the equation and the coefficients A and B. This relationship is also called a *model*. Thus the model is a description of how the dependent variable, in this case Y, will behave given the independent variable X. Schematically this same relationship might be shown as

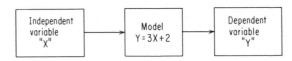

FIG. 6.1   A simple model.

in Fig 6.1 Another way to look at this relationship is to consider the independent variable as an input to the model and the dependent variable as the output from the model, as shown in Fig. 6.2. Thus for a given input we expect a certain output. This relationship of course exists in all business situations. For a given capital expenditure we can build a plant of a certain capacity. For a given advertising expenditure, we can expect a given increase in sales. And so on. The model in this case represents a description of how we can precisely identify the relationship between the independent and dependent variables. In most cases the relationship will be difficult to quantify precisely since in most business cases we are dealing with some form of uncertainty.

Let us proceed to carry our simple example a little further since we really have not introduced control yet.

Usually we are never sure how much of the independent variable

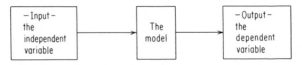

FIG. 6.2   The model restated.

is required to achieve a desired result, the dependent variable. Unless the exact relationship is known, the usual procedure is some form of trial and error. Let us illustrate on our previous example using a direct solution. Let us assume that we want to find how much X is required to produce 23 units of Y. How can we go about our evaluation? We might build a table as shown below and try different assumptions of X and Y.

X	Y
1	5
5	17
9	29
8	26
7	23

What process did we use? We started with a value of X. We saw that the result was too low, and tried a higher value. The result was still too low so we tried a higher value. Then we were too high, and we lowered our assumption until we found the right answer. In other words we went through the process shown in Fig. 6.3. Thus we see that we have set up a loop that consists of picking a value of X, putting it into the model, obtaining a result Y, evaluating the result, and if it is not the right one, repeating the process until we get the desired result. What we have just done is to set up the simplest form of a control loop.

This control loop, though simple, illustrates the concepts of feedback, model, and independent and dependent variables.

To extend our control concepts, take another very familiar example to see whether our basic ideas are still true. Assume you are taking a shower. Is there a relationship between this everyday act and the concepts just discussed? Let us identify the elements just covered. First, what are the independent variables in this case?

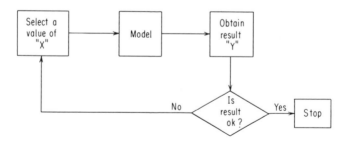

FIG. 6.3 Block diagram of solution.

They are represented by the hot and cold faucets. We can adjust the ratio of hot water to cold water and the volume of each. What are the dependent variables? Basically we could express these as a desired temperature and a desired velocity. What is the model in this case? While an exact mathematical expression could be computed based on the size of the pipes, the heating capacity of the hot-water heater, the ambient temperature, etc., we really do not want to know that much about this model.

Normally we can determine the behavior of the model to suit our needs by trial and error, without worrying about mathematics.

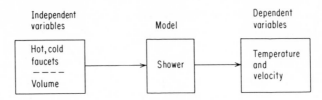

FIG. 6.4   Block diagram of shower problem.

And this raises the interesting point that in many situations we can obtain quite adequate results without a precise knowledge of the facility or its model. Let us now picture our example (Fig. 6.4).

Repeating the evaluation procedure, we go through a series of trial-and-error adjustments on the independent variables until we have the right results. We then take our shower (Fig. 6.5). Here we see the idea of feedback illustrated; i.e., the output is evaluated to determine how to adjust the input to obtain a final desired result. This principle also allows us to close our basic control loop.

This brings out another interesting idea concerning the method

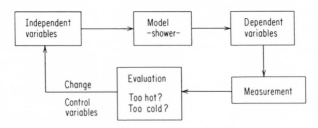

FIG. 6.5   The shower feedback loop.

used to make corrections to the independent variables. In essence there are two basic ways to make corrections in a control system, at least in this simple illustration. These are shown in Fig. 6.6.

In the first case we make large corrections until we pass the target. Corrections are then made in the other direction until the result is passed again. This process is repeated with finer corrections until the target is hit. In the second case the target is approached from one direction until it is met. Which correction procedure to use in reality will depend upon the situation. Each method has its advantages and disadvantages. We shall say more about this later.

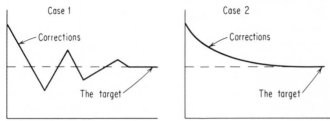

FIG. 6.6 Corrections methods control systems.

Another element will illustrate the importance of control in any system. Assume you are taking an enjoyable shower and, as so often happens, someone else starts to run water to do the dishes or the wash. What happens? Your shower suddenly becomes unpleasant. And what do you do? You hurry to the faucets to make adjustments

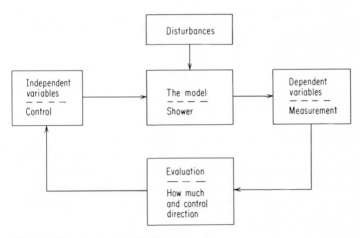

FIG. 6.7 The shower control scheme.

to compensate for the change. In control theory, this departure from a given state is said to be caused by a *disturbance* to the system, as shown in Fig. 6.7.

We are now ready to summarize in concise terms what control

is about in a given system. It is (1) to get on a target and (2) to stay on target.

These two statements are illustrated in the shower example. We used the basic concept to get on target, i.e., to get the shower the way we wanted it. We then used control to keep on target when disturbances to the system caused our results to get off target. In the remainder of this book we shall be talking about the issue of information and control systems to achieve these two objectives.

Another point should be made about the model of the system. In our first example our model was well defined, a single equation. In most situations, however, the model will be very difficult to describe in pure mathematical terms, i.e., the shower. In fact, from this point on, when we use the term we shall include not only a mathematical description of the system, but even more important the information that we have about the system. This distinction should be clearly understood, for in most systems the information base will be the model of the system, and the behavior of the system must be deduced from the information. This is analogous to the shower example, where our only real knowledge about the system was obtained by feeling the water.

A final point to consider in our discussion of the basic control cycle is a factor that seems obvious but is often overlooked—*time*. Time is the factor that converts a control cycle from a static condition to a dynamic condition. Any activity we deal with in the business world normally changes its condition with time. If it did not, we would have a static system and very little need for applying control concepts. Since most activities are dynamic in nature, i.e., they change as a function of time, we have a much greater need for control. Whether we are talking about the corporation, a department, a section, or a process unit in a plant, the normal situation is that the activity, and the characteristics of the activity, will change over a period of time. In the context of control, as previously discussed, two characteristics pertaining to time must be considered when determining the control strategy of the system. They are usually referred to as the response time and the frequency of the control cycle.

Response time is the measure of total time required to complete the basic control cycle, i.e., the total time required to measure the status of the activity, analyze the status, and execute a control decision. *Frequency* is the measure of how often the cycle is completed, i.e., how often we measure, analyze, and execute a control decision. These two descriptions are somewhat oversimplified, but they give the basic definitions of the terms. Now let us look at each of these time factors in more detail, since both will have great importance in later discussions.

RESPONSE TIME

Response time is the time it takes to complete the basic control cycle. In each system there is a best response time as measured by the value of response and the cost to achieve response. In some cases, an extremely short response cycle may be required, measured in seconds. A short response time is well illustrated by the control of a process unit in a chemical plant, using a control computer. In other cases, a fairly long response time may be adequate. For example, a plant manager primarily concerned with setting weekly production schedules may require a response time measured in hours or days. The time value of response usually has the general relationship shown in Fig. 6.8.

Although each different activity has its own value curve, the curve usually has the characteristic shape shown in Fig. 6.8. Note that in the range of very short response times, the curve tends to have a flat portion; then as response time lengthens, we see a more rapid drop-off in the value, until we reach a point where the curve

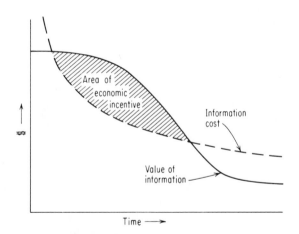

FIG. 6.8 Information cost-value relationship.

begins to flatten out, usually at a very low value. In general this means that when we are dealing with very short response time, it is immaterial whether the response is, say, 1 or 2 seconds. However, as we lengthen the response time value begins to drop because the system is less able to supply information required for control decisions in the time required. Finally, in any system there is a point beyond which the response time is so slow that the system is essentially useless in terms of supplying information in time for the implementation of control decisions. Along with the value curve we have also plotted the general curve representing the cost to achieve a given response time. We see that this curve is very steep, as we would imagine, for very short response time. Then, as response time lengthens, the curve drops off rapidly, until it reaches the point where it begins to flatten out. The behavior of this curve is easily explained. As response time approaches zero, the cost to achieve this response becomes quite expensive. For example, if we wished to have a response time of 1 day in a sales department, the cost to achieve this response would be quite high. Suppose we shortened this response time to 1 second. The cost would go almost out of sight. Fortunately in this case we do not need this kind of response. Also it is easy to visualize in this example that as we lengthen the response time to an hour, a day, a week, a month, a year, the cost will drop proportionately.

The interesting thing to note in these two curves is that they usually cross, yielding an area in which the value of the response exceeds the cost of the response. Finding this maximum value is one of the major considerations in the design of the control system. The schematic we have been discussing has several excellent lessons. First, these curves show that response time, and therefore information, has a value that must be assigned. Second, these curves show that response time, and hence information, costs money. Thus it is imperative that the manager who wishes to implement a control strategy understand both what the response time is worth to him and what it is going to cost to achieve. Only then can he determine whether the results justify the means.

FREQUENCY

We start with an example familiar to most of us to describe some of the basic concepts of the frequency of the control cycle. In a typical accounting system, data are accumulated on a monthly basis. Then after they are processed, they are usually submitted to the management group anywhere from 1 to 3 weeks after the close of the last month's business. These processed data are then analyzed and certain basic decisions made. These decisions are then conveyed to operating groups for implementation. Then the entire process is repeated. What is the frequency of this cycle? It is essentially one month. The sampling frequency, i.e., the measurement period, is 1 month. Evaluation time is 1 to 3 more weeks, and then decisions are passed on. Is the frequency of this example adequate? That depends. If the people making the decisions are trying to control their operation on a monthly basis, the frequency is too low. Let us look at the other extreme. Suppose this same accounting system was capable of sampling the system every few hours. Would this be desirable? Perhaps not, for the decision maker is not making decisions in that time frame if his basic responsibility is to make monthly planning decisions.

In these two extreme cases we see a frequency that is too low and a frequency that is too high. How do you determine the right frequency? First the frequency must be consistent with the time frame of the decision-making process. If a manager is responsible for monthly planning, he certainly should not be satisfied with quarterly data. Nor would he want to be submerged in a mass of detail that described his operation for the past month every few minutes. Perhaps a daily or weekly frequency would be adequate for his needs. *This point we have been making may seem obvious, yet it is often neglected in system design. And one of the main reasons that it is neglected is that the people designing the system do not know the time requirements of the decision process or the number of data required to support that decision process. Who must specify time requirements? The user of the data, the manager, must!*

Thus we see that when we talk about the frequency of the control cycle we must consider several factors. First we must analyze the frequency with which we must sample the system; i.e., how often must we perform the measurement function? Next we must consider how often we wish to evaluate the data that measure the system. And finally we must consider how often we wish to put a decision back into the system. All these go into the determination of the frequency of the cycle. There is no best rule for determining the frequency, but the following rule should never be violated: *the decision frequency should never be greater than the measuring frequency;* i.e., do not make daily decisions on weekly or monthly data. Make daily decisions on at least daily data plus summary data.

Another point to consider is that both the frequency of the cycle and the response time must be in balance. The proper response time with the wrong frequency, or vice versa, will not do. For example, imagine that you are a sales manager who must make daily decisions and that your system provides you with daily information regarding yesterday's sales, inventory, and prices. However, you do not receive these data until 1 P.M., 5 hours after you have made your decisions for that day's activity. You had the right frequency but the wrong response time. Or conversely suppose that your system could provide you with data at 8 A.M. but only at the start of each week. Again we have the wrong balance.

In this discussion we have, in effect, been trying to indicate the

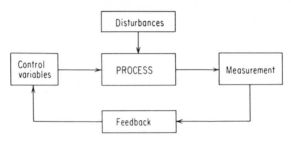

FIG. 6.9 Basic control cycle.

time value of information. The chart of Fig. 6.8 shows a typical characteristic of the time value in terms of response and frequency, considering both value and cost.

APPLIED CONTROL CYCLE

Part 1 discussed two basic control cycles. One, shown in Fig. 6.9, described the basic control-theory cycle, which is scientific and can be defined in such scientific terms as independent and dependent

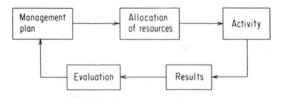

FIG. 6.10 Management control cycle.

variables, process dynamics, etc. The second type of control cycle discussed earlier, the fundamental management control cycle, is shown in Fig. 6.10. That these two control cycles are basically equivalent becomes obvious when we compose the elements as shown below:

Physical Control Cycle	*Management Control Cycle*
Process	Activity
Measurement	Results
Feedback	Evaluation
Control variables	Allocation of resources
Disturbances	Plan

A comparison of a physical and management control cycle element by element shows this equivalence. Thus we can equate process with activity. Both involve and pertain to the facility or operation to be controlled, which might be a process unit, a sales force, a plant, a work force, or even an entire corporation.

Measurement and results are of course one and the same thing. Once the process has been put into operation, we must measure the results, and this measurement will always generate some form of data-gathering system.

Feedback and evaluation are essentially the same in concept. Both involve the analysis of the data gathered in the measurement, or result, phase of the cycle. Using this analysis, certain actions are then taken, based on some form of decision criteria. In control systems with feedback, the decision criteria usually involve some predetermined performance target, such as unit production, product quality, etc. In the management control cycle, the evaluation and decision criteria are normally involved with a budget or some other economic criteria. Regardless, the two are certainly equivalent.

Control variables and allocation of resources are equivalent also in that they are both the point in the cycle at which the decisions are applied. Control variables are the temperatures, pressures, etc., that are manipulated to run the process. Allocation of resources represents the point where the manager allocates his sales force, or his capital, or his budgets to achieve his objectives.

Disturbances are always discussed and accounted for in control theory, which deals with physical processes. They seem to be seldom isolated and identified in a management cycle. They should be. By forcing recognition of disturbances and classifying them we shall find we are better able to define problems to be solved in the computer system.

Conversely, the plan is always specified and identified in a management cycle and usually implied in a control cycle as a target or objective. In both cycles, without the plan, the control aspect disappears.

After this brief comparison of the two basic control cycles let us

see whether we can merge the two, taking the best of each, to develop a new control cycle which can be used to analyze management
system requirements.

Let us examine each of these elements in this modified control
cycle (Fig. 6.11), looking at each of them from the manager's view-

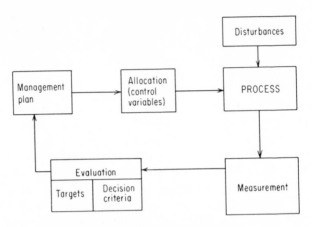

FIG. 6.11   The new management control cycle.

point. In doing this we shall highlight the points the manager
should be aware of and be looking for when he is trying to analyze
his management system requirements.

PROCESS (ACTIVITY)

When the manager looks at this portion of the control cycle, he
should identify what part of the process he is trying to control. At
first glance this may seem to be an easy task, when in fact it is quite
difficult. Later we shall go into more detail on how to analyze the
process.

At this point let us simply state that the manager must identify
the process to be controlled. This identification should include:

1. A description of the process and its major elements
2. Parts of the process requiring particular emphasis
3. The bounds of the process
4. The dynamics of the process

For example, a sales manager of a manufacturing concern might
describe his process as the entire sales department, including the
sales force, wholesale and retail outlets, inventories, and customers.
Relative to point (2) though, the control elements he might be most

concerned about are the allocation of the sales force and inventories. Hence, from a system standpoint, he may wish to concentrate on the parts of the process that pertain to these two items. Another sales manager may be concerned primarily with retail outlets and wish to concentrate on this item. Each manager must describe his area of concern since he is the one responsible for proper functioning of the process.

Broad definitions of a process are generally quite useless. Later we shall see the steps to go through in describing the bounds of the process.

Examples of what might constitute a process as we are defining it include:

1. A manufacturing plant
    a. A division of a plant
    b. A unit or piece of equipment within the plant
2. A marketing division
    a. A marketing district
    b. A product segment within a division
    c. A customer segment within a division or district
3. A financial unit, such as an accounting division
    a. A facility covered by a capital budget
    b. A facility covered by an expense budget
    c. A profit center

Obviously, depending on the type of industry and company, there are many other examples of facilities that meet the definition of a process. The main test to use, when defining a process, is to be sure that the bounds of the process are under the manager's control.

MEASUREMENT (RESULTS)

Measurement of a control cycle is, again from the management viewpoint, quite difficult. In a physical control system a predominant amount of time is spent in the evaluation of which variables to measure, when to measure the variable, and how to accumulate the data. In many management systems this aspect is, curiously enough, overlooked or neglected, or even worse the wrong measurements are taken, and then management becomes disenchanted with system results.

In fact, in many "management systems" the *measurement* phase is the weakest part of the system. This does not mean these systems do not generate lots of data. They do. In fact, often they generate too many. But the data are of the wrong type or in the wrong form.

To answer the question of what data to measure, management

must look at all other parts of the control cycle. Measurement must be related to the type of process, the resources involved, the management plan, and the evaluation method to be used.

In a control system environment, measurement cannot be sloughed off as a necessary evil. The manager must learn from the experience of the physical control system where measurement is a vital part of the system.

Each measurement taken in a physical control system is taken because it is needed to evaluate or describe some aspect of the process being controlled. How many data-processing systems can make this same claim, particularly from the standpoint of the manager, the final user? Is this shortcoming in many of today's systems the fault of the computer expert? In many cases, no. The fault lies often with the manager who assumed the computer expert would know what he needed or gave the expert vague specifications about his information needs.

The manager should be able to specify the detail levels he requires for all sets of data, how the data are to be summarized, when they are to be gathered, how accurate they must be, and how they will be used for evaluation. These requirements are somewhat more stringent than having the manager say that he needs a couple of reports to show him where he stands year-to-date on sales. What is the necessary content of these reports?

Regarding these specifications, it should be stressed that the information the manager gives to the computer expert is basically in the manager's terminology. He need not be a computer expert to tell someone else the kinds of information he needs to run his business. In fact at this stage of problem analysis the manager should not even concern himself with the computer aspects of the problem but should state his requirements with an open mind, regardless of implementation methods. At later stages he will have to make concessions, mainly on a cost basis, but at the early stages of analysis he should not concern himself with this point.

ALLOCATION OF RESOURCES (CONTROL VARIABLES)

In most problems that apply to the MICS concept, we are dealing with the allocation and control of resources, and more specifically we are looking for methods of control that ultimately will yield the greatest profit, performance, and efficiency for the business. The allocation-of-resources problem has been studied and classified by many people. Traditionally the resources of a firm are broken down into the M's: manpower, money, machinery, and material. Most systems with which we are concerned will involve some form or combinations of these resources. The result of using the resource is what we measure. How we allocate or control the resource is what causes the result.

It is amazing how many problems reduce to an allocation-of-resources problem. The difficulty in many management areas, however, is that an optimum allocation of resources is extremely difficult in all but a classical set of problems. Thus in many cases we must satisfy ourselves with partial solutions. This is not as bad as it seems, because in many cases a partial solution may lead to enormous improvements in performance. For the problems that do lend themselves to classical analysis to determine an optimum, we should strive to carry out this analysis and make it an integral part of the system.

Many significant results have been achieved using mathematical methods for this class of problems, particularly the method known as *linear programming,** which is ideally suited to allocation-of-resources problems, specifically those involving linear conditions. Examples where this method has been successfully used in solving management problems are:

Petroleum:
  Gasoline blending
  Refinery scheduling
  Crude selection
  Unit control
  Multirefinery scheduling
  Transportation analysis
Chemicals:
  Site location
  Product selection
Lumber:
  Pulp-mill scheduling
Agriculture:
  Farm allocation

In the cases listed, these problems have a particular set of conditions: a limited amount of resources must be allocated between competing facilities, etc. The problem is made up of *linear constraints* and the *objective function.* Many other mathematical methods can be applied for other types of allocation-of-resources problems. Where

---

* See example at the end of the chapter for an explanation of linear programming.

these methods apply, we should try to use them because they have been shown, time and again, to be successful, but we should remember that not all problems lend themselves to this type of analysis.

Another view of the allocation of resources treats these resources as the control variables. Let us take a simple case. In inventory control experience teaches that in an inventory usually no more than 15 percent of the items account for 75 percent of the volume. One of the major control variables is the list of these items. Once this list is obtained, we can focus our attention on these items and by controlling them, control the entire inventory or resource. Next the major parameters that will give us control must be identified. In inventory these have been defined as reorder points, lead time, etc. Thus for a good inventory-control system we see that the major control variables are: orders requested, orders lost, orders shipped, current cost of lost orders, current cost of inventory, and current cost of ordering. Granting that inventory is a fairly well defined area, we can see that this same basic idea will apply to budgets, production schedules, expenses, sales performance, etc. The job of the manager is to define and recognize the control variables. In some problems there may only be one major variable; in other cases there may be dozens. It is still the manager who must set the ground rules by defining major variables. He is the problem solver in the final sense. It is he who must define whether it is sales, inventory, production, etc., that he wishes to control.

In this sense the major control variables always relate to the ultimate management objective. For example, a sales manager who is trying to control sales performance must specify his objective clearly in order to define the primary control variable. This is really nothing more than defining the problem area.

Another major point is that the manager must identify specifics and not merely generalize. For example, "I want to control profits" is hardly a good definition of a control variable. We must be more precise. A good illustration of management control variables is given in Fig. 6.12, which is a summarization of a Du Pont control scheme. Here we see that departmental "rate of return" is the ultimate control variable. This variable is, however, fully quantized, as can be seen in the chart, and all variables that go to make up rate of return are well and precisely defined. In effect, this chart shows a complete set of control variables for a particular management control system.

One of the problems frequently encountered is that management assumes that other people will be able to identify the control variables that it recognizes. This is a serious mistake.

Disturbing elements, in a sense, are the most important of all control characteristics. If there were no disturbances, there would be no need for control, and for that matter, if there were no disturbances in business, there would be little need for management. It is the disturbances, both internal and external, that create the need for management control systems. This is easily proved. In a steel mill, for example, if all units behaved the same each month, if the feed stocks were always uniform, if the end-product requirements were always the same, and if there were no emergency breakdowns, the optimum production schedule could be computed once and the mill run on that basis now and forevermore. The manager could then spend all his time on industrial relations and community affairs. It is because disturbances are constantly occurring that man-

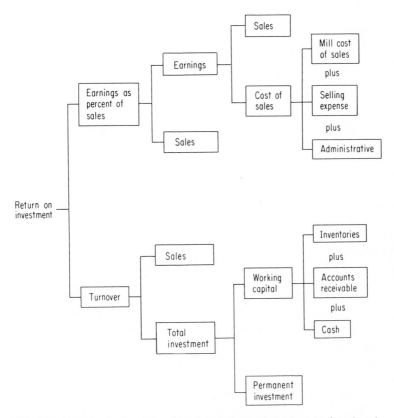

FIG. 6.12 Formula chart—relationship of factors affecting return on investment.

agement must constantly react to a set of varying operating conditions.

Disturbances normally can be classified into two major groups, internal and external. *External disturbances* are those which enter the system from outside and in a sense are completely beyond the control of the manager until they occur, e.g.:

Weather

National economy

Competition

Consumer behavior

Government

Internal disturbances are those which occur within the bounds of the process under control. These disturbances may or may not have been omitted or controlled prior to their occurrence. Examples of internal disturbances are:

Equipment failure

Equipment performance

Raw-material variation

Regardless of the type and severity, the disturbing element must be recognized and control action taken for correction. A basic problem of management is that often disturbances are not obvious, especially when they are gradual and difficult to detect. These types of disturbance, however, are exactly the ones that management must look for, *and find*. Again, this job cannot be delegated.

EVALUATION (FEEDBACK)

Evaluation, in the control sense, is the element that closes the control loop. It is time-dependent and relates to the concept of feedback control. The rate of feedback defines the dynamic response of the system. Feedback is also the element that converts a measured result into a new decision that is put back into the system.

From a management standpoint, then, we are concerned primarily with evaluation as it applies to time dependency and decision making.

Let us look at some examples of feedback in a management environment. At the corporate level, feedback can be illustrated by monthly operating and financial reports, which describe what happened during the last time period. As this information is accumulated month by month, corporate management makes decisions that affect activities throughout the company, and these new actions in turn generate new results, which lead to new decisions, and so on goes the feedback loop. At the corporate level, most response is on a fairly long time scale. Most decisions are strategic in nature.

As we move down through the corporation, we see the response time shortened, until we get down to the actual level of operations, where, in the case of a process, we may have almost instantaneous feedback. As a generalization we can say that as detail gets more precise and specific, the time responsiveness of the system tends to shorten. Hence, in any system of this type, there is a balance between detail and time response.

Stating this another way, we can see that if a vice-president is making decisions that affect results several months or years in the future, the information on which he bases his decision will be based on a slower time response. In other words, corporate executives do not base decisions about next year's budget on all the meter readings in all plants taken 30 minutes ago. On the other hand, a process-unit operator who must decide how to run a unit for the next half hour can hardly base his decision on data that were taken on the unit at the end of the month, or even yesterday. He must base his decision on how the unit behaved during the past hour. This is not to say he will not use last month's data, but he will base his decisions on recent performance, biased by past history.

This means that management must determine how responsive this system is, and then set up a proper feedback loop with the correct time dependency.

There has been a real danger in the past in applying this concept. Many management systems tend, particularly at the higher levels, to have too long a response time, caused probably by the existing reporting systems based on a monthly reporting cycle. For many problems encountered at middle- and top-management levels this is too slow, much too slow. But since many data-processing systems are geared to a monthly cycle, management seems to assume that this is correct. This is not true. The response factor should be examined with great intensity. Setting a proper response time is vital to success.

The other element is decision making. In control systems at the unit level, this is usually accomplished with a mathematical model, and as we adopt this method we shall use some of the same procedures. Of course, often we shall not be able to reduce our decision process to a quantifiable model, and often we should not even try, but where possible, we should formalize in mathematical terms as many of the decisions as possible. Later we shall see how powerful this method can be.

Many successful managers have made their decisions by intuition, "crystal ball," or the "seat of the pants." This will always continue to be one of the marks of a good manager: up to a point, there will always be a class of problem that requires solution by these time-honored methods.

Modern management realizes that many decisions of the past that were handled by intuition can now be quantified, and a "best" decision reached. This is not to say that all decisions can be quantified. We are looking for those which can. By properly defining these decisions in quantifiable terms, we improve the decision process and thereby improve management control.

This statement leads to a basic principle. A decision, whether intuitive or highly analytical, is a selection of alternatives. Even a simple yes or no decision is a selection of alternatives. For example, a production manager has a bottleneck in his production line that could be solved by replacing a particular piece of equipment. After analyzing the cost of replacement, the manager may decide to leave things as they are, which means he has decided to do nothing. Even this decision, which does nothing to alter a current situation, is a selection of an alternate choice, namely, to buy a new piece of equipment or struggle along. This situation must be clearly understood because often the decision to do nothing has an associated cost or penalty that should be quantified when using decision models.

There are many degrees to which we may quantify a decision and its alternates. Some of the important decision analysis and modeling methods with which the manager and his staff will be concerned are:

Decision tables
Statistical decision models
Bayesian statistics models
Linear programming
Dynamic programming

Another dimension to the decision process is the element of certainty (or conversely risk) involved. Here again we have many degrees. On one end of the scale the alternates are clearly defined, as are the outcomes, with little or no risk involved. On the other end of the scale is decision making under uncertainty*

Although management usually is not involved in generating a decision model mathematically, it should at least be aware of the capabilities and limitations of such models and should remember that it will be trying to express decision criteria so that they can be quantified whenever possible. In the past this has not been easy, perhaps because of a severe communications problem between the model builders and the manager. Neither has understood the other.

* An entire field of mathematics has evolved in this area; see the brief discussion of linear programming at the end of this chapter; for further discussion see R. L. Ackoff, "A Manager's Guide to Operations Research," John Wiley & Sons, Inc., New York, 1963.

However, where communication has been established, the results have often been remarkable. One of the best examples of this is the emergence of a critical-path method,* which is basically a planning and decision analysis model.

MANAGEMENT PLAN

We now come to the focal point of the system, the target, or management plan, which is one of the main functions of management, whether we are talking about computers or not. Here we are talking about a particular type of plan in the context of the management control system.

First we must recognize that the creation of a plan is a one-time effort followed by many other actions. The plan itself is a continuous effort and a part of a continuous cycle, as shown in Fig. 6.13.

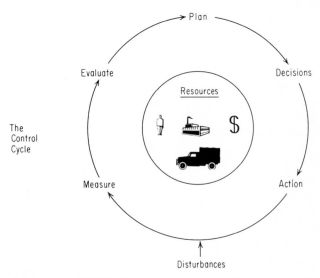

FIG. 6.13 The planning cycle.

In a continuous cycle such as we have been discussing, the plan may be a dynamic element in the system. This does not mean that the overall plan is constantly adjusted but rather that a master plan will be adhered to with modifications as required in the control

---

* Critical-path method (CPM) is a computer program that aids the manager in analyzing trouble spots and pointing out interrelations of elements or activities that depend on each other. Major uses are in construction and maintenance scheduling.

cycle. As a simple example, suppose we establish a budgeting plan for the next 12 months, which is for some total amount set by corporate management. As we proceed through the year we adhere to the total annual figure, but we may want to make monthly adjustments based on over- or underexpenditures.

This dynamic nature means that we must have the flexibility to be able to adjust the plan.

Another way to look at a management plan is to consider it as a forecast, which in fact it is. A forecast is, of course, a prediction in the future and usually one for several time periods. In plans of this type we shall normally want to set the plan, or forecast, several time periods in the future. This will be an important factor when we touch on a multiperiod optimization.

The next factor in the planning phase is that the plan must be quantifiable, usually in the form of targets or objectives. The targets (or the forecast) will be the set of basic data that management will be supplying to the system. Without the target, and some related decision-making criteria, we lose the element of control in the evaluation part of the control cycle.

Since the target is the standard against which performance is measured, obviously without a target there can be no measure of performance. Again let us take a very simple example, the budget. Suppose we have a total budget of 12 million units, giving us a monthly target of 1 million units. The standard of budgetary performance each month is then 1 million units. This rather trivial example of comparison of actual expenditures to budget gives us the measure of performance. (If this were all we were trying to do, we would hardly have a management control system. Our present example is passive, i.e., it indicates only what has happened compared to a standard, but it does not indicate what to do about it. This shows that setting a plan helps, but does not achieve, management control. We must expand the planning function to get control.)

One thing we can do is to establish a procedure for recomputing a pseudo plan based on the actual results. If we are 6 months into our example budget and 20 percent over budget, we can have the system recompute the budget for the rest of the year to stay on target. Normally such a procedure is simple. It can be made more elaborate by applying weighting factors, seasonal trends, and other forecasting procedures to readjust the plan. All these methods involve the principle of dynamic change to a plan to achieve control.

Another simple method in the planning phase is to develop

limits, which function as boundaries for the targets and serve to alert management to deviations. (This is also known as the *exception method* of reporting.) This method is extensively used where there are large masses of data to be analyzed by management. The use of limits and out-of-bounds conditions flags those areas on which management should concentrate.

THE MANAGER'S QUESTIONS

Let us now summarize what we have just said about MICS. Such a system will normally be computer-dependent and have some degree of real-time computing capability, plus a man-machine interface. The types of problems with which we are concerned will contain control elements, i.e. the system will have control variables, time dependence, feedback, disturbance, and measurement. In the pure management aspect we were concerned with the allocation of resources, decision criteria, and management planning in the form of targets.

If most of these elements are present, we are truly dealing with a MICS. Obviously, we shall encounter all degrees of these systems, depending not only on the class of problem, but on the level in the corporation at which we are trying to solve the problem. The reader by now will probably have recognized some problem of his own that falls within this category. Some areas that have lent themselves particularly well to this approach have been:

Control of unit process
Plant production control
Plant maintenance
Inventory control
Budgetary control
Sales performance
Multilevel gasoline blending
Paper-plant scheduling

All these areas of application contain most of the elements previously discussed. To help in using the principles outlined in this chapter, a list of questions to be answered before actual system design has been developed. By forcing himself to answer as many of these questions as possible, and as completely as possible, the manager should be able to present his requirements to an experienced system designer. The questions have been grouped as far as possible by the elements of control covered in this chapter. The sequence presented, while not the only way to answer the questions, is a suggested order to follow.

PROCESS (ACTIVITY)

1. What is the basic process or activity?
    a. Does it include manpower, machines, money, material?
    b. Is the entire process to receive attention or just part of it?
    c. What parts are to receive special attention?
2. What are the bounds of the process?
    a. Is it geographically concentrated or dispersed?
    b. Is part of the process external; i.e., does the process include consumers or competitors?
3. What are the dynamics of the process?
    a. Does the process change rapidly or slowly?
    b. Do changes with time have a trend? If so, can this trend be predicted?
4. Is the process as defined above truly controllable by the manager?
    a. What actions can he now take to control the process?
    b. Are there actions he would like to take but cannot at the present time because of poor information?
5. What parts of the process are essentially not controllable by the manager?

ALLOCATION OF RESOURCES (INDEPENDENT VARIABLES)

1. What are the major independent variables that enter the process and their rank in order of importance?
2. What effect does the manager exert over each of these variables and are there limits he must observe in controlling them?
3. If the manager could exercise perfect control over the variables stated above, would he truly be able to control the process; if not, what other factors have been omitted?
4. What is the time dependency for allocation of resources?
    a. Are all resources allocated at one time for a specified period, as in an annual budget?
    b. Does the manager have the ability to modify his allocation of resources within a given time period? What degree of modification is allowed?
    c. If he can make corrections to the independent variables within a time period, would his corrections tend to be large or gradual? In other words, can the system stand large corrections?
5. Does the allocation of one resource imply allocation of other resources? What are these interactions?

MEASUREMENT (DEPENDENT VARIABLES)

1. What are the important dependent variables?
2. Can all the relationships between the independent and dependent variables be stated?
   a. List those relationships which are precisely known.
   b. List those which are qualitative in nature.
   c. List those which are strongly influenced by the environment i.e., those affected by consumer behavior, weather, national economy, etc.
3. At what level of detail must the dependent variables be measured?
4. Which measurements must be combined to provide meaningful information?
5. How often must measurements be taken on each variable?
6. Over what time period should the measurements be made?
7. Must information be taken outside the system and combined with the measured dependent variables for evaluation? If so, what is this information, and do means exist for getting it?
8. What are the basic units of measurement?
9. What errors might be expected to appear in the measured variables? Can they be detected? Might they tend to obscure valid information?

DISTURBANCES

1. Are there known disturbances to the process?
   a. Are they external?
   b. Are they internal?
   c. Is the frequency of disturbances known?
   d. Can any of the disturbances be predicted?
2. Can the effect of a disturbance be identified in the measurement phase?
3. What action can the manager take to correct for each disturbance? Does he have alternative actions?

EVALUATION

1. Can the entire management plan be stated as targets to be used in evaluation?
2. State these targets.
3. Are there performance limits on the targets?
4. What is the response time required for evaluation?
5. What is the frequency of evaluation?

6. Can a model of the process be constructed for use in evaluation?

   a. Can the type of model be identified?

   b. Are all data required for a model of the process going to be available from the measurement phase?

7. What level of detail is required to carry out the different forms of evaluation?

8. What summary levels will be required?

9. What type, form, and content of reports is desired?

10. How are exceptions to be flagged?

11. Are all necessary dependent variables being measured for evaluation?

12. Are all necessary items identified for evaluation that will enable the manager to control the process?

MANAGEMENT PLAN

1. What are the quantifiable plans that will guide the performance of the process?

2. Does this plan coincide with the independent variables that were identified?

3. Is the plan broken down into detail levels that can be used to set targets for the dependent variables?

4. Over what time period does the plan function?

5. Are there subplans within this time period?

6. Are there limits of performance for the plan?

7. Can the results that are measured and evaluated be applied to the plan?

8. Is the plan dynamic; i.e., does the ability to modify the plan exist?

9. Into how many levels must the plan be broken down before implementation takes place in the process (the control hierarchy)?

10. Does the plan consider the possibility of disturbances entering the process? Does it account for them?

Assuming the manager answers the majority of these questions, he must still cover one more point, the figure showing the balance between the cost and the value of a system. The computer expert, using the answers to the questions just covered, can provide an estimate of what such a system would cost. The manager, however, is the *only* person who can answer the question of value of the system. He must determine how much a system would be worth to him if it could provide the kind of control over his operation implied in the answers to the questions above. The answer to this question is not easy because the results one might expect from a system of this type tend to be intangible. The user—the manager—must be the one to place an economic value on the system.

The basic concepts of control theory have now been discussed as they pertain to a MICS. Using control principles to analyze a management problem forces the manager to focus on those aspects of his operation which are important to him and over which he can exercise control. What is the net effect of this when designing an information system? In general, these methods will compress the information needs of the manager. One of the major complaints heard from management is not that they do not get enough information (in many cases just the opposite is true) but that the information provided does not adequately describe the problem or pinpoint areas that require action. Too often this information is buried in a maze of reports that are at best difficult to analyze.

By using control principles, the manager can at least draw attention to those variables and areas which are vital to his operation. The superfluous tends to be eliminated. Traditionally this has been true in classical control areas, e.g., control of a continuous-process unit. It has been equally true where these principles have been used in a management environment. The reason is obvious. *The use of control methods requires the formal documentation of independent and dependent variables, disturbances, correction procedures, evaluation methods, targets, and system models.* This documentation details the key variables. Superfluous information tends to fall by the wayside.

CASE STUDY

To more clearly illustrate how management can apply the principles of the control cycle to particular areas, let us examine a situation that one would rarely think of analyzing in terms of control principles, i.e., the maintenance operation, more specifically, the plant maintenance operation.

Before analyzing it from a control standpoint, we shall first describe the problem. In most manufacturing companies that carry on production operations in a plant a large percentage of the manpower and expense is devoted to plant maintenance. This is particularly true in the continuous- and semicontinuous-process industries, such as chemicals, petroleum, steel, and paper. In many plants in these industries, as much as one-half the manpower may be involved with plant maintenance.

Plant maintenance has lent itself to mechanization in the computer sense because of the enormous amount of detail and paperwork involved, but in spite of this, it is extremely difficult for management to control for maximum results. A survey made several years ago in the chemical industry showed that the industry average for manpower efficiency was 40 percent, as opposed to a maximum potential efficiency of around 85 percent. Even more interesting, in many of the facilities examined, the manager had thought the efficiency was much higher.

In plant maintenance we are dealing with three major resources: manpower, material, and equipment. They are usually monitored under an annual maintenance budget, the objective being basically to keep the plant running at maximum up time for some minimum expenditure.

Within the scope of plant maintenance there are many questions management must ask, such as:

- What is the effectiveness of the work force?
- Does the work force have the proper balance of craft types?
- What high-priority jobs are behind schedule?
- In what area are costs rising?
- Are spare parts and stores inventories too high? Too low?
- Is reliability of service too low?
- What is the best preventive-maintenance schedule?
- Are safety and lubrication schedules being met?
- When is the time to schedule major maintenance projects?
- Can emergencies be reduced by preventive maintenance?
- Are men assigned to jobs without available materials?
- What vendors are supplying the best equipment at the least overall system costs?

It is imperative that all the information used in answering these questions be accurate and timely if resulting decisions are to be effective. For example, in order to reassign men to handle an emergency without interrupting important jobs, information is often required within minutes, not hours, and it must indicate which jobs can be interrupted to handle the emergency. At present, management has neither the time nor the personnel to analyze the mass of information that should be considered in reaching decisions. Without data-processing equipment, it is extremely difficult to provide management with this necessary information.

It is also imperative that management make the system designer aware of such questions, since they highlight the aspect of control.

As further definition we should identify the basic maintenance process in terms of information flow. This is shown in Fig. 6.14, which is highly simplified but does show the basic process. Work requests are initiated by maintenance forces throughout the plant and sent into a central scheduler. The scheduler accumulates all work requests into a master record and assigns, usually daily or weekly, the next series of projects to be worked on. He does this by issuing the basic document in maintenance, the work order, which not only describes the work to be performed but usually contains estimates of manpower and material and serves as the authorizing document to begin work. After manpower and material are assigned for the job in question, usually by an area foreman, the work is performed. The work order is then closed out by the foremen and returned to Accounting. There are many variations, but this is the basic scheme.

With this brief background, let us see how we might examine the maintenance activity from the control cycle standpoint, to pinpoint and identify the major control elements. Remember, we shall be categorizing this activity using the control elements of:

1. Process
2. Allocation of resources
3. Plan
4. Disturbances
5. Measurement
6. Evaluation

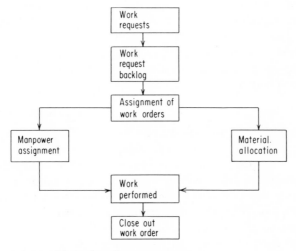

FIG. 6.14 The basic maintenance process.

PROCESS

By definition the process, or activity, is plant maintenance; but since this is a very broad category, let us suppose we are concerned mainly with the manpower aspect. Thus the process we are dealing with is manpower, material and equipment having been eliminated for simplicity. Elements of process definition then may become:

1. *Basic Description of the Process.* The basic process is plant maintenance. The preventive-maintenance (PM) work force is to be scheduled and controlled within the existing expense budget. The process will include only the work force and not materials and spare parts. It will include all equipment which is to receive PM.

2. *Parts of Process Requiring Control.* The process will not include the remainder of the work force or outside contract labor. It will not include the materials and spare parts inventory. Special attention should be paid to the development of job standards.

3. *Bounds of the Process.* The process will include all equipment within the plant site that receives or will receive PM. The process includes the entire work force allocated to PM.

4. *Process Dynamics.* The dynamics of this process is determined by the frequency of emergency repairs and the existing PM schedules. These schedules change with time as experience and equipment history are developed. Too high an emergency rate tends to indicate too low a PM frequency. Too low a rate tends to indicate too frequent a schedule.

5. *Basic Control Actions.* This process can be controlled by the size of the PM work force and the frequency of PM schedules on each piece of equipment. Further control can be exercised by the use of job standards for each PM job. Further control is exercised by the expense budget.

6. *Process Activities That Are Not Controllable.* There may be emergency breakdowns due to faulty equipment or old equipment; emergency breakdowns due to extreme operating conditions.

ALLOCATION OF RESOURCES

The resource we are allocating, or controlling, namely, manpower, can be allocated in many ways. A simple assignment of manpower to work requests as they occur will not suffice. For example, decisions must be made regarding such questions as:

1. What percentage of the work force should be assigned to PM?

2. Do we have the right distribution of skills (welders, carpenters, electricians, etc.)?

3. Do we have the proper size work force?

4. Should we schedule overtime or second shift?

5. What is the current manpower efficiency?

It is in this phase that the control variables should be identified. From the above questions these variables become size of work force, skill distribution, PM, distribution, contract labor, overtime labor, etc.

Each manager in his own right must determine which of these

variables are important or whether all are important. He must then guarantee that other parts of the system generate proper information, so that he can adjust his resources. Elements of resource allocation may be stated as:

1. *Identification of Independent Variables.*
    a. Expense budget
    b. Size of work force
    c. Frequency of PM schedules
    d. Distribution of skills in work force
    e. Equipment to receive PM
2. *Limits on Control of Resources*
    a. *Expense Budget.* The manager has the ability to modify the total amount spent on PM each month.
    b. *Size of Work Force.* The manager can raise the size of the work force within the bounds of his expense budget. He cannot reduce the size of the work force unless he can place the manpower in other maintenance areas.
    c. *Frequency of PM Schedules.* Setting PM schedules is entirely in the hands of the manager. However, he is expected to meet his expense budget and limit emergency breakdowns to 30 percent.
    d. *Distribution of Skills.* This variable is totally under the manager's control.
    e. *Equipment to Receive PM.* This is determined by the manager. He can add or remove equipment from PM. Hence the size of the process to be controlled is determined by the manager.
3. *Dynamics of Independent Variables.* The expense budget is set annually. The manager may modify this budget on a monthly basis so long as he stays within the annual figure at year end. The size of the work force is also set annually. This too may be modified within the bounds of the expense budget. PM schedules are reviewed quarterly, and required changes are made at that time. Equipment to receive PM is also analyzed quarterly. Scheduling of work force is carried out weekly within a monthly forecast, with daily updating.
4. *Interaction of Variables.* The expense budget is the overriding variable. Its modification implies that the work force or the size of the process is modified.

PLAN

The plan in our maintenance example might be made up of several levels. One level certainly would be the maintenance expense budget. The budget might be broken down between (1) internal manpower and (2) contract labor.

Within internal manpower the budget could be broken down by other categories such as:

1. Major turnarounds
2. Preventive maintenance
3. Safety and lubricant maintenance
4. Regular maintenance

The overall plan might be set for a 1-year period, broken down by months.

Within this overall plan, though, it might be necessary, from a control standpoint, to have a second-level plan, or even a third-level plan. The second-level plan may be a plan generated each month, by weeks, and include both an expense and manpower forecast based on the work backlog, scheduled turnarounds, and PM schedules. If still more control is required, it may be necessary to develop a weekly plan, by days, or shifts. The main consideration is that if management wishes to control maintenance on an 8-hour-shift basis, they need an 8-hour-shift plan. The time period involved in the control cycle must be consistent with the plan and with the data gathered for evaluation.

In some plants a monthly control cycle may be adequate. In others, an 8-hour cycle may be too long. Again management must understand and classify the dynamics, which must relate to the planning cycle.

DISTURBANCES

Disturbances to a maintenance system can take many forms. Extreme weather conditions, a major emergency failure, a shortage of skilled workers, increased production, or material shortage all constitute disturbances.

In our hypothetical maintenance system shortage of workers or a major emergency would certainly be potential disturbances. Even more important, though, are the gradual disturbances that may be difficult to detect, such as gradual need to add more electricians or to add more men to PM as emergency repairs increase.

Remember, in a control cycle, that if everything goes exactly according to plan, it is because the system didn't encounter any disturbances. Disturbances are what upset the system and what management must react to. If they can be anticipated and planned for, the control system will function more effectively.

Disturbance variables are:

External:
Modification of expense budget
Extreme operating conditions
Weather
Internal:
Emergency breakdowns
Equipment replacement

MEASUREMENT

Analysis of control variables to be measured must consider time dependency and the decisions criteria to be used for evaluation, plus the nature of the plan. If we are doing daily maintenance scheduling, we must gather data that enable the scheduler to be effective. This means that work in progress must be reported daily, work orders completed must be reported daily, skill assignments must be known daily, and expenses must be accumulated daily.

If, instead, we are on a weekly scheduling basis, our frequency of measurement may decrease, but we still need to know the disposition of the labor force (size, work in process, etc.) at the point in time of scheduling.

We may also want to use job standards as a measurement criterion. The dependent measurement variables are:
Equipment receiving PM
Emergency breakdowns
Equipment replacement
Manpower efficiency
Equipment history

EVALUATION

Evaluation is the point in the system where we combine the data we have measured and compare them to the targets.

In maintenance, this would mean comparison of budget versus actual expense, efficiency of the work force, percentage of scheduled versus unscheduled maintenance, utilization of skills, current status of the backlog, current status of work in process, etc.

Evaluation of this type will enable the manager to decide on a new plan, to determine whether to adjust control variables (reallocate resources), and to recognize disturbances.

It is in this stage also that management should specify its decision criteria. For example, it may want to set out-of-limit conditions on expenses, frequency of emergencies, or manpower efficiency.

Evaluation, particularly in analyzing various decision criteria, lends itself to computer analysis. For example, in maintenance control we might want to use a CPM scheduling and manpower-leveling model to study the best allocation of manpower.

By reducing the previous analysis to capsule form, a maintenance manager might describe the major control elements in his system as shown in Fig. 6.15.

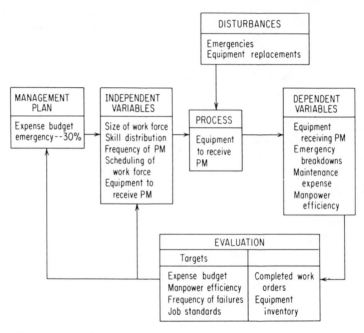

FIG. 6.15   The maintenance control system.

The plant maintenance management system may be block-diagrammed as shown in Fig. 6.16. The disk files represent the needed data bank. The elements within the dotted lines represent the four major phases of the management control cycle for maintenance. The cards represent needed input information.

SUMMARY

In this chapter we have attempted to show the application of control theory to develop a MICS. Every MICS has a different *content* and a basic *form* which the manager must identify. The application of control theory allows the manager to use this tool or technique in constructing a *model* of his activity. Response time of the system must be included because of the dynamic nature of present-day business. The *frequency* of calculations depends upon the response time of the activity.

There is a direct relationship between the elements of a management control cycle. When we recognize this and equate these elements, we may see where control theory applies to our management control structure.

For a system to be effective, a means of *measurement* must be

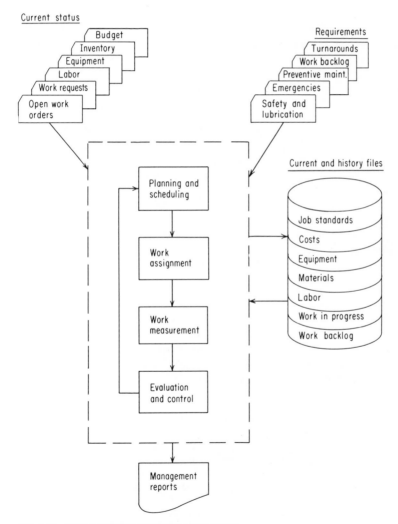

FIG. 6.16 Plant maintenance management system.

available and defined. The frequency of measurement must be related to the response time of the activity.

The use of control methods requires the formal documentation of independent and dependent variables, disturbances, correction procedures, evaluation methods, targets or objectives, and a system model.

LINEAR PROGRAMMING—
AN EXPLANATION AND EXAMPLE

Programming problems are concerned with the efficient use or allocation of limited resources to meet desired objectives. These problems are characterized by the large number of solutions that satisfy the basic conditions of each problem. The selection of a particular solution as the best solution to a problem depends on some aim or overall objective that is implied in the statement of the problem. A solution that satisfied both the conditions of the problem and the given objective is termed an *optimum solution*.

One special subclass of mathematical programming problems consists of linear-programming problems, which differ from the general variety in that a mathematical model or description of the problem can be stated using straight-line, or linear, relationships. The mathematical statement of a linear-programming problem includes a set of simultaneous linear equations, which represent the conditions of the problem, and a linear function, which expresses the objectives of the problem. To take full advantage of this powerful mathematical tool requires an understanding of its foundation.* For an example, consider the following:

A company makes two grades of fuel, gasoline and jet fuel. Restrictions under which most profitable operations are to be decided are:

Crude Oil. Of this raw material a maximum of 10,000 barrels per day is available.

Gasoline. You must supply at least 2,000 barrels per day to a distributor 30 miles away. Profit is 20 cents per barrel.

Jet Fuel. You must supply at least 1,000 barrels per day to another distributor located at an airport 10 miles away. Profit is 10 cents per barrel.

---

* Additional reading is recommended from the following: A. Charnes and W. W. Cooper, "Management Models and Industrial Applications of Linear Programming," John Wiley & Sons, Inc., New York, 1960 (excellent for the manager); S. I. Gass, "Linear Programming," 2d ed., McGraw-Hill Book Company, New York, 1964 (several applications discussed); G. H. Symonds, "Linear Programming: The Solution of Refinery Problems," Esso Standard Oil Company, New York, 1955; R. L. Ackoff and P. Rivett, "A Manager's Guide to Operations Research," John Wiley & Sons, Inc., New York, 1963 (very easy to read).

Trucks. Capacity for 180,000 barrel miles per day.

PROBLEM: What is the mix of gasoline and jet fuel you should make for maximum profit?

SOLUTION: Define the set of linear equations that represent the model and objective function. If

X = barrels of jet fuel

and

Y = barrels of gasoline

then the following relations must hold:

$X + Y \leq 10,000$ barrels	maximum crude supply
$Y \geq 2,000$ barrels	minimum gasoline
$X \geq 1,000$ barrels	minimum jet fuel
$30Y + 10X \leq 180,000$ barrels	truck capacity

The objective function is:

Profit $= 20Y + 10X$ dollars

In graphical form, this may be represented as shown in Fig. 6.17.

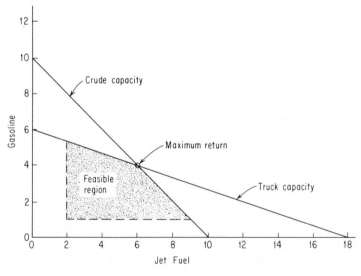

FIG. 6.17 Graphic solution to linear-programming problem.

The solution in this simple case is at a node and from the graph gives a jet-fuel production of 6,000 barrels and gasoline of 4,000 barrels. This solution optimizes profit and meets the constraints of the system.

Linear programming is a mathematical method of solving this and more complex problems directly to arrive at the optimum solution.

CHAPTER SEVEN

Management System
Elements or
Building Blocks

In the preceding chapter the use of control-theory principles and concepts to analyze and classify management problems was illustrated. The close correspondence between a theoretical control cycle and a management control cycle was shown. A method transforming a management problem statement into a format useful for a computer expert was developed. Hopefully, by this time the reader has been able to think of pertinent examples from his own experience that can be analyzed using the concepts of control theory. The methods shown represent a new way of looking at a problem. Our prime concern is that the reader be able to think of his problems in the frame of reference we have been describing. If he can, he will find that he is getting closer to a better description of his problem area, and this in turn should enable him to communicate his needs to the computer analyst. The improvement in communication between the manager and the computer specialist this method provides will justify the additional effort required by its application.

If we were to stop at this point and use only the ideas covered so far, a decided improvement in problem definition should result. However, there is still one missing piece that the manager requires if he is to truly participate in the levels of system design and implementation described earlier. This additional factor pertains to MICS characteristics. By understanding certain basic "system" characteristics the manager should then be able to take his basic area of concern, analyze it using the control principles covered earlier, relate this analysis to a set of system characteristics, and thereby provide the system analyst with a complete and definitive set of requirements for a management control system.

In this chapter we shall explain the basic elements, or building blocks, of a management control system present in any true man-

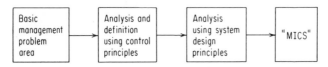

FIG. 7.1   Steps to a MICS.

agement control system. Through knowledge of these elements, the manager should be able to guide the computer experts in the ultimate design of a MICS. The reader will observe, as he reads, the close tie with principles already covered. In other words, we are going through a transition, schematically shown in Fig. 7.1.

This schematic, by inference leads to the following steps:

1. We recognize a management problem area.

2. We analyze and define the problem and its elements using control theory.

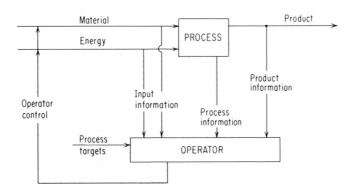

FIG. 7.2   Basic process control loop.

3. We take the control elements and relate them to system characteristics.

4. The computer analyst designs and installs the system.

Fig. 7.2 depicts a basic process control loop. The control activity is expanded by adding information as to current process status and predictions of plant operations at some future time (Fig. 7.3). The physical control loop is completed (Fig. 7.4) by adding the function of optimization. The completed control loop may be com-

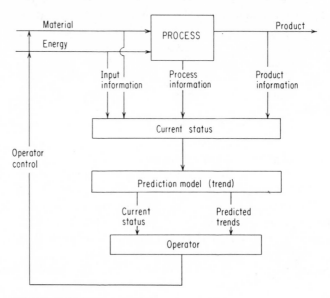

FIG. 7.3   Control loop expanded.

pared (Fig. 7.5) to the block diagram of the elements of a management control system. Let us now see how we convert our control description into a system description.

First, we must realize that there are several dimensions to a MICS. One we have already touched on, namely, the control elements required to define a system of this type. Another dimension is the *structure* of the system. The structure of these systems can be looked upon as consisting of building blocks, which are the fundamental parts of the system. They are related to the basic control loop or cycle discussed earlier. However, to create a simpler explanation let us look at the building blocks out of the context of the control cycle for the time being.

The basic building blocks we are concerned with are:

1. Planning
2. Present position
3. Current plan
4. Forward look
5. Optimization

The first three blocks must be present in any system. The last two blocks represent degrees of sophistication. The control cycle can be completed to some degree from any block. Hence in a very sophisticated system we may have several levels of control cycles. Let us

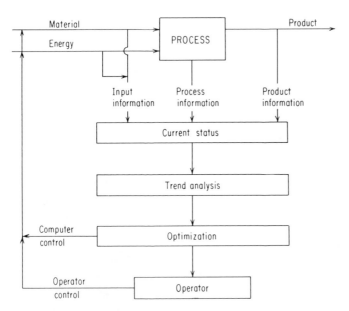

FIG. 7.4   Completed control loop.

now take a look at what each of these building blocks contributes to the system.

PLANNING

This building block must be the first one in the system. As stated earlier, if a plan, or a target, cannot be specified, we lose the element of control.

The plan with which the system is working may be either internally or externally generated. An external plan will be one entered periodically from outside the particular system by higher-level management. This may be a representation of a corporate plan on a gross basis, or it may be very detailed, dealing with the next 24 hours in the case of a plant. The main thing to remember is that there must be some numbers in the system that represent this plan. The plan may be very simple (one number) or very complex (many numbers). It may be an arbitrary set of numbers, or it may have been determined using a very elaborate optimization model. As stated earlier, we must recognize that the system will be constantly reacting against this plan, and hence the plan may be frequently modified to handle the disturbances in the system.

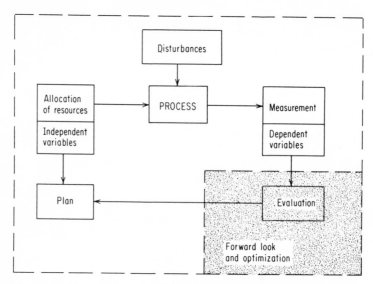

FIG. 7.5 Building blocks of a management control system.

PRESENT POSITION

In a process control environment the present position is usually represented by the on-line monitoring of a series of instruments; i.e., the system is hooked up to the instrument action of the unit under control, and the continuous reading of these instruments gives the current status, or present position of the unit. In process control the present position may also be defined as a data-logging procedure. In either case the function is the same. Hence, by having on-line measurements of the process, we can usually obtain in seconds the status of the process.

In a management control environment the concept of the present position is often neglected. Granted that management may get monthly performance reports, rarely will these be oriented to give a management view of the present position of the system. Unfortunately, management too often assumes that reports of this type represent the present position of the system and hence makes decisions on very incomplete or inaccurate information. Examine the necessity of the present position shown in Fig. 7.6. Bear in mind that we are in a management environment where decisions must be made on a continuing basis.

In this figure, point *C* represents both the current point of time

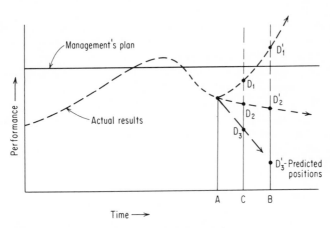

FIG. 7.6   Effect of performance and measuring time.

and the time when a decision must be made on how to control the system to time *B*. Assume that the point in time *A* is the last known position of the system. Hence at the point in time *C*, management has available a description of where the system was at time *A*. The increment of time between *A* and *C* could be looked upon as the *lag time* required to report the results at time *A*. (In the previous chapter, for ease of illustration, we neglected this time increment of response characteristics.) The difficulty arises when one considers that in a dynamic system its position will probably have changed between *A* and *C*. Hence, management is constantly faced with the problem of making a decision based on where the system was, not where it is.

Let us see what effect this has on the decision. If the system continues its current trend to point *D*2 (see Fig. 7.6) the decision will probably be the correct one, all other things being equal. If, however, the system has moved to *D*1, the corrective action will probably be too severe, and an overcorrection will result. If the system has moved to *D*3, the correction will probably be too weak, and an undercorrection will result. In neither case will management see a satisfactory behavior in the system. In the case of going to *D*1 and overcorrecting, it will be very easy to create a highly oscillating system, which most managers have probably encountered at some time. The $D3$ position may create a system which continually degenerates performance until extreme corrective action must be taken. At this time the system will begin to oscillate as in $D1$. The reader can see the obvious difficulty that arises as the time between A and C is increased to the point where management really has no good description of the current state of the system.

The other extreme occurs if points A and C coincide. This would occur only if we have a perfect data-gathering and data-reporting system that could report at any instant the present position. In the management sense this situation is not desirable or necessary. So what is the answer to the present position?

Let us look at the problem from an economic standpoint. In Fig. 7.7 we see illustrated the balance between cost of the present position and value of the present position. The figures shown are based on actual studies made in the steel industry,* but they have been made relative rather than absolute to illustrate the principle.

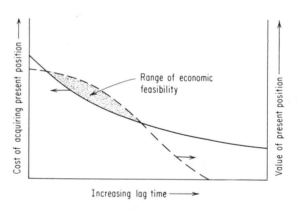

FIG. 7.7   Relationship of value of present position to cost of acquiring.

Let us see just what this figure implies. Analysis of the cost of the present position curve shows that one end, instantaneous (no lag time), present position is extremely expensive. The other end of the scale, a very large lag time (probably months), has relatively low cost. Information costs money. This cost seems to climb exponentially as we shorten the lag time.

From the other view, the value of present position, or more importantly the value of information, has a definite plateau when we

* IBM case studies on data collection.

move into the range of very short lag time. In a normal management situation the same decision would probably be reached whether the information is 1 minute or 1 hour old. As the lag time is extended, the value of the present position begins to diminish, until a point is finally reached where the value goes to zero. Notice that this point is reached even though the cost curve may continue. The importance of this behavior is that beyond some point, which will vary widely, the definition of the present position fails to have any value or meaning.

The range of interest, called the *range of economic feasibility,* is the one with which we are concerned. Traditionally this has been a difficult range to find. One of the major reasons is the difficulty of assigning economic values to the management need for the present position. We shall discuss some of the methods of determining value later.

Before leaving this analysis of the economics of present position we should discuss one other major factor that influences the economics enormously, namely the level of detail required to describe the present position. If we examine the present position description at a particular point on our previous figure, we see a certain cost and value associated. To be completely accurate we should add another dimension to the analysis. In Fig. 7.8 we see another economic dimension added for any particular time lag.

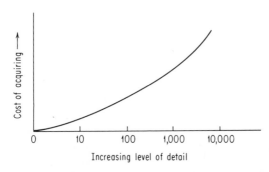

FIG. 7.8 Relationship of cost of acquiring increased detail information.

This chart implies that a choice of a suitable time lag for the present position still has associated with it a choice in the amount of detail needed to describe that position. This level of detail is very deceptive. For example, in the control of a refinery process unit, we normally consider 300 or 400 variables an adequate description of the status of the unit. One might assume that if we want to control an entire refinery in an on-line sense we would require 300 or 400 variables times the number of units, plus other data. This need not be the case at all. Bear in mind that the time responsiveness, disturbances, feedback, etc., are at a different level and hence the objectives of the system are different. Experience has shown that to obtain a meaningful description of the present position of a refinery may require only the same number of variables as a unit, 300 to 400. In other words the control variables from the refinery manager's standpoint are different from the control variables of the unit operator. Likewise, at the next higher level of control—the manufacturing department—we require only 300 to 400 variables for a meaningful description of several plants.

The unit operator, to carry out his level of decision making, may require a very detailed description of the variables in his unit. The refinery manager, on the other hand, is looking at a somewhat larger picture, and hence he may require only 20 or 30 variables to describe the performance of that same unit for his decisions. That this is normally going to be true is well illustrated by the summarization levels that exist in most data-processing systems. As information moves up through the corporation it is summarized and aggregated to meet the needs of each level of management. This is of course a desirable occurrence since it is rather pointless to assume that the corporate executives need to know the readings of all the pressure gauges in the company to make a decision.

In our economic analysis of present position we are looking for the most suitable time lag and the most suitable level of detail to provide the most valuable information to the decision makers—this is not an easy task.

Perhaps a final example, with which we are all familiar, will illustrate the value of information and cost in decision making. Our example is the weather. If your company is planning a picnic for employees and their families and you are in charge of selecting a date, about the most detail you would need would be your knowledge that it is hot in the summer months and that it usually rains in June. You might check with the weather bureau to get their latest long-range forecast. If, on the other hand, you were a farmer who needed to bring crops in at the best time you would probably keep in close touch with the weather bureau on a day-by-day basis as harvest time approached. If you were a pilot for a commercial airline about to take off on a flight you would need the latest current weather data and forecasts. Once in the air you would need to reaffirm your analysis even further by using radar during the flight to avoid turbulence. Each of these cases represents a different type of decision. Each decision required a different type (level of detail) of data. As the decision time (reaction) shortened, we went to more elaborate and expensive data-handling methods. This is what we have been stressing. *Management must classify its objectives and decisions and identify data time dependency and the economic value of gathering the data.*

The determination of present position is more than just a description of where the system is at a specific point in time. It must include factors other than the exact physical status at a single instant of time. For example, in a continuous-process plant present position normally will include the following factors:

1. Historical behavior
2. Current material balance
   a. Qualitative
   b. Quantitative
3. Current plan
4. Scheduled commitments
5. Existing commitments

In a given system all these factors may not be necessary, but an analysis of them will show the relationship to the allocation of resources and the performance of the system. These factors are designed to answer the management questions of:

How are my resources currently committed?

Which resources are currently available?

Are my resources generating the required performance?

Can my resources meet the future plans?

Have my resources been properly used over the last control period?

Do I need to change the plan?

We shall now examine in more detail the five factors of present position and see how they may be applied.

For illustration assume the plant maintenance case previously discussed in Chap. 6.

Historical Behavior. Historical behavior is used to generate the original figures for the critical-path chart. These figures would be generated from existing work-order systems.

Current Material Balance. At any point in time, say at the end of a shift, reports are generated to show the amount of effort and type of effort used.

(Note that the material balance covers a discrete time period. In other words it may show the status as of 4 P.M., but it shows it in terms of the last 8 hours. This is why we say the report is for an increment of time.)

Current Plan. This is simply the existing critical-path method (CPM).

Scheduled Commitments. This is the part of the job that is unfinished but scheduled.

Existing Commitments. This is the part of the job that is unfinished.

All this information when supplied to the maintenance superintendent will allow him to schedule his resources (men and materials) for the next activity.

With this simple example in mind, let us proceed to a more elaborate analysis of each aspect of the present position.

Historical Block. The historical behavior of any system to be controlled must be analyzed. The analysis should be much more than a cursory glance at past events. Significance must be gleaned from historical data. Control variables must be found. Standards of performance must be sought. Correlations must be developed. Trends must be studied. And finally, data must be selected to create the data files needed in the system.

Regardless of the age of the system under study we have some form of historical data available as a base of information. What about, you may say, a completely new system where there is no history? No matter how new a system we shall have available a data base. For example, take a new plant with a new process. Even in this case there are data available. Pilot-plant data, process evaluations, and design specifications all provide a starting point, even though sometimes it is minimal.

In an older system, one that has been in existence for many years, there is a wealth of data. The danger, however, is that these data may not truly describe the history of the system, as management has defined it for control. Even worse, the historical data from an established system many times create an improper description of the system. With problems of this type how can management analyze historical data? As a starting point, we return to the requirements of management describing the objectives of the system. The objectives of the system provide a good insight into the analysis of historical data. Identification of the control variables provides a further clue to the analysis.

Of all the methods of analyzing historical behavior perhaps the best is to look ahead to the actual design of the system to see what types of historical data it will be desirable to accommodate. The difficulty of this approach is that it is more or less a "chicken or the egg" proposition. But there is an important principle here; i.e., any MICS will generate and rely heavily on historical data. Today's present position becomes tomorrow's historical data file. And these data files must be compatible with operation of the system. There is nothing worse than a system that generates reams of historical data that go into a file drawer and are never used again! Historical data must be treated as a dynamic and powerful part of the system. If they are not, we do not have a MICS.

ENVIRONMENTAL DATA AND MATERIAL BALANCE

1. *Environmental Data.* We have been talking largely thus far about internal historical data, i.e., data generated within the system. We must realize that there is another class of data developed outside the bounds of the system which has, in many cases, a dominant effect on the data generated within the system. This class we call *environmental data.* The reader will recall that disturbances are both internal and external. External disturbances certainly represent a major category of environmental historical data.

For example, if we are dealing with a marketing system that has many seasonal products, an examination of sales performance alone, say by product, may be very deceptive. Obviously, if we have a company that sells bathing suits and the summer was very cold, the information on seasonal temperatures is important to an analysis of the sales situation.

Once we select the major categories of historical data to be analyzed and identified and the types of historical files to be generated, there is still a tremendous amount of information to be developed from the historical data that can be useful in the present position calculation.

Some of the types of data analysis that might be needed are:

Regression analysis (correlation)
Probability distributions
Trend analysis
Exponential smoothing
Time series
Seasonal variations

A final note should be made regarding the size and organization of the files. Much of this task is in the realm of detailed system design. However, management must be aware of certain factors. There are two extremes that should be avoided, too many data and too few. Too many data tend to bog down a system and make it difficult to use and maintain. Computers have the ability to process large amounts of data rapidly, but bear in mind we are interested in the right data and not all the data. Too few data make a system inoperative because of inadequate information for decision making. How do you select the right amount?

Management can help by recognizing the major classes of information in which they are interested. Information normally falls into indexable patterns, and it is the indexing scheme that describes the volume of the data files.

2. *Indexing*. Indexing in the computer sense is a complex subject requiring special and detailed analysis. Indexing from the management viewpoint, however, reduces to a fairly simple question: "What data shall I be requiring for decisions (present position), and in what categories shall I want them summarized?" This question means that management must identify the summary levels and the basic level of details.

To illustrate the concept of indexing, consider this simple example. Suppose a marketing manager is in charge of a regional territory with districts and branches under the regional level. The manager keeping track of the sales performance of a particular product obviously will want to know the performance by region, district, and branch. Graphically this example looks like that in Fig. 7.9. Each of these summary levels represents an index. The more detail the manager desires, the deeper must be the indexing, i.e., in this case, down to sales by customer category, location, etc. In other words, for each category or summary level for which we desire information, we must establish an index. Management must indicate to the system designers what these desirable categories are.

FIG. 7.9 Sales aggregation levels.

In the above example the summarization levels were based on organizational units, which is one of the major categories. Other examples are:

Geographic

Physical units

Legal units

Financial units

Product units

The point for management to remember is that data not indexed cannot be retrieved or referred to directly. For example, if the sales manager in the example just given desired information on product by customer and the data did not contain an index category for customer, he obviously could not obtain this information. This point is probably one of the least understood by management.

3. *Material Balance.* The present position of a system requires some form of material balance. The term material balance is normally considered as an engineering term, but it can be applied in a broader sense.

The physical items for which the material balance is used may be money, inventory, production, manpower, etc. A cash flow statement is a material balance, and so is a production operation. The fundamental principles of a material balance are:

1. Current balance plus input minus output equals change.

2. A material balance requires that the bounds of the system be defined.

3. A material balance implies a closed system.

4. A material balance accounts for all material in the system.

5. A material balance can be both qualitative and quantitative.

Examples of material balances are:

In chemical engineering, heat or mass balance

In petroleum, a reservoir material balance

In accounting, a yield and cost balance

Schematically, we can look at a material-balance description as in Fig. 7.10. The material balance describes the bounds of the facility. This does not mean the facility cannot grow, for it can and still be within the bounds of the facility. For example, suppose the facility for which we wish to set up a material balance is an entire refinery. The bounds of the facility are in a sense the fence around the refinery. However, through the addition of capital to the facility, we may add a new unit. Our material balance must now account for this unit, but the bounds have not changed. Or suppose that we wish to add a new tank farm to the refinery, requiring additional land. We must now in concept move the bounds (the fence) of the facility to account for the addition. While we have made a physical movement of the material-balance boundary, the boundary has really remained unchanged in that it is still a plant material balance. In each case the boundary always represents the plant facility.

Now let us look at the inputs and outputs of the material balance.

First we must describe what they are inputs and outputs to, since, as indicated earlier, our material balance for present position may involve money, material, products, etc. For illustration, let us assume we are describing a product material balance. In our refinery example, this means that we take raw crude oil or semirefined stocks,

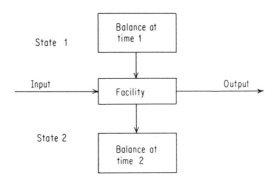

FIG. 7.10   Material-balance description.

process them, and turn out a variety of petroleum products, i.e., gasoline, motor oil, etc. Hence, in a material balance of this type we must account for the status of all products in the system.

Obviously, then, one of the major items in our material balance will be the amounts of products that have entered and left the system. These amounts will be accounted for by receipts and shipment statements. Knowing these amounts, we must now account for the product within the system. An adequate description of the product balance may require many classifications. For example, we will want to know the following:

Raw-material (crude-oil) inventory

Semirefined inventory

In-process inventory

Unit processing volumes

Refined-products inventory

Since in our example we are dealing with a continuous process, we must normally compute these volumes for a particular time period. This tells where they were at the start of the period and where they stand at the end of the period. The value of present position (material balance) is proved here, since most refineries are managed today using this information as the basic decision point.

In many cases, in addition to the quantitative data, we must add qualitative information on product quality, specifications, reliability, etc. Data of this type will be supplied by the laboratory, inspectors, and on-stream analyzers. Too often this aspect is overlooked when in actuality it is the dominant part of the system.

The final point regarding material balance is that the time period for gathering the data and performing the computation must be consistent with the management decision criteria. The refinery manager in our example, who must make daily scheduling decisions, would derive little benefit from a system that gave him only a monthly material balance. This leads us to the next important element of the present position calculation.

CURRENT PLAN

All managers are indoctrinated with the importance of the planning function. All managers set plans. Yet how many follow through and monitor the plan to see that it is being implemented? Unfortunately, this seems to be extremely difficult for many managers. The standard practice seems to be to spend a considerable amount of time laying out a monthly or annual plan, and then being forced to abandon it gradually as the press of day-to-day crisis grows. Perhaps if the plan were followed and modified as time progressed, there would be fewer day-to-day crises.

In the MICS philosophy the establishment of a plan and the subsequent monitoring and adjustment of the plan are essential. Without a plan, or target, or some measure of performance we do not have a management system. This point is so important we shall repeat it. If the present position does not incorporate the management plan, the entire system concept falls apart. Now let us see just what we mean by plan.

There are several terms that may be used to define a plan. Most familiar are forecast, budget, standards, schedule. Each of these terms implies a slightly different type of plan, however, and each has certain basic characteristics. A management plan from our viewpoint will comprise:

1. *Comparative Measure.* This consists of:
   a. Historical comparison
   b. Problem of changing historical basis
   c. Extrapolation
2. *Time Dependence:*
   a. Levels of time
   b. Response time

3. *Units of Measure:*
   a. Related to results
   b. Present status
4. *Modification to Plan* as needed
5. *Following the Plan.* Control of plan and the elements of the plan stated as:
   a. Resources
   b. Results
   c. Requirements
   with consistency between levels of the plan

FORWARD LOOK

Once management has developed a system using the concepts outlined in the previous section of present position, with the material balance, data requirements, and current plan defined, we can examine a next stage of sophistication. This is defined as *forward look.*

Forward look, as the name implies, is a method of projecting where the system under management control will be at some future time. In one sense, then, this method is another form of forecasting; however, it is different from the forecasting mentioned under the section dealing with current planning and has a different use.

Perhaps we can show the concept more easily with a simple

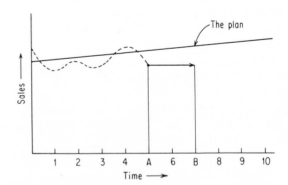

FIG. 7.10A   Product A marketing system.

example. Suppose we are dealing with a marketing system and are concerned with a particular product, product A. In Fig. 7.10A we see plotted (1) the annual sales forecast and (2) the actual results for the first 5 months.

Point *A* represents the present position. Point *B*, which can be estimated using several different means, represents the forward look. With gross figures such as we are using here the forward look is basically the sales forecast for the next 2 months. This figure can be arrived at by averaging the sales over the last 5 months. Another more advanced method that could be used is exponential smoothing, which gives more weight to recent entries. Hence, in its simplest form the forward look is a forecast or projection of where the system will be in the future based usually on where it has been in the past. If the systems we were dealing with were as simple as the one in our example, we could conclude our discussion of forward look. However, in the real world most systems are more elaborate and cannot be projected merely using an extrapolation of past results. So how is forward look projected? In the discussion of present position, we identified a material-balance description of the system, which is in effect a mathematical model of the system. If we have a model of the system, we can usually extend it to generate a forecast of its own future performance. This procedure is more involved than the simple extrapolation we performed in a simple example of forward look.

The next extension to forward look is even more important from the standpoint of management control. If we have a model that can predict the next level of performance in time under current operating conditions, we can extend this concept so that the model will show how an alternate course of action will affect the system. Remember that we are dealing, by definition, with systems that have control elements. So wouldn't it be logical to see the effect of controlling these elements under certain conditions? We can also see the effect of external disturbances, e.g., weather, competition, etc.

In other words, the forward-look concept will allow a manager to test alternate courses of action in the systems he is controlling and then choose the best course of action.

Forward look can also be used to analyze performance in reverse. In other words, how must the system behave if we are to meet our market plan, etc. (e.g., simulation for control decision)?

OPTIMIZATION

After establishing a management control system that incorporates the principles of (1) present position and (2) forward look, we are ready to look at the final level of sophistication, *optimization*. We should stress that here we are speaking of system optimization. This distinction is pointed out, because optimization as a method to solve discrete problems has been used successfully for many years. It does not seem to be used extensively as an integral part of a management system.

The reason is threefold:

1. *Complexity.* It is admittedly difficult to implement an optimization model into a dynamic management system.

2. *Data.* Data for models of this type are difficult to acquire, and until recently systems were not geared to supply these data.

3. *Need.* Some problems do not lend themselves to optimization or require it.

With these three difficulties, why explore optimization? Because in many management systems there is a need; they lend themselves to optimization, and with sufficient data optimization can be incorporated.

Before looking at how we use optimization, let us take a quick look at what it is. For our purposes we can view optimization as *some method of mathematical analysis (of a system) that will enable the analyst to select a "best" alternative from several alternatives.* Some methods that have been used are statistical analysis, linear programming, nonlinear programming, dynamic programming, and simulation.

Most optimization problems have these characteristics:

1. Allocation of resources
2. Control variables
3. Alternate ways of using resources
4. An objective function

(For a simple example, see the discussion of linear programming at the end of Chap. 6.)

If the system in question has a need for optimization, based on the above criteria, then there are many other factors to consider, such as:

1. How many of the resources should we attempt to optimize?
2. Over what time period should we optimize?
3. What method of optimization should be used?
4. What data are needed?
5. How often should we optimize?

To help answer some of these questions let us examine a case where optimization models were first used in a system environment, namely, unit process control in the continuous-process industries.

Control computers have in a sense gone through the entire process we have been describing, the same process that business systems are now going through.

Early control computers were first used to monitor and gather data and compute a material balance. Since these systems were on line, they were capable of computing a present position on a unit in a matter of minutes. The present position was essentially a heat and/or material balance on product flowing through the unit in question. This provided a qualitative and quantitative report on the current status of the unit.

After this capability was developed, people started using the control computer to project unit status, perhaps for the next hour or the next day. This forecast, or projection, was usually based on a physical model of the process unit considering both past performance and current status.

The next stage was to add an optimization scheme, usually stated as a linear program, to develop an optimum set of conditions for running the unit.

The optimum conditions were then printed out as a set of operator guides to help the operator run the unit for the next time period. When a system of this type was proved reliable, the computer

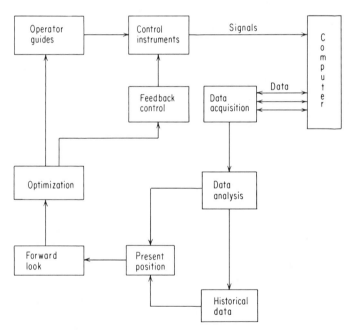

FIG. 7.11   Control schematic.

began sending control instructions directly to the control instruments, and the loop was closed.

This brief description is interesting in that it involves the same principles we are advocating in a management system (see Fig. 7.11).

In our example we were looking at a precisely defined closed system. There are external disturbances, but these are mostly techno-logical in nature and can be planned for in the system. In a man-agement system, we are dealing with an entity that is less precisely defined and is not as closed as our example. There are many more undefinable external disturbances. For this reason, when we speak of optimization in a system for management, we are not really looking for the model to control the system. We are looking for the model to assist in planning and scheduling and to present suggested courses of action.

Let us now return and try to answer the questions raised earlier. First there is the question of how much of the system (resources) we should try to optimize. This is pertinent because rarely shall we want (or be able) to optimize our entire system. We may want to concentrate only on products or selected products. We may want to optimize our marketing effort. We may want to optimize manpower. And so on. We must identify those items which are optimizable and those which we want to optimize.

A related question is: "Over what time period do we wish to opti-mize?" In our control example we may optimize hourly. At the top corporate level we may want to optimize over a 5-year period. The selection of time period depends on the dynamics of the system, as discussed earlier. A rapidly changing system may require more fre-quent optimization than a fairly static one.

Another question raised earlier involved the selection of the method of optimization. Once the manager has supplied the neces-sary information, a specialist must select the best optimization technique. His choice may be obvious, or it may require the trial-and-error application of several methods.

The next question was concerned with data requirements. The identification and gathering of data for an optimization scheme are often more difficult than the formulation of the model itself. The manager can assist here with a clear statement of management ob-jectives and decision criteria. The manager should also be aware that some data that are required in an optimization model may not be readily available in the present information system.

How often we should optimize again comes back to both manage-ment requirements and the dynamics of the system. A regional sales manager, concerned with meeting monthly sales quotas and ex-penses, would hardly be interested in a model that optimizes sales effort every 5 minutes. On the other hand, an optimization every month may be too infrequent. The manager must determine the best frequency, based on his ability to apply the optimized results of a model.

SUMMARY

In this chapter we have covered the basic modules, or building blocks, of MICS. Any time-control system may be structured using these modules. The manager, by thinking of his problem in terms of these modules, should be able to explain his requirements to the computer analyst in meaningful terms.

CHAPTER EIGHT

The Concept
of Mathematical
Models

When we discussed control theory and its application to problem definition, system design, and implementation, we saw an essential tool mentioned again and again, the mathematical model. A model is the statement of the interrelations between the problem variables that permits determination of the cause and effect of disturbing influences that change the management plan. Since the reader should have some understanding of models, this chapter deals with them.

In the technical literature, the system of equations that describes a business problem is referred to as the *mathematical model* of the business problem. A mathematical model can be looked upon as an approximate description of a business problem in the language of mathematics.

The most difficult problem, when applying management-science and mathematical techniques to business situations, is to establish the mathematical model. An understanding of the concept of mathematical models, how to develop and test them, is essential for a clear understanding on how and where to use them. It is difficult to explain what a mathematical model is, what it does, and how one should go about setting one up. Numerous books are available for depth study of different aspects of model building, modeling techniques, and model use.* Knowing some of the advantages of using

---

* See the selected bibliography at the back of the book.

models may help in the understanding process. The mathematical model offers these advantages:

1. It makes it possible to describe and comprehend the facts of the situation better than any verbal description could hope to do by forcing a logical examination and analysis of the problem.

2. It uncovers relations between the various aspects of the problem that may not be apparent in a verbal description.

3. It indicates what data should be collected with what frequency to deal with the problem quantitatively.

4. It establishes measures of effectiveness.

5. It explains situations that have been left unexplained in the past by giving cause-and-effect relationships.

6. It makes it possible to deal with the problem in its entirety and allows a consideration of all the major variables of the problem simultaneously.

7. It is capable of being enlarged step by step to a more comprehensive model to include factors that might be neglected in verbal descriptions.

8. It makes it possible to use management-science and mathematical techniques that otherwise might appear inapplicable to the problem.

9. It frequently leads to solutions that may be adequately described and justified on the basis of verbal descriptions.

10. It forms an immediate bridge to the use of digital computers as an aid to problem solutions, thus allowing the computer to be used as a tool in problem solution.

The first phase of the use of mathematical models is to establish a frame of reference. The problem solver has to get a feel for the problem and determine the strategy to be followed. The second phase is the establishment of a conceptual model, which usually can be best expressed in the form of a mathematical model. The model's validity must be tested to find out whether it does what it is supposed to do. Does the model describe the situation? Does it indicate what data are needed? The third phase of the process is obtaining acceptance of the model by operating management and designing the control system required to put the mathematical model into action. The final phase consists of the indoctrination of personnel concerned and the introduction of the new control system into operational practice for decision making and operational control.

MANAGEMENT CONTROL
STRUCTURE MODELING

After planning, organizing, leading, and staffing comes the last of a manager's fundamental responsibilities, *controlling*. Control is the process of checking to determine whether plans are being adhered to and proper progress being made toward the objectives and goals, and acting, if necessary, to correct any deviations. Planning sets up programs; controlling accomplishes them.

Controlling is definitely a manager's function. From chief executive officers down to the foremen on the production line, managers are responsible for performing by the standards by which the next level of authority measures them. For example, plant managers are responsible for:

- Production control
- Materials control, both purchasing and inventories
- Budgetary control
- Inspection and quality control
- Overall cost control

They are responsible for the overall profit picture of their plant in relation to the corporate objectives.

Managerial control is like a thermostat. Both operate on the feedback principle, which means they report the actual conditions (measurements) to the manager, giving him the data on which to act. Controlling consists of four essential steps:

1. Setting the standard (the basis for control)
2. Measuring performance
3. Determining how well the standard has been met by finding the difference between it and performance
4. Applying remedial action

A manager, whatever his place in the managerial hierarchy, must realize that good controls are forward looking. In addition to being forward looking, a control system should be understandable, not only by the manager but also by the people responsible for the activities controlled. Controls must also be appropriate and adequate, economical and flexible. Deviations must be quickly spotted and corrective action taken. Only by taking corrective action is control really exercised.

THE USE OF CORPORATE
MODELING METHODS

In this section we give illustrative examples of the use of corporate modeling methods. Although they are not exhaustive and cannot demonstrate all the possibilities, these illustrations do show particular types of application that can be studied and the types of result that can be expected. In conjunction with the general descriptions of management control in earlier sections, these examples should serve to convey some idea of the usefulness of corporate modeling methods.

Modeling methods, in general, are optimistic in that they seek solutions. They represent a perspective of the world around us in some form definably distinct from personal perceptions of the actual world. Generally, human perception of business problems tends toward increasing pessimism with increasing number and complexity of problems. Quite frequently, thresholds are reached beyond which we say the problems are insoluble. Computers have extended these thresholds. And modeling methods are optimistic tools used for seeking solutions. The language of the modeling method merely defines the problem as a starting point from which to seek a solution. The whole attitude of modeling is solution-oriented or optimistic. In fact, models are often formulated which are unnecessarily complex or detailed for the problems to be investigated. Perhaps this is due to a sense of art, a secret hope that the computer will fail, or (more commonly) an optimistic belief that the computer is entitled to have the most sophisticated models we can give it so that we can confidently demonstrate its ability to overcome complex problems and develop solutions. Modeling is a perception or perspective of a problem; simulation is a tool for finding answers.

The response sensitivity of a corporation to its own operations as well as to external forces is frequently a critical factor not only in the cost of doing business but also in increasing sales, gross income, and the returns on investments. Models can be developed to study precisely what response sensitivity is worth, both in acquiring the data and in using them.

The typical corporate entity undertakes generally a series of distinct activities, e.g., raw-materials procurement and transport and storage of these raw materials; some manufacturing, fabrication, or production; storage of the finished products at one or more plants; coordination of interplant operations for multiplant corporations; supply and distribution to wholesalers, retailers, customers, warehouses; and various marketing or sales functions. Usually, each one of these activities or operations tends or seeks to improve its own efficiency; this is a sign of good management trying to do a better job for the company (sometimes at the expense of the other activities). Often, computer applications are developed to enhance the operation of one or more of these activities: for example, the use of linear programming in plant scheduling, transportation codes for distribution problems, inventory systems for warehouses or storage control, sales analysis to study marketing methods. But 100 percent efficiency in any one of these multiple activities does not necessarily contribute any more to the corporate objectives than 85 percent efficiency. It is the totality of corporate activities that counts, not the individual corporate activities, except where the individual activities will affect, directly or indirectly, and materially, the corporate objectives. Is is possible that moneys invested in upgrading a particular activity do not result in the attainment of particular general corporate objectives and can, conversely, degrade the operation of another activity to the extent that the overall corporate operations are degraded rather than improved. One perhaps unrealistically simple example of this is an instance in which a plant operating at peak efficiency or capacity produces more product than can be sold, resulting in a tie-up of storage facilities, distress sales, or perhaps complete loss. As long as the corporate activities are studied or improved or controlled vacuously and not in the clear perspective of the ultimate corporate scheme or objectives, certain inefficiencies between activities as viewed from a total corporate perspective are possible. A new tool or technique to aid the manager in the understanding of corporate activities and interrelationships is the dynamic corporate simulators * (DCS). These techniques permit the study of each of the corporate activities individually or collectively and their relationship with one another and the corporate objectives within the framework of a total corporate model, thus allowing a means of reducing, if not eliminating, the interactivity inefficiencies.

The DCS models can be used experimentally by management to determine in advance through simulation the effect of certain changes in operating decision rules, increases in capacity or capability of specified activities, or additional warehouses or other facilities, likely sales trends, or competitive activity. Several possible changes can be studied or investigated and investments made in the most promising or critical areas. Particularly valuable in this regard is the probabilistic use of the simulator so that the probabilities

* Application programs for computer available from **IBM** reference library.

of success or the degree of risk inherent in a prospective course of action or investment can be measured against the probabilities of returns or improvements. This probabilistic method can be employed in evaluating certain prospective risks, e.g., the risk of inadequate plant capacity, from sales forecast data and the like. Management decisions to combat these risks can be simulated so that the action actually taken in the present is reasonably related to the risk at that time. Reevaluation of the present action can be made periodically as the realities of the prospective risks materialize or evaporate and further appropriate action taken in reasonable relation to the current probability of the risk.

In the design of a total MICS, corporate simulation can be employed to determine what information is actually required to better manage the corporation. In this fashion, the simulation constitutes a means of finding new computer applications to fulfill corporate objectives or to achieve them more effectively. The necessity or value of particular pieces of information and the use to which they can be put can be demonstrated through simulation.

Through the construction of corporate models and simulations, a better understanding of the corporate actvities is possible. Through this better understanding or better information, management can more effectively manage the corporation as a single entity, rather than a collection of individual activities bonded together by a common name. Particularly illustrative in this connection is a recurring problem in the interplay between sales forecasts, inventory levels, distribution capabilities, and plant scheduling. Through corporate modeling methods, such as a DCS, these activities can be planned or scheduled as a single integrated operation taking advantage of combinatorial efficiencies rather than individual efficiencies. Such problems would generally require a sales-forecasting routine, an inventory simulator, a transportation code, and a linear program or some single combination of all these related by a DCS. In addition, some analysis of probabilities would be worthwhile and highly desirable. Where profitability of operations is quite critical, the analysis of probabilities may be essential.

All the above possible applications allow closer control of the corporation by management. Such closer control, better information as to the actual corporate activities, and simulation systems to evaluate prospective courses of action offer management a new weapon in running the company, the ability to evaluate and seize opportunities: for example, the ability to evaluate quickly whether the purchase of large quantities of raw materials at particularly attractive distressed prices can be effectively exploited, whether excess plant capacity can be utilized effectively to defer fixed costs or even make a small profit by increasing sales through advertising or special promotions, whether peculiar conditions or transportation facilities and existing inventories can be better deployed to achieve sales or profits, etc.

Although clearly beyond the present capabilities of corporate simulation today,* no discussion of corporate modeling possibilities would be complete without at least some mention of closed-loop controls; where source data are teleprocessed directly to the computer, the computer continuously analyzes all available data, and through preestablished decision rules the computer responds as is required, again through teleprocessing devices, to those locations where some affirmative action is required. Such applications are analogous to process-control applications, but here the process is the operation of the corporation. Exceptional cases or decisions requiring human intervention can also be reported to the responsible parties for some appropriate action. Basic to the implementation of such ambitious projects is the creation of adequate models of the corporate activities. Judging from the advances in teleprocessing equipment, computers, process-control applications, and software, such closed-loop systems are a great deal closer in time than we might imagine.

DYNAMIC CORPORATE SIMULATION

Recent successes indicate that dynamic model simulation methods can be quite effectively used on a corporate level, something considered theoretically possible but very impractical just a few years ago.

Those lofty objectives so eloquently and abundantly discussed in recent years under the various headings of total Management Information Systems, management by exception, management Operating Systems, etc., are now at least capable of some practical degree of implementation through computer modeling techniques on a large scale. Modeling methods, game theory, heuristics, and the like can be put to the acid tests of actual practice.

Areas of prospective application transcend the corporate entity which the project title would suggest as a limit. The same techniques used in corporate simulation have application in social, economic,

---

* Present-day computer simulation programs do not include feedback or feedforward control theory; work under way may soon offer solution to the inclusion of control theory in corporate simulators.

political, national, international, and scientific planning and endeavors; they have application to that vast array of unsolved problems often too complex for practical human comprehension.

These problems are still capable of reasonable description in non-mathematical languages (using "language" in its broadest sense), as long as adequate description disciplines are provided. Furthermore, many of these elusive problems are soluble through simulation employing more in the way of logic and reason systems than mathematical algorithms. This does not exclude mathematical methods or imply that mathematical methods are neither reasonable nor logical, but merely holds that mathematical methods for solving complex problems are often themselves the insurmountable obstacles for the practitioner in other fields.

In a sense, the methodology is a hodgepodge of many techniques which through disciplined, logical, and reasonable use can be used in a single organized structure to solve significant problems that are incapable or impractical of adequate solution by any one method in particular. The most significant attribute of this approach is that it works.

Vast areas of science, engineering, medicine, law, economics, sociology, political science, and national and supranational goverment operations have consistently evaded modeling in a mathematical sense because adequate mathematical notation or identification of the mechanisms or even the ability to quantize the relationships between factors has not been possible. By employing simulation techniques and drawing upon the vast wealth of solution methods employed successfully in other fields, in conjunction with purely mathematical modeling methods, we begin to approach the utilization of the best of all methods in a single method and begin to solve these epic problems. The cohesive element is reason. Long before man invented mathematics, he discovered reason; neither mathematics nor any other solution method, for all their benefits, has yet repealed the law of reason.

The dynamic relationships between solutions from any of the individual, traditionally independent, applications can be studied.

Forecasting, transportation, inventory planning, supply and distribution, raw-material procurement, plant or manufacturing scheduling, management decision flow and management information systems analysis, job shop scheduling or optimization, to mention a few, have been traditionally treated as independent applications to solve particular problems, assuming that certain solutions that could be developed would fulfill the ultimate corporate objectives. In many cases, these methods have been overused, in the sense that their great success has motivated employment in marginal areas where other techniques might be better utilized. DCS treats them all as one application package for the solution of the ultimate corporate problems or the fulfillment of the ultimate corporate objectives. By necessity, therefore, it allows the use of a particular technique where it is deemed appropriate but does not preclude the employment of another technique where it is felt to be more appropriate in some other identifiable segment of the overall problem or model. This, of course, obviates the need to assume that the solution to any one facet of the overall problem independent of the others is in fact the best means in this particular area for the furtherance of overall corporate objectives. A particularly fruitful area of study is the dynamic relationship between various facets of the business: for example, planning the output of production facilities and planning sales drives in conjunction with transportation capabilities, considerations of by-product capabilities, storage or inventory possibilities, probable competitive activity, and pricing structure.

DCS employs a teamwork approach to these corporate or business problems in a structured environment, structured in much the same way that the problems are viewed in the world external to the computer. This permits easy identification of a particular segment of the model and the related tactical solution with the real world. Such structuring produces a certain inherent simplicity which benefits the utilization of the system in correlating a reasonable solution method with a particular problem segment and the credibility of the results and the confidence that may be placed upon them. The teamwork method is analogous to certain nonlinear-programming application packages, e.g., the employment of mathematical algorithms to supplement the linear programming.

The simple, pictorial, flow-chart language of the general-purpose systems simulator (GPSS)* has a universal appeal for problem description. Flow charting, in general, is rather readily learned. The particular flow-charting notations or conventions used in GPSS are not a particularly unreasonable or difficult discipline. The basic programming language of a DSC might be a flow chart in which the model user could identify the basic structure of the business or corporation in the material environment of the problems to be studied or simulated as well as certain sets of solution strategies. In essence, this flow chart becomes a picture of the problem, and a picture is worth a thousand words. This is particularly true when the thousand words are in a machine-recognizable language.

* An IBM available general purpose program for simulation of business systems; see the description which follows in footnote on page 173.

Pictorial language forms enhance the development of models as well as implementation of major changes to the model in the way of changes to the description of the real world or the solution strategy. In addition, the outputs from the simulation can be better analyzed in the presence of a pictorial representation of how those answers were developed, thus enhancing the credibility of the results and confidence in them. This is particularly valuable in such complex or large problems as the running of a corporation. Further, it does not require the acceptance as fact of certain numbers produced by a machine without full appreciation of their import or value. Still further, considerably less training is required to draw these primitive pictures or perspectives of problems than to define them in a detailed mnemonic of linguistic form or in any form in which the problem cannot be readily related. Problem solvers are thus better able to solve their problems rather than wrestling with the mechanics of methods in varying degrees foreign to them.

For present computer systems, there seems to be no reason why generalized linear-programming formulations cannot be described in terms of requirements, capacities, costs, or profits, etc., instead of the totally problem-unrelated description mechanics currently in use, right-hand sides, columns, rows, objective functions, etc. (These expressions are method-oriented.*)

OPTIMAL CONTROL MODELS

Most of the literature on control deals with production units or plants. The literature on optimal control presupposes exact knowledge of a valid mathematical description of the plant, exact knowledge of the momentary state, precise and valid mathematical description of the "cost" of performance and of constraints, etc. Typically the sources of such information are excluded from optimal control consideration. To keep in the same context as the literature we shall examine an approach for optimal control modeling of management control functions in terms of a plant.

In some simple plants, e.g., attitude control of spacecraft, a priori information on a mathematical model is available for the structure of the equipment. More customarily even the form of a mathematical model is highly questionable because of the immense complexity of the actual equipment. Even if a model can be ob-

* An example of a general-purpose simulation system is IBM's GPSS, which is available from IBM libraries. This simulator is basically a tool for modeling the operations of a business enterprise in a simple flow charting, pictorial language, easily implemented without extensive training.

tained from a priori structural information, the coefficients of the model are subject to variations and uncertainties.

The state has to be identified from measurements on such inputs and outputs as are accessible. These same measurements can be used as bases for identifying uncertain aspects of the mathematical model. Some signals are not accessible to measurements, and all measurements are subject to errors and contamination by noise. Mathematical descriptions of "costs" or criteria of performance are subject to as many difficulties as obtaining models for the plant itself.

In this situation a search for a comprehensive outlook on the entire situation is required. There are obvious possibilities for trade-offs. Exact a priori knowledge of a mathematical plant model abets the extraction of the pertinent components of poorly measured signals. On the other hand, exact measurement of signals permits firm conclusions on the unknown aspects of the plant model. The quality of information of the plant model, the quality of measurements, and the realism of the cost function will jointly determine, along with a number of other factors, how actually optimal control can be.

These considerations seem to point toward the existence of some quantity or concept which sets the bounds within which control can approach optimal for any given situation. Further, the existence of a best balance of utilizing the heterogeneous sources for achieving an overall optimal control operation is implied.

Signal measurements can be used for identifying the plant model and the state of the system, thus providing the data required for the usual phrasing of the optimal control problem. Yet this may well be a roundabout route which is of questionable value in view of the limitations of models, identifications, and state vectors. We can investigate the feasibility of a more direct approach of deriving from available signal measurements only such information as is necessary for the immediate control aim without depending on any preconceived ideas on the characteristics of the controlled plant. For immediate "optimal" control the present response of the plant and its present sensitivity to control forces are needed, and these are the data utilized. The limitations established for this investigation also restrict somewhat the mathematical tools available for carrying out the control operation. Nevertheless, the conclusion seems to be that it is not only possible to carry out successful control within these limitations, but that it has some strong practical advantages. Most notable are a simplicity of the operation and the elimination of the necessity of establishing specific mathematical models for the plant.

SUMMARY

The most difficult problem in defining, designing, and implementing a Management Information and Control System is in establishing the mathematical model describing the control situation. Models offer another technique in analyzing data and often uncover relationships between various aspects of the problem not readily apparent. Models are the bridges that allow the modern digital computer to become an effective management tool. Many modeling methods have been successfully used and are now available in computer program libraries.

Simulation may be considered as an additional method of model manipulation. We shall expand this theme in the next chapter.

CHAPTER NINE

Dynamic Analysis and Simulation of Management Control Functions

The dynamic behavior of management may be treated as a feed-back control system with the mathematical functions of management to plan, staff, organize, direct, and control an organization. Analysis and simulation of management decision-making functions, coupled with the dynamic functions of the organization, provide a means of displaying future trends for advanced planning and decisions.

In a nontechnical sense, control systems techniques and tools have been applied for many years to management problems of guiding and controlling industrial operations. Management's ability to design the organizational structure, to assign functions and responsibilities, and to establish procedures, methods, and reporting channels has been obtained through experience in the necessary requirements for control methods and profitable operations. Alterations in the design of the organizational system and modifications of the procedures and reporting methods are continually being made to improve the overall performance of the organization. At present, management's experience in cause and effect is the keynote of dynamic control. Good communications and feedback are recognized as essential elements of good management.

The combination of known principles and fundamentals of communications, computers, and controls used in engineering science provides the foundations for management as a science. The management and operation of the industrial organization is a control process to which the dynamics analysis and simulation, as used in the control system technology, provide an approach to organizational structure, performance evaluation, and prediction. The industrial organization is a dynamic response, and the organization may be treated as a feedback control system with all control techniques of analysis and synthesis applied for control within the boundaries of technical tasks, schedules, and cost requirements as a three-dimensional control problem. The concept of applying feedback control techniques to engineering operations is one of relating parameters and their function of time as applied to machines with equivalent types of parameters and time functions of the organizational structure. Once this is determined, the analogy is revealing. Investigation shows that the organization operates as a machine and follows natural laws of motion. This fact is the basic principle of management dynamics.

The application of feedback control technology to organizations and management shows that the combined resources of machines, materials, men, and money for performing tasks may be expressed as a mathematical model. Computer simulation of the time predictions of accomplishment and performance may be analyzed and evaluated so that decisions and corrective action can be taken in the early phases of the program to counteract possible trouble areas before it is too late. By using mathematical model syntheses, the effect of varying resource allocation can be simulated and future plans selected that satisfy requirements in support of management decision making and control.

The organization is a complex machine in which feedback control is a predominant characteristic. The dynamic functions such as time lags, natural frequency, dead time, lead time compensation, and other familiar control-theory terms may be expressed as performance operators, and the development of a mathematical model provides a more exacting treatment by use of control system techniques and simulation to determine the effects of various courses of action. Sampled data and adaptive control techniques are inherent in management control systems.

The basic management control function measures the degree and rate of progressive accomplishment toward objectives at any given time. Feedback information may be compared with the objective requirements to establish deviations between the desired and the actual accomplishment. The deviation information may be passed on to the functional operations doing the work by means of two management channels: (1) the experience channel, which takes immediate and proportional corrective action required by the deviation, and (2) the analysis and evaluation channel, which requires more time to consider the situation but provides a more accurate picture; i.e., management "sums up" the situation by integration. Analysis will show that the preceding functions result in the anticipation or lead-time action of management. In effect we introduce feed-forward corrective actions.

The association of feedback control techniques with cybernetics by Wiener, economy by Tustin, and industrial dynamics by Forrester supports the use of control technology applied to organization and management to do work by a definite dynamic pattern. The mathematical concept of management control may be applied to the fulfillment of other types of requirements which, in general, are controllable events. The scope of controllable events extends from the individual, group, and company, through major national and international events related to the control of economy, labor and effort, product and growth. Investigation indicates that the dynamic behavior of controllable events may be analyzed and simulated by the control theory developed for mechanized systems.

Computers and network control theory such as PERT have aided greatly in organizing the logical steps of management control. The human being is a part of the total organization, and his behavior is tailored to organizational demands.

Mathematical models of the management control functions have been developed and simulated using analog and digital computers. The application of these functions shows that synthetic techniques, when taken by management, improve the design of the organization and its performance.

CHAPTER TEN

Tools and Models

The manager should have a familiarity with the computer analyst's tools and techniques. This familiarity will greatly aid in communicating the problem definition to the analyst and make it easier for the manager to comprehend the design and solution techniques proposed by the computer specialist.

THE TOOLS OF MATHEMATICS

The mathematician carries in his kit four basic tools, plus a mixture of special models. His basic tools are *matrix algebra, calculus, probability theory,* and *simulation.*

MATRIX ALGEBRA

Matrix algebra is a tool by means of which large arrays of numbers in the form of *vectors* and *matrices* can be manipulated by rules similar to those found in ordinary algebra.

As a miniature example, suppose (3,000 2,200 2,100) is a *vector* (for our purposes, a single array of numbers) whose component numbers represent sales targets in three geographical markets, say, West, Midwest, and South, respectively. Past records show that on the average it takes 1 hour of sales effort and $1 of advertising expenditure to produce a sale in the first market; $\frac{1}{2}$ hour of sales effort and $1 of advertising expenditure to produce a sale in the second market; and $\frac{1}{3}$ hour of sales effort and $1 of advertising expenditure to produce a sale in the third market. This information can be summarized in a *matrix* (for our purposes, a rectangular array of numbers):

	Sales effort (hours)	Advertising expenditure
West	1	$1
Midwest	½	1
South	⅓	1

To find the total hours of sales effort and dollars of advertising expenditure required to achieve the geographical sales targets, we multiply the vector by the matrix:

$$(3,000 \quad 2,200 \quad 2,100) \quad \begin{matrix} 1 & 1 \\ \frac{1}{2} & 1 \\ \frac{1}{3} & 1 \end{matrix}$$

For example, we can call the vector A and the matrix B, and we then proceed to find their product, $B \cdot A$.

There are definite rules for the multiplication of a vector by a matrix (and, for that matter, for the multiplication of two vectors or two matrices, etc.). In the example above, the product $A \cdot B$ is $(3,000 \times 1 + 2,200 \times \frac{1}{2} + 2,100 \times \frac{1}{3} \quad 3,000 \times 1 + 2,200 \times 1 + 2,100 \times 1)$ or, collecting terms, $(4,800 \quad \$7,300)$. This new vector is the solution; and it means that the company must have enough salesmen to make 4,800 hours of calls and an advertising budget of at least $7,300.

Matrix algebra is essentially a symbolic shorthand for the manipulation of large arrays of data. It affords the advantage of economy in quantitative expression.

For example, matrix analysis, a branch of operations research, provides a convenient method of tabulating and analyzing input/output relationships for complex systems. This technique regards a system as a transformation unit that receives certain inputs—raw materials, semifinished parts, labor, energy, etc.—and converts the inputs into certain useful outputs. Methods of mathematical notation and display, developed for matrix analysis, are readily adaptable to manufacturing systems synthesis.

CALCULUS

The second tool which the mathematician brings to management is calculus. Using differential calculus, the mathematician can, among other things, determine what combination of inputs will maximize some output.

A marketing mix is a combination of inputs, such as price and advertising. Suppose that it were possible experimentally to vary the price input and the advertising input while controlling other factors. The effect of these variations on sales could then be recorded, and the profit implied by each level of sales estimated.

The task is to find an equation which best describes how profit varies with variations in price and advertising. A form for such an equation as well as a method of estimating the coefficients (usually "least squares" regression) must be decided upon. Suppose the following equation is found to give a good fit to the data:

$$I = 100 + 2P^2 + 6P - 3PA + 4A^2 - 60A$$

On the left side of the equation is income (represented by I). Income is treated as the *dependent variable,* because its value is conceived to depend upon the values taken on by variables listed on the right side of the equation. These *independent variables* are price P and advertising A. The particular numbers in the equation are constants and coefficients, which are estimated by an appropriate statistical method.

If such an equation can be found, what unique mix of price and advertising would maximize profit? The nonmathematician can use trial and error to arrive at the income-maximizing mix, but this will be frustrating and time-consuming. The mathematician can determine this mix in a very short time by using calculus. Although this is not the place to explain the procedure, his calculations will show that the optimum price is $5.60 and the optimum advertising budget is $9.65 (in some appropriate unit).

The chief contribution of differential calculus to marketing is to make possible a direct determination of optimal action where differentiable functions are involved. In fact, *marginal analysis,* which is applied by economics to all kinds of decision situations such as determination of the best price or the number of salesmen, actually is a gross application of differential calculus.

Integral calculus, representing the other branch of calculus, is not used to find the maximum and minimum values of a function but rather the *area* under a function, among other things. An area can have a meaningful management interpretation.

Suppose that on a particular billing date a petroleum company ranks all its credit card accounts by dollar size. These charge accounts range from $0 to $100. The frequency distribution of all the accounts by dollar size is shown in Fig. 10.1. The shaded area under the curve between $25 and $75 represents the percentage of all accounts falling in this range. How can this area be measured? It does not have the simplicity of a rectangle, triangle, or circle. This area, or other areas under the curve, can be readily measured through integral calculus, provided that the frequency distribution can be represented by a mathematical equation with certain properties.

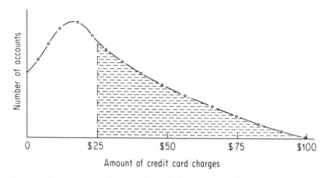

FIG. 10.1 Frequency distribution of charge accounts.

The third important tool of the mathematician is probability theory.

How should a manager handle the uncertainty that surrounds legislation, consumer intentions, and competitors' acts? He can try to list all the possible consequences of a business move, along with their probabilities. The probabilities can be based on the frequency distribution of past outcomes for similar business moves or on personal judgment. The assigned probability numbers must satisfy only two requirements:

1. The probability that a particular consequence will occur is given numerically by some number between 0 and 1 inclusive.

2. The sum of the probabilities of all possible consequences is 1.

Probability numbers can serve as "weights" for appraising various money (or utility) outcomes. Suppose a manufacturer has developed a new product and must hire and train a special sales force to sell it. The number of salesmen to hire will depend upon his estimate of market potential, among other things.

Suppose that he is uncertain whether there is a potential of 1,000, 2,000, or 3,000 units, and he is trying to decide whether to hire 50 or 100 salesmen. Too few salesmen will mean that some potential sales are never realized, and too many salesmen will mean that excess selling costs are incurred. It would help to estimate the profits under different assumptions of market potential and sales-force size. The estimates will depend upon an appropriate set of assumptions about product price, production costs, the effect of the number of salesmen on sales, and selling costs. A hypothetical set of profit estimates is shown in Table 10.1.

TABLE 10.1 Estimated Profits for Different Combinations of Market Potential and Sales-force Size

Decision?	Market potential		
	1,000 units	2,000 units	3,000 units
50	−$10,000	$60,000	$ 60,000
100	− 40,000	40,000	100,000

If market potential is 1,000 units, the manufacturer will lose $10,000 with 50 salesmen and $40,000 with 100 salesmen. If market potential is 2,000 units, the manufacturer will earn $60,000 with 50 salesmen and $4,000 with 100 salesmen. Finally if market potential is 3,000 units, he will earn still larger profits. In this last case, the profit is higher with 100 salesmen because 50 salesmen are inadequate to tap the full potential.

Should the manufacturer hire 50 or 100 salesmen? By hiring 100 he has the opportunity to gain more but also to lose more. His decision will depend upon the personal probabilities he assigns to the three estimates of market potential. Suppose he quantifies his beliefs as follows: there is a 0.2 probability that the market potential is 1,000 units, a 0.5 probability that it is 2,000 units, and a 0.3 probability that it is 3,000 units. If this were a game of chance which the manufacturer could play repeatedly, facing the same payoffs and the same probabilities, and if he had adequate funds, it would be easy to define a good decision rule: choose the act which has the highest *expected monetary value* (EMV). EMV is a weighted average of the alternative profit consequences of an act, the weights being the probabilities assigned to the alternatives. For the example we have:

$$\text{EMV (50)} = -\$10,000 \times 0.2 + \$60,000 \times 0.5 + \$60,000 \times 0.3 = \$46,000$$

$$\text{EMV (100)} = -\$40,000 \times 0.2 + \$40,000 \times 0.5 + \$100,000 \times 0.3 = \$42,000$$

The results present an interesting paradox. The manufacturer is optimistic about the market potential, and yet EMV is higher with 50 salesmen. His optimism is not quite strong enough.

The use of EMV as a decision criterion in a once-only decision is generally acceptable, if the best consequence is not too great and the worst consequence not too bad. Were money stakes unusually high for the decision maker, it would be necessary to employ a utility index instead of a money index. The utility index can be constructed from preferences expressed by the decision maker between given sums of money and certain gambles. Instead of the maximization of EMV, the decision criterion would be the maximization of expected utility. Many excellent texts on probability and statistics in business are available in most libraries for further study.

SIMULATION

The great majority of managers' problems remain intractable to ordinary mathematical solution. For example, the correct price to charge depends upon such elements as the future sales outlook, the possible reactions of competitors, the time lags of these reactions, the intended level of advertising support, ad infinitum. A complex phenomenon is characterized by feedbacks, distributed lags, uncommon probability distributions, and other features which render exact mathematical solutions difficult or impossible. But mathematicians are undaunted. "When all else fails, simulate!"

A simulation is essentially a hypothetical testing, as opposed to a field testing, of the consequences of alternative business decisions. The first step is the construction of a model which spells out how the key variables interact in the situation. The second step is the testing of alternative decisions on the model. Simulations can range from simple paper-and-pencil exercises to full-scale computer analyses. The purpose is to speculate on the consequences of changing a price, or dropping small distributors, or introducing a new pattern of trade deals, before risking the irrevocable judgment of the marketplace.

The model used in the simulation may be *exact* or *probabilistic*. In an exact model, the effect of one variable upon another is known with certainty. In a probabilistic model, one of several effects might take place, and we presume to know only their respective probabilities.

For a better insight, we shall illustrate a probabilistic model. Study of a system such as retail inventory control shows that the problem is to adopt purchasing rules which will balance inventory losses against sales losses. Either an analytic or heuristic study should reveal a description of the input and output phenomena. After a determination that these phenomena are probabilistic in nature, a substitution for a synthetic distribution is possible. Suppose a service station desires to reconsider its present purchasing policy with respect to one product, e.g., lube oil. The daily demand for lube oil fluctuates, and each day of the week has its own demand distribution. Suppose that on a sample of past Saturdays the number of oil changes demanded has varied between none and four, according to the probabilities shown in Table 10.2.

T A B L E 10.2 Probability Distribution of Demand for Oil Changes on Saturdays

Number of changes demanded	Probability	Monte Carlo numbers
0	0.07	00–06
1	0.20	07–26
2	0.22	27–48
3	0.33	49–81
4	0.18	82–99
	1.00	

The third column of the table consists of an allocation of 100 two-digit numbers (between 00 and 99) to all possible events in proportion to their probabilities. Thus, on 7 percent of the Saturdays no lube changes will be demanded; so we assign 7 different two-digit numbers (00 to 06 inclusive) to this event. Likewise, we assign 20 different two-digit numbers (07 to 26 inclusive) to the event of one change being demanded, and so forth.

We now make use of a table of *random* digits, in which the digits are listed in no apparent pattern. Each digit had the same chance of appearing on each trial. While there is no pattern, we know that all the digits will be approximately equally represented in a large sample of such digits.

We draw two digits at a time. If the first two-digit number is 43, this is looked up in the Monte Carlo column of the table and would be interpreted as two lube changes. In other words, on this Saturday the demand at the station is two lube changes. By repeatedly drawing two-digit random numbers, we can generate a characteristic picture of demand for a succession of Saturdays.

We can use a different demand distribution, based on station records, for each day of the week. Then we can make assumptions about supply, such as a delivery period every other day and a decision rule to purchase sufficient lube oil for three changes. With this information, we can manually or mechanically generate daily demand-and-supply quantities to learn the likely magnitude and frequency of excess inventories and shortages. We compare the average losses incurred under different purchasing rules and choose the loss-minimizing rule.

The use of probability gives realism to the problem and has given us the name of Monte Carlo simulations. In more complex simulations, a computer is used to produce the random numbers, interpret the events, make the necessary computations, and summarize the results. Such marketing problems as media selection, department-store ordering and pricing, site location for retail outlets, and customer facility planning in retail outlets have used computers for simulation.

THE MAJOR MODELS

Matrix algebra, calculus, probability theory, and simulation are fundamental tools used in setting up and solving many of the models developed to aid executives in decision making. Some models are designed for setting standards for decision making and others for the analysis of a process. Most of these models have originated from operations research (OR) activities.

Some models which have been used sufficiently to acquire names are:

1. Allocation models
2. Competitive-strategy models.
3. Brand-switching models
4. Waiting-line models
5. Critical-path scheduling models

Some of the examples below were contrived to be simple for illustrative purposes. Model building is not just a "fun" exercise for those who like to solve puzzles but can be a serious attack on decision making in business.

The final model for a real decision problem can be quite elaborate and represent a hooking together of several more elementary models and techniques. We shall discuss each of these five models in the context of a marketing department for ease of illustration. Similar analogies would hold in production or manufacturing or almost any area of a business.

ALLOCATION MODELS

The economic aspect of business decision making is the "allocation of scarce resources to competing ends." A decision must be made on how to allocate or *program* these limited resources to product lines, classes of customers, or inventories. An example of these scarce resources may be advertising dollars to be spent or salesmen to be assigned.

We shall illustrate allocation of resources by the development of a media plan. The number of available media is very great. But when a particular product is considered, a number of constraints severely limit the range of media choice.

We can define, in our example, some of these constraints. First, the advertising budget is finite. Second, the message must be directed at specific market segments; and certain media are more effective than others in reaching these segments. Third, the geographical distribution of the market segments imposes restrictions on the choice of media. Finally, the media or the advertiser, or both, may impose restrictions.

Usually we find that a large number of different media plans satisfy all our constraints. But of those media plans, which will be the most effective? An *effectiveness criterion* needs to be developed against which every feasible plan can be rated. In media selection, the criterion is the number of expected effective exposures, or some variant of this. *Programming* is one of the mathematical models that can be used for the discovery of an exposure-maximizing media plan.

As an example, suppose that a petroleum company wishes to select a media plan consisting of the purchase of X_1 advertising units of medium 1 (radio) and X_2 advertising units of medium 2 (television). Table 10.3 indicates the relevant characteristics of the two media.

The following constraints are made explicit in a discussion between the media planner and the advertiser:

1. The total advertising budget is $1 million.

2. At least 30 million exposures are to be achieved in the New York, Boston, and Washington areas (region 1) and 20 million exposures on the West Coast (region 2).

3. No more than 2 million exposures are to take place among non-sports-minded people.

4. At least 40 million are to take place among automobile drivers.

T A B L E 10.3 Selected
Characteristics of Two Media

	Medium 1 (radio)	Medium 2 (TV)
Cost of an advertising unit (football game)	$25,000	$100,000
Maximum number of units	40	10
Minimum number of units	10	3
Total number of effective exposures per unit	1,000,000	6,000,000
Number of effective exposures in region 1 per unit	600,000	3,000,000
Number of effective exposures in region 2 per unit	400,000	3,000,000
Number of exposures to non-sports-minded people per unit	75,000	80,000
Number of exposures to automobile drivers	800,000	4,500,000

T A B L E 10.4 Mathematical
Statement of Media-selection Problem

Maximize	$1{,}000{,}000\ X_1 + 6{,}000{,}000\ X_2$		
Subject to			Budget
(1)	$25{,}000\ X_1 + 100{,}000\ X_2 \leq 1{,}000{,}000$		constraint
(2)	$X_1 \leq 40$		Individual
(3)	$X_2 \leq 10$		medium
(4)	$X_1 \geq 10$		Usage
(5)	$X_2 \geq 3$		constraint
(6)	$600{,}000\ X_1 + 3{,}000{,}000\ X_2 \geq 30{,}000{,}000$		Regional
(7)	$400{,}000\ X_1 + 3{,}000{,}000\ X_2 \geq 20{,}000{,}000$		constraint
(8)	$75{,}000\ X_1 + 80{,}000\ X_2 \leq 2{,}000{,}000$		Customer characteristic
(9)	$800{,}000\ X_1 + 4{,}500{,}000\ X_2 \geq 40{,}000{,}000$		constraint

The problem is to find the number of programs of the two media which would maximize the total number of effective exposures subject to the various constraints. A mathematical statement of the problem is given in Table 10.4.

Each constraint has been expressed as a mathematical inequality. For example, the budget constraint reads: the number of advertisements purchased in medium 1 (X_1) times their unit cost ($25,000), plus the number purchased in medium 2 (X_2) times their unit cost ($100,000), must be less than or equal to the budget of $1 million.

The second constraint reads: the number of advertisements placed in medium 1 must not exceed 40. We interpret the other inequalities in the same manner.

The constraints have the effect of eliminating most combinations of X_2 and X_1 but there still remain a large number of combinations which would satisfy all the inequalities. But only one of these (usually) will also maximize the total number of effective exposures. Mathematical programming is the technique for finding the best solution.

In this simple case, the inequalities could be drawn on graph paper; this would help to delimit the set of media plans (points) which would satisfy all the constraints. Then there is a procedure for locating the best plan, the details of which are beyond the scope of this book.

The best plan calls for seven advertisements in medium 2, and twelve advertisements in medium 1. This plan will cost exactly $1 million and yield 54 million exposures.

There are several types of mathematical programming. Linear programming implies that the criteria and the constraints in the problem can be represented by straight-line segments. For a straight-line segment the slope is constant, which means that the ratio of a change in one variable to a change in the other is constant. For example, a linear cost function means that the cost of an additional unit is constant; and a linear exposure function means that the cost of an additional advertising exposure is constant. In other words, diminishing or increasing returns are ruled out in strictly linear models.

Linear-programming models are popular because linear assumptions are the easiest to work with and solve. Many important functions are linear or nearly linear over much of their range.

A number of techniques are available for solving a linear-programming problem, once it is expressed mathematically. For not more than three variables, graphical solutions are possible. Alternatively, Dansig's *simplex algorithm* is an all-purpose method. The word simplex has nothing to do with simple but is a well-defined mathematical concept which has a geometric interpretation. An algorithm is a systematic method for testing various solutions; it guarantees that each successive solution represents an improvement until the best solution is reached.

The term *nonlinear programming* is reserved for problem formulation where some constraint(s) or the effectiveness criterion, or both, are not linear. An example is quadratic programming, which uses a second-degree (quadratic) curve for some of the constraints or effectiveness criterion. or both.

Integer programming is a variant so named because the optimal solution is constrained to consist of whole numbers. For example, suppose X_1 represents the number of salesmen that should be hired. If the answer *is not* constrained to be an integer, it could be a mixed decimal such as 100.7. What does it mean to hire 0.7 of a salesman? Should the answer be rounded to 100 salesmen or 101 salesmen? The solution is not obvious, and the decision may involve a difference of many thousands of dollars. Integer programming is a way of avoiding the ambiguities of fractional answers.

Dynamic programming is applied to problems where a series of consecutive interdependent decisions have to be made. It is the most complicated of the programming methods. For example, purchasing decisions must be made throughout the year; today's decision must be made in terms of what it implies for the decision choices in the next period. This in turn affects the decision choices in the following period, and so on.

In summary, a programming model is applied to problems where there appear to be many different ways to allocate resources. Constraints (usually in the form of mathematical inequalities) are introduced to reduce the number of admissible solutions. A search is then made for that solution among the feasible set which selects an optimum in terms of some stated effectiveness criterion. Programming models hold great promise for aiding in the solution of such important marketing problems as media selection, allocation of sales force, determination of the best product line in terms of a firm's resource base, site location, and selection of channels of distribution.

Specialized versions of programming models are useful in a marketing context. One of these is the *transportation model* which defines the existence of several origins (such as warehouses) and destinations (such as retail stores) and the unit cost of shipping from every origin to every destination. The amount of goods available for shipment from each warehouse and the amount of goods ordered by each retail store are specified. Under the constraints given, the problem is to find which supplies should be shipped from which warehouse to which store in order to minimize overall costs of transportation.

A sample problem is shown in Table 10.5. Mathematical analysis shows that there is a shipment allocation which costs only $580,000. This problem could be converted into a standard linear-programming problem and then solved by the simplex method. Special techniques have been developed to solve problems of the format in Table 10.5 directly.

Some large companies have used the transportation model for a number of years to develop shipping schedules. There is a useful variant called the *assignment model,* with promising applications to problems other than transportation. In the assignment model, the number of origins equals the number of destinations and each

T A B L E 10.5 Unit Shipping Costs
from Various Warehouses to
Various Stores

Warehouse	Store 1	Store 2	Store 3	Warehouse availabilities
A	$40	$10	$60	5,000
B	$80	$70	$30	6,000
C	$40	$90	$20	2,000
D	$60	$30	$50	3,000
Store requirements, units	4,000	10,000	2,000	16,000

origin is associated with only one destination.

As an example, suppose four salesmen are to be assigned to four territories. The salesmen differ in skills, and territories differ in stage of development. An estimate of the expected annual sales that would result from each man's being assigned to each territory is made by the sales manager. This information is summarized in Table 10.6.

T A B L E 10.6 Estimated Annual Sales
from the Assignment of Different
Salesmen to Different Territories

Salesman	Territory 1	Territory 2	Territory 3	Territory 4
Andy	$170,000	$ 75,000	$140,000	$195,000
Bill	75,000	51,000	35,000	51,000
Cecil	151,000	140,000	140,000	100,000
Dan	145,000	182,000	140,000	120,000

There are 24 (4X3X2X1) different possible assignments. Because this is a small-scale example it is not difficult to arrive at the total sales-maximizing assignment by trial and error: *A*4; *B*1; *C*3; *D*2; total sales, $592,000.

In more complex examples, the number of possible solutions increases factorially, and a mathematical analysis is necessary. (For 10 salesmen, there are 3,628,000 combinations). The same mathematical technique used in the model could be used for assignment of salesmen to other than territories, e.g., to different company products or to different types of customers.

Another classic problem is known as the traveling-salesman problem. Although allocation is not involved, the traveling-salesman problem is similar to an assignment problem. A salesman must make calls in n cities. This means that there are n factorial possible routes. One of these routes has a minimum total travel cost; another route (possibly the same) has a minimum total travel time. The problem is to find the best route in terms of total travel cost or total travel time, whichever is the stated objective. At present, general solutions are lacking, but important theorems have been discovered, such as the fact that the best route never involves any crossing of paths; and mathematical solutions are available where special simplifying assumptions are made. A simulation approach also can be used to search for a reasonable solution.

COMPETITIVE-STRATEGY MODELS

Profit outcomes are a function of the decision of a firm, but the decision of a firm is affected by the competitors' decision. A marketing decision must be based on an estimate of what competitors are likely to do, even though their intentions may not be known in advance.

Game theory is the name given to the systematic investigation of rational decision making in the context of uncertainty concerning the moves of competitors. The theory of games has provided a conceptual framework within which most competitive problems can be formulated. In most real competitive situations, statistical decision theory can be more successfully applied. Competitive theory has been used effectively to develop bidding tactics, pricing policies, advertising strategies, and timing of new models into the marketplace. Competitive behavior and reaction are more predictable with generally available data than most managers realize.

There are some interesting marketing possibilities for game models designed for a variety of military and political situations. One is a game of timing involving two competitors (duelists) who at a signal are to begin approaching each other at some constant uniform rate. Each has only one available bullet (a new product) and is free to fire it at will, with the knowledge that his chance of hitting the opponent improves as the distance narrows. When should the duelist fire?

Another interesting game involves distributing an army over several battlefields, with the knowledge that each territory is "won" by the side which has disposed more troops in that territory. How should an army distribute its troops (or a company distribute its salesmen) in this situation?

Another game, gambler's ruin, involves two competitors with different initial endowments of capital. A coin is tossed repeatedly with a probability p that competitor A will win and a probability $1-p$ that competitor B will win. When the capital of one competitor is exhausted, the game ends. Given specific data, it is possible to estimate such things as the probability of "ruin" for each gambler and the likely duration of the game.

Game models suggest a useful analytical approach to such competitive problems as pricing, sales-force allocation, and advertising outlays. Their value is in clarifying the strategic implications of such moves as surprise, threat, and coalition.

Game theory and operational gaming should be distinguished. The latter term describes the modeling of a game around a realistic situation, where the participants actually make decisions (often in teams, as in the IBM Management Game) and where the results of their interacting decisions are reported and become the data inputs for the next round of decisions. A large number of management and marketing games are available and used both in formal management-training programs and in research settings.

BRAND-SWITCHING MODELS

Market share must be watched by marketing executives just as much as profits. Present customers can never be taken for granted.

The attitude of marketing executives toward brand switching is quite simple: the switching-out rate must be slowed down, and the switching-in rate must be increased. Brand choice factors must be analyzed, and this knowledge applied where possible in order to alter existing brand-switching rates.

An estimate of switching rates can be made from data showing the individual brand choices made over a period of time by a representative sample of consumers. These data can then be used to construct a brand-switching matrix that provides information about:

1. The *repeat-purchase* rate for each brand, indicated by the principal diagonal numbers. Under certain assumptions, the repeat-purchase rate can be interpreted as a measure of brand loyalty.

2. The *switching-in and switching-out* rate for each brand, represented by the off-diagonal numbers.

If the switching rates remain constant, at least for a short period, the matrix may become a useful tool in predicting the magnitude and velocity of change in future market shares on the basis of the present market shares. If the switching rates change in a predictable way, a forecast of market shares is possible.

Waiting appears in many situations, e.g., in marketing, customers wait for service, and companies wait for both customers and deliveries. In a machine shop, lathes may wait for material, and in a warehouse, movement of goods waits on transportation. Waiting is of interest because it imposes a cost. The customer who waits in a queue in a supermarket bears a cost in terms of more desirable alternative use of his time. If he regards the waiting time as excessive, he may leave and buy elsewhere, and the cost of his waiting would be shifted to the supermarket.

Waiting time imposes a cost, but so does the effort to reduce waiting time. The supermarket might reduce waiting time by adding more counters or personnel, or both. The decision problem is one of balancing the cost of lost sales against the cost of additional facilities for service up to the point where the cost of an additional facility would just balance the profits lost because of customer impatience.

The decision problem is illustrated graphically in Fig. 10.2. The higher the average waiting time in the system, the greater the cost

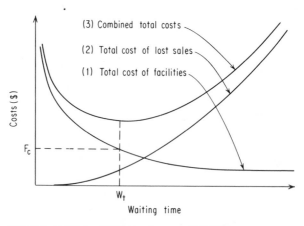

FIG. 10.2   Costs as related to average waiting time.

of lost sales (curve 2) but the lower the cost of facilities and personnel (curve 1). The two cost curves are added vertically to derive a combined cost curve (curve 3). The lowest point on this combined cost curve indicates the average waiting time W_t which will minimize combined costs. The implied investment in service facilities is F_c. The lowest point on curve 3 can be found graphically or through differential calculus if appropriate cost equations can be found.

The cost of additional facilities is not difficult to measure; but it is very difficult to measure the value of lost sales which result from customer impatience. People vary considerably in their attitudes toward waiting; customer impatience is also a function of the difference between anticipated and actual waiting time, and anticipated waiting varies by situations. Also, customers who feel impatient may decide not to abandon the store if they think that alternative stores are no better.

Queuing theory (or waiting-line theory) is not designed to answer how much waiting time should be built into a system. This is primarily an economic question, as shown in Fig. 10.2.

Queuing theory is designed to handle two preliminary questions: what amount of waiting time may be expected in a particular system, and how can this waiting time be altered?

The waiting time will depend on four dimensions of the system:

1. *The Interarrival Time.* The time between arrivals into the system has a probability distribution, estimated from frequency data. The mean, standard deviation, and other characteristics of interarrival time can be derived from the probability distribution.

2. *The Service Time.* The time between initiating a service and its completion can be viewed as having a probability distribution.

3. *The Number of Service Facilities.* The number affects the amount of waiting time.

4. *The Service Method.* Usually customers are serviced in the order in which they arrive (called first-in, first-out). But other methods are to give service to the most "important" customers first, to service the shortest orders first, to service at random, or combinations of these methods.

With these four dimensions specified for a particular system, it is possible to estimate queuing characteristics. These are expected waiting time, expected queue length, and the variability of waiting time and queue length. For certain simple queuing situations, it is possible to derive these answers mathematically; for more complicated systems, simulation can be used to derive these estimates.

The decision maker can simulate the effects of different hypothetical changes when the system breeds long queues. In the case of a service station with a serious queuing problem on Saturday, four possible attacks are indicated by the dimensions. The manager can try to influence his customers to have their automobiles serviced on other days—this would have the effect of increasing the time between arrivals on Saturdays. Or the service station can decrease the service times, as by employing assistants to aid the mechanics. Or another service area can be added. Or, if the business is large enough, the manager can go to specialized service with particular employees. For example, two men can lubricate one car, one in front, the other in the rear, at the same time.

Most of the literature about queuing deals with facility planning for telephone exchanges, highways and toll roads, docks, and airline terminals. Yet retailing institutions such as supermarkets, service stations, and airline ticket offices also face critical queuing problems; marketing executives of such organizations are showing increased interest in waiting-line models.

CRITICAL-PATH SCHEDULING MODELS

A technique called PERT (program evaluation and review technique) deals with the tactical questions of managing a complex project. As an example, suppose that management has just finished reviewing and approving ideas for a new product. Important tactical questions are: (1) What is the one best sequence for the various activities which must be performed? (2) With normal departmental resources, how long will it be before the product is ready for sale? (3) What extra resources would be necessary to complete the project x weeks earlier?

Each new product will require the starting and completion of hundreds of different activities. The completion of an *activity* is called an *event*. As a simplified illustration, suppose the following six events must take place:

1. Corporate approval granted
2. Engineering and styling completed
3. Marketing analysis completed
4. Advertising campaign plans completed
5. Manufacturing preparation completed
6. Market testing completed

After these events are identified, a PERT analysis consists of:

1. *Preparing a Program Network.* In what order should the above events take place? Certain events will be in a priority relationship and others in a concurrent relationship.

The best way to see this distinction is to work backward from the terminal event. Before a market test can be started, let alone completed, two prior events must take place. The advertising campaign plans must be completed, and the product must be manufactured.

But these two prior events are themselves in a concurrent relationship—the activities leading to the completion of each can be carried on concurrently. The next step would be to examine each of these events separately, to determine what events must precede each. When there are hundreds of events, the task of preparing a "network" for these events is neither easy nor free from ambiguity. But for the six events listed above, the most efficient network is fairly straightforward. By representing the events as circles and the activities as arrows connecting the circles, we would prepare the network showing the order of events.

2. *Estimating Activity Times.* The department responsible for each activity is asked to estimate the most likely time to complete that activity, given the department's normal resources. This estimate is supplemented by both an optimistic and a pessimistic estimate, again assuming normal departmental resources. For convenience, three estimates are connected by commas and placed alongside the activity arrows.

These simple explanations on major models and tools have been given in order that the manager may understand a little better the problem solutions put forth by the specialist. Also they may aid the manager in recognizing possible solution techniques for his problems.

PART THREE

Applications

CHAPTER ELEVEN

Marketing Management Information and Control System

WHAT A MARKETING MICS IS

An information and control system for marketing management may be defined as a set of procedures and methods for the regular, planned collection, analysis, and presentation of information for use in making and carrying out marketing decisions. Notice that this is a step beyond a logistics system, which would handle inventory control, purchasing, and so forth.

An information and control system has two major components: (1) a support system and (2) an operating system. In this definition support systems include those activities required to generate and manipulate the data. Examples of activities may be market research, data gathering, and programming of the computer for data processing to convert the data into information. The operating system uses the information as aids to planning and controlling marketing activities.

In this discussion, we are concerned mainly with the development of three types of marketing operating systems, those designed for basic research, planning, and control.

In basic research, we try to find, develop, and test sophisticated decision rules and to hypothesize cause and effect, which should improve our ability to assess effects of actions and permit learning from experience. An example of basic research is the application of Leontief's input/output tables to a business concern. Such a model begins to relate the true sources and sinks of material movement.

As information is collected and processed, an advanced market-planning model can be assembled by any company.

Planning systems furnish in convenient form information the marketing executive requires for planning marketing and sales programs. A data bank enables product managers in a group or division to base their plans on the same data. Higher-level management then is able to review comparable information more quickly when considering plans for approval. Simulation (see Chaps. 9 and 10) allows a more sophisticated analysis of alternate plans to effect a better decision. From such market planning systems, several large retailing organizations are now advancing to the ultimate sophistication, a system that reviews sales trends and inventories and then places orders for merchandise.

Control systems provide management with continuous monitoring (sometimes through exception reporting) and rapid setting of trends, problems, and marketing opportunities. Control systems allow better anticipation of problems, a more comprehensive and detailed review of performance of lower echelons against plans, and a greater degree of response. IBM's marketing division has developed an information and control system that allows district sales managers to interrogate the data bank for such information as:

- Sales or rental to date, broken down by product, type of customer, and branch office making the sale
- Sales in relation to marketing targets
- Various combinations of information relating to sales, customer classifications, products, applications sold, etc.

Current information allows the manager to keep up to date on marketing problems and opportunities and on progress in relation to sales goals.

AN EXAMPLE OF MICS IN A PETROLEUM COMPANY

With today's knowledge of hardware, both in computers and memory capacity and in data acquisition and transmittal, and programming technology together with management science techniques in use in other areas of the business environment, a marketing MICS is feasible and offers a high degree of economic payout. For example, let us look at a major petrochemical company. Such a system could provide a data-storage facility, communications, and data processing capability for all wholesale and retail data processing for sales detail, stock control, and customer receivables. The facility for detail demand forecasting on a regular basis and periodic consumer market surveys or complex sales analysis are system by-products. Marketing management could have the means to establish and control sales effort by market potential rather than considering performance in relation to last year's activity. With the facility of having access to, and control over, bulk terminal stations through communication features, all information from the original data recording through all levels of processing would be available to management at all levels as required. Accurate data in real time could facilitate the developing of realistic inventory control, market forecast, and consumer potential through modern mathematical modeling techniques.

We shall examine three of the many elements of the marketing system in more detail for illustration. First, look at market forecast planning activity. Such a system could systemize, speed up, and integrate sales forecasting by displaying the information needed for forecasting and providing the on-line tools for improving, updating, communicating, and organizing the forecast. Management-science tools and techniques such as statistical smoothing, trend analysis, and regressions are in common use today in other business areas. Such techniques as Bayesian statistics aid in generating forecasting models that take into account user judgment, converting demographical data to total market forecast and converting strategy changes and historical data into market share projections.

For the petroleum company, the system may be structured as follows: a company marketing history file containing strategic changes, sales volumes, and prices by product, geographic area, and type of customer as major account. Environmental data files would consist of segmented industry sales and demographical data and projections such as population, income, number of cars registered, and so on. A competitive-action file could contain estimates of competitive sales volume and action with measures of size, timing, and approximate commitment. Another system section may be an exception control and display program which would reexamine forecast projections when actual results differed by a control limit set by management. A forecast model generator, under the direction of the forecaster, could derive model equations relating designated data from the corporate files to price, sales, or market share in a particular market segment, then generate a market forecast based on these derived equations.

With such a system, forecasting could change from a cyclic project to a continuous change-as-required process. As history files are updated, forecasts can be compared with actual results. The next step would be a tie-in of the above forecasting system to corporate planning models allowing the inclusion of sales objectives with sales forecast and calculation of profitability indexes. This updated forecast could be automatically incorporated into the operations planning models in the manufacturing, distribution, and financial areas. Increased efficiency in forecast personnel would probably pay for the system's hardware.

The second element of the marketing management control system we wish to examine is market strategy planning. Its purpose would be to monitor marketing expenditures and sales in order to provide assistance to marketing management in sales decisions, pricing policy, and the allocation of marketing resources such as promotion, manpower recruiting and assignment, services, and investing funds. A program forecast allocation could take sales and marketing expenditure data periodically from the corporate data banks and allocate expenses to sales segments by products, geographic area, organizational area, customer class, etc. The marketing history and expenditure files could be augmented by a transfer-price file containing transfer prices for each product at each possible location where marketing obtains ownership and assumes all further expenses. These transfer prices may be set by optimization simulation on manufacturing and distribution models. A forecast file could contain company sales volume and price by product, area, and customer types. The marketing executive might probe the files to examine the latest realized price, i.e., transfer price versus expense allocations. This updated information would aid the executive in decision making when setting up or changing budgets or approving marketing expenditures or investments. The most profitable routes for market expansion could be determined and prices for new market opportunities assessed. Often large sums of company money or resources may be committed in a short negotiation, often with poor or inadequate information. Accessible, timely, easily manipulated information including multiple products, multiple delivery points, and sliding-scale prices would enable the negotiator to deal from strength, i.e., from knowledge of profitability to his company.

A third element may be a control system for competitive tactics. Such a system could serve marketing management by providing an automatic means of evaluating results of company tactics and decreasing reaction time to meet competition's actions. A competitive model including action and reaction cycles between competitors indicating new equilibrium points may be included as a management decision tool. This allows other criteria besides sales volume to be used in choosing alternate courses of action. Some of the decision maker's emotional factors could be downgraded by factual information.

MANAGEMENT SCIENCE IN MARKETING

The modern marketing man has to be multilingual, for he obtains his material from many disciplines. He must be able to converse with economists about marginal analysis, elasticity, and diminishing returns; with psychologists about projective techniques, latent needs, and nonrational behavior; with sociologists about acculturation, social norms, and correlation. Now another language, that of higher mathematics, is needed. Many marketing men are uncomfortable about this. They do not look askance at mathematical concepts, but they are a bit anxious because of a language barrier. Fortunately, the language barrier is not insurmountable. Linear programming, queuing theory, and the like are simply unfamiliar names for some significant ideas.

We have tried to reduce some of the mystery by defining the mathematics vocabulary and illustrating ideas in a marketing concept in the previous discussion. These discussions are also valid for all areas of the business environment.

DECISION MAKING

Quantitative analysis is not alien to the field of marketing. For many decades marketing research departments have conducted consumer surveys, prepared sales forecasts, and analyzed sales reports. A few practitioners have even used higher mathematics for complex problem solving in marketing. But until recently the mathematical "sophistication" underlying the typical research project could be found between the covers of a textbook in elementary statistics. And much of the research has amounted to routine information gathering.

Today the emphasis is changing. The focus of research is on *decision making* and not fact gathering for its own sake. The belief is spreading that models can be built which identify and relate the key factors in a problem situation, and which offer explicit directions for decision making.

Today a marketing executive is asked to distinguish carefully between alternative strategies in making a major decision. Each strategy will lead to one of several outcomes, depending in part upon events beyond the firm's control; and the possible outcomes for each strategy must somehow be weighed to achieve an estimated value for that strategy. The values of the various strategies must be compared, and the executive must then attempt to select the strategy promising the highest value or payoff.

THE STATUS OF MANAGEMENT SCIENCE IN MARKETING

The accomplishments of management science in the marketing field can be viewed in terms of four classes of effort. Many of the approaches that will be mentioned have been in use for a long time. They have been expanded, modified, and brought into sharper focus by management-science practitioners.

DATA REDUCTION

Masses of data must be reduced to a practical level if they are to be of use to the marketing decision maker. Management science helps to increase the validity of such information by insisting upon the careful design of experiments. Frequently, data collection has preceded a knowledge of how the data were to be used. Reliability has been improved by paying careful attention to the sampling problems. Much effort has been expended in this direction.

PREDICTIONS

The ability to predict has been improved. Using multiple correlation, autocorrelation, regression analysis, and new smoothing techniques, greater predictive strength has been developed. On the other hand, predictive techniques based on causal relations of variables have been essentially nonexistent. Functional systems of marketing variables that are developed by means of correlation analysis seldom appear to hold with time. They are, therefore, only useful in explaining what has happened in the past—what was observed—not what will happen in the future. It can be conjectured that the selected independent variables are not fundamental to the dependent variables. Brand-switching analysis has been applied to the prediction problem with some success. This model permits prediction and at the same time presents a new way of looking at the marketing process.

MARKETING SYSTEMS MODELS

The mechanics of marketing will be understood only when reasonable models of the marketing process are developed. The functional relationships that describe the way in which the system operates are required if such models are to be built. The brand-switching model is a management-science development that succeeds in describing certain aspects of consumer behavior. Simulation models are being used for the same purposes. They provide a reasonable way to explore consumer dynamics based on hypothetical functional relationships.

In another mechanical area, that of competition, game theory has great conceptual importance. For practical problem resolution, it has always been and continues to be something of a toy. There are sufficient reasons to doubt the applicability of classical game theory, including the fact that the payoff matrix is dynamic and that competitors have only bounded rationality.

With respect to a third mechanical area, communication channels, a media model variant has been developed that is based on simulation. These models constitute a way of organizing great quantities of information that is vital to the media-selection process. For this type of media model, the individual specifies a number of media schedules which he considers both feasible and desirable. These alternatives are then tested and compared. Each schedule is measured or characterized in a number of different ways. The decision maker is the final arbiter; he makes the selection.

DECISION-MAKING MODELS

In this fourth area, decision-making (or optimum-seeking) models in marketing, little has been accomplished. The only exception is in the media-selection area. Here, both linear- and dynamic-programming systems are being used. While these models qualify as optimum-seeking models, it must be pointed out that they are totally dependent on estimations of the critical marketing factors, and these are derived by judgment. Because these models use operator intervention during the course of the solution, they are far from being "true" optimum-producing models. Instead, they produce an organized set of data upon which the decision maker can operate from time to time, as he deems necessary. Many media models are available as computer programs. The computations can be stopped from time to time to permit operator intervention. (This sort of interaction provides an excellent example of man-machine interfaces.)

MANAGEMENT SCIENCE AND THE MARKETING MANAGER

Operations research and management scientists are strongly motivated to produce decision-making models where the objective is to find the optimal solution. Yet this type of achievement in the marketing field is almost negligible. In fact, although there have been some real accomplishments in marketing science, they have been quite different from those which management science has achieved in other areas. We should apply experience, knowledge, and techniques so useful in other business areas to marketing.

Traditionally, management science states that it is the executives' responsibility to develop strategies. The problems associated with creating strategies cannot be delegated to scientists if understanding and respect are ultimately desired by the marketer. Strategy development is fundamental to the marketing process.

Several approaches suggest ways in which management science can help in marketing. First, we can attempt to identify all the relevant variables that combine to produce strategic alternatives. The various combinations may then be obtained by random simulation with a set of rules to filter out undesirable strategies. As these rules are improved by some learning process connected with judgment, fewer rejects get through the net. The process is akin to a chess-learning program. As the evaluation rules are tightened, exceptional strategies begin to appear.

Random creation within the set of variables would be wasteful. Instead, an efficient creative system should be able to explore the historical evolution of events. Each previous marketing effort can be viewed as a cluster of points in the n-dimensional space that scientists use to characterize it. Where gaps appear in these clusters, unique opportunities might exist. Although this discussion is quite abstract, it should be easy enough to see how one might inventory the character of an existing product market.

When we choose a strategy, we would like it to coincide with our actions for the immediate present and over a reasonable period of time. In this way we would hope to avoid serious, in-time suboptimization. Precisely because of the complexity of marketing strategies, management science may be able to provide help in their formation. Simulation techniques, rather than analysis, seem most promising. The computer is a great ally of the management scientist in his efforts to help produce creative strategies.

We must begin to analyze marketing problems in terms of the competitors' value systems, and we must be able to identify those factors which trigger various competitive behaviors. The search for a reasonable decision criterion under conditions of competition leads us to recognize that although we seldom know what a competitor will do, if we can enumerate everything that he might do, we can then take steps to prepare ourselves for each and every eventuality. This is a system of "thrust and parry" which may well follow the lines of classical control theory. Simulation techniques prove to be of considerable benefit in this area.

The development and application of new marketing "optimization" techniques hinge on the establishment of a working rapport with behaviorists, economists, statisticians, and people with marketing experience. The problem of conflicting cultures within the marketing management field cannot be resolved until those concerned recognize that one cannot proceed without the other. The buying consumer is forcing even further shrinkage of decision time.

Forcing marketing problems into production-type models will, in the long run, create a most serious problem. We must become conscious of the cost of studying a problem. When it appears that a traditional approach is more rewarding, it should be followed. We must have a willingness to accept improvement instead of optimization—for the time being. This is realistic and necessary, but optimization should remain the goal of management science.

Using new techniques and approaches such as graph theory, information theory, mathematical topology, and simulation techniques and by developing cybernetic models, epidemic models, prey-predator models, and addiction models, to name just a few possibilities, we shall be able to move ahead.

CONCLUSION

The present lack of adequate information-handling techniques in the marketing area demonstrates the failure to deal more than superficially with the "total" corporate enterprise. Within the last decade, the concepts and methods of integrated information handling have altered completely management's approaches to decision making and control. But the vital marketing function has been almost completely untouched. In no area of business operations have the new techniques and tools been more neglected. The unrealized profit potential for a company is as large in marketing as in any other area of business. Applications are possible now to such fundamental areas of marketing as product line development, pricing structure, distribution operation, sales force management, advertising, and sales forecasting. Information handling and manipulation in a systematic manner can help find answers to some basic questions. What level of advertising expenditures is realistic in a specific market situation? What is the preferred salesman distribution in a given sales situation? Should the sales force be geographic or product-oriented? What is a valid measure of the salesman's use of his line? What are reliable measures of marketing effectiveness?

The reasons why marketing systems have not developed to the same extent as production, logistics, or financial systems are not technical. Marketing research technology (data gathering), computer technology (data handling), and analytical procedures (e.g., model building) are all sufficiently advanced to permit companies to build an effective marketing MICS.

Experience has shown that development of MICS requires management to accept the responsibility. The user group, such as the marketing department, must define and be responsible for the system. The system sophistication must be balanced with the sophistication of the using managers.

CHAPTER TWELVE

An Inventory Control Process

Concepts that have an adaptive-control aspect to them may be found in a number of fields separate from the more conventional areas of automatic control systems. For illustration, we shall look at the control of stock inventory, as such, as an area where adaptive-control ideas may be considered. It may be explanatory to describe some of the prominent features of such an inventory control scheme and to identify some of the adaptive-control features.

We shall describe the control of inventory in a manufacturing plant and make some observations about it. The particular characteristics considered for the inventory control process are representative of a consistent inventory policy. They are not cited because they necessarily represent a better inventory policy. This system is outside the class of control of physical systems with which most automatic control engineers are concerned. Thus this illustration may give an increased insight into various adaptive-control features. Control engineers and managers may gain a further appreciation of the capabilities and areas of usefulness of adaptive control. It should become apparent that there are a number of adaptive-control features present in this illustration which contribute to its effectiveness.

This illustration may lead the control system designer to recognize that by using sound adaptive-control principles, even if he is not thoroughly familiar with all the details of the process being controlled, he may work with someone who has the prerequisite information of process capabilities and limitations to do a more effective job of synthesizing a good control system. This description may also illustrate that thorough understanding and knowledge of a process can lead the control system designer to employ adaptive-control features later useful for interpretation of models in terms of their adaptive-control characteristics.

For illustration a simplified block diagram of an inventory control process is shown in Fig. 12.1. This illustration depicts the relationship and interaction of some of the major portions of inventory control. Blocks in the illustration are used to show pictorially the qualitative relationships that exist among the various parts of the inventory system.

Orders may be received at any time but usually are serviced at regular ordering-time intervals. The order requests then proceed directly to the present stock area. The present stock status is updated by subtraction of requested orders. The shipping policy accepts requested orders together with the difference between order requests and the present stock. This then determines the orders ac-

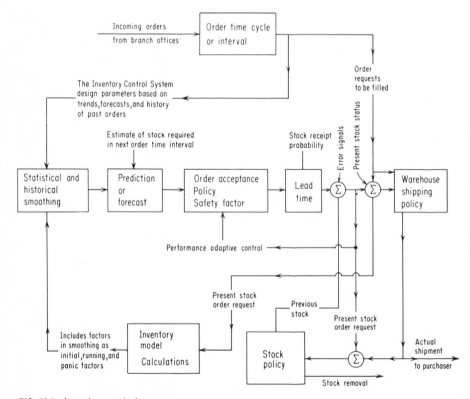

FIG. 12.1 Inventory control process.

tually shipped. The shipped amount is subtracted from present stock. The result provides information regarding the value of stock at the beginning of the new ordering interval.

A computation performed by using the difference between present stock and orders actually shipped together with orders actually received is used for averaging past and present order values. These calculations are called *smoothing*. Smoothing factors may include an initial factor, a running factor, or a panic factor (out of stock).

An estimate of the value of stock required at the end of the next interval can be predicted using the smoothed values of the present average and the trend. This estimate, in effect, represents an input adaptive feature in which an effort is made to use the invariance principle on the orders received to better estimate future stock requirements.

The effectiveness of these calculations is dependent on the validity of the assumptions made regarding the statistical properties of the orders received as well as the occurrence of the sampling, smoothing, and predicting calculations. In themselves, the smoothing and predictive processes are not inherently accurate.

To determine what stock should be requested for the coming period, the order policy uses information such as the present amount of stock, the predicted increment during the upcoming interval, and the safety factor. This has the effect of providing a predictive control feature which serves to represent a form of performance adaptive control.

The lead time affects the stock requests and also influences whether the stock requested will be stock received by the end of the ordering interval. This last question is probabilistic and relatively uncontrollable. Lead time has great significance in determining whether stock is received in sufficient time to become part of present stock at the start of the next interval. By improving the probability of receiving the requested stock, the value of the present stock can be controlled better. For example, a closer check on requested stock may prove valuable when significant-sized orders have been received.

Stock policy may relate to the way of removing obsolete or outmoded stock, or other regulations regarding the handling of stock. Other factors going to make up stock policy are the amount of present stock, the current shipments, incoming order rates, etc.

From data on the difference between the present stock and order requests together with the inventory model, the logic rules and appropriate smoothing and prediction factors are generated for forecasting.

The differences, shown by Fig. 12.2, are essentially the actuating error signals of the system. From these differences, the performance adaptive function generates control for the system. Estimating future stock requirements (smoothing and prediction) is responsive to the improving values of the smoothing and forecasting variables.

Figure 12.2 depicts the costs of running the inventory control. This diagram shows some of the relationships existing between the variables in the inventory system. The principal inputs are the stock and order requested; the output is the actual orders shipped.

Delays due to sampling-time intervals depend upon the probability of filling an order. Some of the cost factors, e.g., cost of orders actually shipped, cost of lost orders, and stock available at the next interval, are quite different depending on whether the present stock is greater or less than the requested orders. Three cost com-

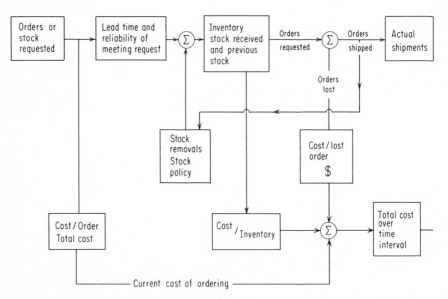

FIG. 12.2   Cost diagram of the inventory process.

ponents making up the current total cost are (1) current cost of lost orders, (2) current cost of inventory, and (3) current cost of ordering. These may be stated as proportional to orders lost, present stock, and stock requested. The total overall cost for this inventory control method is these factors integrated over the current time interval of sampling.

These diagrams provide insight to the operation of inventory control. We may summarize them as:

1. The smoothing and prediction calculations offer significant possibilities by which cost performance can be improved. If a closer analysis is made of the orders received with different time intervals, it may be that the ordering frequency can be changed in a manner that will reduce cost when certain orders are incoming.

2. The adaptive-control feature analysis may allow decisions on safety factors that will change panic conditions to a smoother-running condition. Variable safety factors may be incorporated and improved with each succeeding time interval.

3. The inability to depend on the receipt of stock that has been requested can be one of the major contributing factors to losing orders. This is depicted by a probability factor associated with each time interval or successive intervals. This analysis may point to better control of incoming stock, thus changing the probability.

4. A better knowledge of the cost factors value would permit a better determination of system parameters and smoothing and predicting factors.

The similarities of this inventory control problem to a sampled-data problem having adaptive-control capability with stochastic features make it an attractive subject for modeling by persons with automatic-control training and interests. Such modeling reveals the sensitivity of total costs of control to the system—design parameters, the order policy, and the smoothing and predicting model computation factors. The orders received and the probability of receiving the stock requested at the start of the current interval are vital factors in establishing overall total costs of inventory. Better vendor control may be exerted.

Adaptive control is not a cure-all, but together with other methods for a better understanding and identification of process characteristics it should allow better control of the inventory process.

An understanding of adaptive control applied to such an application as inventory should lead the imaginative manager to other problem solutions relating to other facets of his business, e.g., a real-time control model of cash flow.

CHAPTER THIRTEEN

Management Information
and Control System
for Process and Plant

INTRODUCTION

Since the topic of this case study is MICS for process and plant, we shall digress long enough to define a few terms and establish some boundaries.

The highest level of management we shall consider is the individual responsible for the entire manufacturing operation as shown in Fig. 13.1. Let us call him the general manager of manufacturing. To further clarify his area of responsibility, let us consider an integrated petroleum company as a specific example. The man we are considering would have the complete responsibility for all refining operations, and we shall assume, as shown in the figure, that he has several plants which are geographically dispersed. We are not speaking of the higher-level manager who has the overall responsibility for such disperse manufacturing operations as crude-oil production, refining, chemical manufacturing, etc.

At the lowest level of management, we shall consider those individuals who make routine decisions affecting the operation of individual process units under normal circumstances, specifically the foremen of those process units (plus service units) shown at the bottom of the figure.

The foremen frequently adjust operating conditions to keep them within predetermined limits or to lower costs for achieving a predetermined result. Obviously, there are several levels of managers (or decision makers) between the department manager and the foreman.

The primary responsibility of all these managers is essentially: (1) to operate the existing facilities under their direct control so that they will turn out an externally specified slate of products at

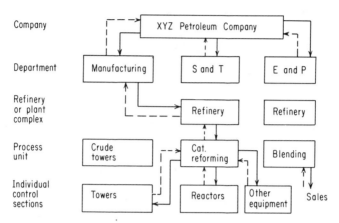

FIG. 13.1 Schematic of a petroleum company.

minimum cost, recognizing both current and near-term factors; (2) to contribute to, or actually select, the type and size of new facilities (or expansion of existing facilities) to maximize future profit at an acceptable return on investment; (3) to provide timely, complete, and reliable information to managers of other functional organizations such as marketing, research, supply, and (at any except the general-manager level) other parts of the manufacturing organization so that each can evaluate and plan their activities in a manner which will minimize current costs and maximize future profits for the total company. As a converse to this last objective, they must advise the other parts of the organization of their information needs so that other departments can structure their information systems properly.

With this brief definition of the management involved and our conception of its responsibilities, we should be able to discuss intelligently their information needs.

PRESENT INFORMATION SYSTEMS

Certain inadequacies exist in present information systems. If you discuss the problem with almost any manager of a manufacturing operation, he can probably list these inadequacies even if he knows nothing about information systems or data processing.

1. There is timeliness. All managers need to know where they stand now and not how they performed, on the average, for a 30-day period ending about a month previously.

2. The data are far too summarized and clouded by allocation of costs, over which managers have no direct control, but still are buried in stacks of relatively worthless paper. Managers do not want to know, in total, merely *that* they are off target: they want to know *where* they are off target, particularly in the places where they can do something about it. For example, how much of their poor performance was caused by increased volume or inferior feed quality as dictated to them by others?

3. They want assurance that their operations are now (and as planned at least in the near term) coordinated with the operations of other organizations with which they abut. There is little point in striving to increase the yield of a more valuable product by changing operating conditions if market conditions will not allow its increased sales, whereas there is an unlimited market for the less profitable product. What is the optimum operation of the manager's particular segment from a total company viewpoint?

4. Managers want an ability to look ahead and determine the impact of present activities on future performance. There is no point in operating at peak efficiency today if it results in a future shortage of feed from an associated unit and forces either a shutdown or high-cost operation at reduced capacity. Perhaps the better choice would be to sacrifice some efficiency in current operations to gain efficiency later on. After all, the manager is judged on an average, and not a spot basis, of performance.

5. Managers want all the assistance possible in determining the best method of operation. They have all heard of sophisticated computer techniques that can provide such assistance, especially when they have a choice between many feasible methods of operation. There must be a "best" way. When they discover that even better yields than predicted by available process correlations are possible, they want these findings to be recognized and integrated into the planning of research and other technical activities.

6. They want the ability to look back and measure their performance against the best that was possible considering all the restraints under which they operated—again in sufficient detail to ascertain where they went wrong. Almost all current information systems, even the more sophisticated, have many of these inadequacies.

Until very recently, information systems were designed under the direct control of data-processing personnel structurally organized under a comptroller. Excellent results have been accomplished in building financial systems to pay personnel and invoices promptly, to make adequate reports to higher levels of management regarding profits (measured against budgets and previous years' performance), and to compile statistics for, and payments to, tax and regulatory bodies. For the most part, the degree of detail required in such reporting is not great, and there is little need for up-to-the-minute information. These results are not sufficient for a realistic evaluation, from an operator's viewpoint, of past performance or to serve as the basis for improved planning. But they have performed an excellent job of financial management!

Data-processing personnel have long been aware that additional information of the type needed by operations personnel could be developed at relatively little additional expense as a by-product of the financial information systems. Many have tried to interest the users in actively participating in their systems studies so that operational needs could be incorporated. But line management has been so busy with line responsibilities that it has avoided getting really involved in the difficult chore of thinking through and defining its information needs in the detail required for incorporation in a MICS design. There is no shortcut; the ultimate users of such information systems must get intimately involved.

THE IMPACT OF OPERATIONS RESEARCH ON INFORMATION SYSTEMS

During the past 10 years, another computer-oriented group has slowly matured, usually from a base in research and development organizations, namely, the operations research (OR) specialists. Not too surprisingly, quite a large percentage of them are converted chemical engineers who have acquired a considerable knowledge of mathematics. They first attacked relatively simple problems, constrained to a small segment of the operation, where the required detailed information could be accumulated without an involved data-processing system. After a few false starts and living down of exaggerated claims, it became evident that they really had something to offer. By following their advice, tempered by experience-based judgment, it was possible to find combinations of variables not previously considered which resulted in significant cost reductions.

As the OR analysts dug in deeper and expanded their impact to greater spans of activities (hence higher levels of management), it became evident that the available information systems were not adequate to provide the input to their optimizing techniques. The inadequacies of which they complained show a striking similarity to those noted by the operations managers. However, there is a difference. Whereas the operations manager may have been pleased with 24-hour-old data, the OR analyst was able to show need for much more current, even on-line, availability of data. He wanted a definitive separation of the truly variable and fixed costs and the derivation of a mathematical relationship for those types of costs which varied with throughput but not linearly. He agreed that currently updated projections of requirements and deliveries from other organizations were necessary, but he started to request ranges of these values with probabilities for each segment of the range, and he wanted the projections to extend even farther into the future with corresponding expansion of the range as future time and consequent uncertainty increased. He wanted more precise physical measurements of such values as flows, inventory levels, temperatures, pressures, etc., as a companion part to the more accurate historical cost breakdown. And, finally, as his optimization techniques aided the operating management in finding more economic operating conditions, it was often found that the most profitable mode represented an extremity of existing process correlations. At this point, the need for an experimental program to increase the range in the indicated direction was obvious. He was not concerned with the inability to look ahead, project "best" future operating conditions, or to look back, as the manufacturing manager had been. These were the types of information systems which he thought he and the operations manager could develop if the other data and information were made available.

In an access of zeal to develop the required information systems, it became more and more evident that developers of systems were, to a large degree, paralleling the financial-accounting systems and that a hopeless intermingling of these and other related operating information systems was in the making. Most are about at the stage where they realize that the term management information system means the intelligent integration of all information systems into one whole and that they must combine the previous commercial data-processing and technical computing organizations into one combined group at a relatively high level in the company if such systems are to be developed at all—and that level must take it out of the manufacturing department, or any other department representing a single user.

THE HIERARCHICAL APPROACH TO
INFORMATION NEEDS

Another breakdown of information can be made dependent upon whether the data are developed internally to an organization or just flow into the organization from outside. Any manager needs both types. The internally generated data and information relate to his feasible operating options, costs, and the efficiency of facilities and personnel under his direct control. That generated externally consists of environmental information plus projections from adjacent organizations which provide a basis for the planning of his own operations.

At the lowest level, the process foreman needs accurate and timely information regarding current operations plus a group of technical relationships such as process correlations, capacity restraints, utilities requirements as a function of mode of operation, utility costs, etc. If the unit under his supervision is rather complex, he may desire to have all or most of these technical-economic factors interrelated by a mathematical model. He also requires a recording of historical operating results and costs, with the same breakdown as included in his planned budget, so that he can measure the adequacy of his correlation and the efficiency of his subordinates. Additionally, he requires a projection of feed rates and quality to his unit and of product quantities and quality expected from his unit. If such forward planning is impractical, he at least needs to know feed and product inventories and the individuals with whom he should communicate if unexpected changes in either his own operations or those of abutting organizations occur. Any other information, such as allocation of costs beyond his ability to control or influence, is worse than useless for it masks the information on which he must base his decisions.

Considering the large number of process units in a large manufacturing complex, the total of the information generated at this level of management is very great, as shown by the base of the left pyramid in Fig. 13.2. As we move up the management ladder, the span of operations continually increases and an information system, to be of use, must lose detail. But sufficient detail must be retained at every level to allow the manager to perform his functions of appraisal and planning. The general guidelines are to sacrifice detail in those areas where costs are relatively small and stable and to maintain detail where they are high and volatile. The same guidelines exist in the area of physical restraints although skewed toward more detail in all areas to recognize their importance (although involving only minor costs to remove) on near-term operating limits.

At the top of the pyramid, the general manager for manufacturing needs the same basic types of information. Rather than current information for a single process, he needs highly summarized current information for each of the several plants under his control. Rather than a body (model) of technical-economic information relative to a particular process, he requires highly summarized technical-economic correlations for the several plants, for it is his responsibility to allocate the total manufacturing job among those plants. Also, just as in the case of the process foreman, he needs a periodic recording of historical operating results and costs, again with the same categories as he employed in his planning and budgeting. The abutting organizations from whom he requires projections of supply and demands are the marketing department,

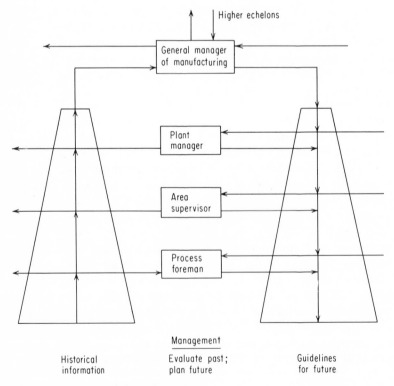

FIG. 13.2   Hierarchical information system.

the purchasing department, etc. He also requires a stream of information from research and other technical organizations in the company upon which to base a wide variety of decisions relating to mode of operation and to capital expenditures. And, like the process foreman, he must be able to appraise the actual performance of his organization, not against an annual budget, but against the best which could have been done considering all his capabilities, restraints, and externally imposed changes to plans since preparation of the budget. This postappraisal of performance, in recognition of unplanned events, should be the basis upon which he judges his plant managers, his own planning procedures, and the entire body of technical-economic information and correlations upon which his planning procedures are grounded. A control budget, prepared at the first of the year, is essential for the financial control of a company. Unless overall company planning is perfect, it is not a valid basis for measuring the performance of parts of the company which are forced by others to deviate from plan.

Higher levels of management have other information needs so that the entire company (marketing, product distribution, manufacturing, purchasing, research, etc.) can plan and operate in harmony. However, we stated in the beginning that we were going to stop at the general manager of manufacturing. Thus, we assume here that higher management has provided a coordinated planning base to the general manager of manufacturing and has, additionally, defined an information system and communication channels which apprise him day to day of deviations and revisions to that plan. Likewise, his own information system automatically advises higher and correlative managers of unexpected developments in the manufacturing area which necessitate revisions in the overall company plan.

If we are to avoid the certainty of incompatible suboptimizations of the separate parts of the manufacturing department, planning and scheduling must start at the top. In every instance, the manager must have just enough information to allow an optimum allocation of effort to his subsidiary managers with sufficient tolerance that infeasible operations are not specified. As shown on the right side of Fig. 13.2, these guidelines from above are combined with the more detailed information available at each management level to develop even more detailed guidelines, which ultimately reach the process foreman level. Each level of management has the responsibility for suboptimization within the imposed guidelines and for specifying that portion of the information system which apprises him and his superiors of the results. Thus the information loop is closed.

In the field of capital expenditures, the same general rule applies. An increase in capacity or the installation of a new process cannot normally be judged based on its effect on the cost performance at the installation site, but rather as it affects the entire manufacturing complex. Consequently, planning for capital expenditures must follow the same hierarchical path with sufficient latitude for suboptimization within guidelines imposed at higher levels.

THE DYNAMIC NATURE OF INFORMATION SYSTEMS

If only we had the capacity to forecast the future accurately, there would be little need for the complex information systems which are now under development by most companies. We do not. Therefore, our information systems must allow us to recognize deviations from plan at the earliest possible moment and to be able to react rapidly in as near an optimum manner as possible. A major reason for the development of sophisticated management information systems is a recognition of the dynamic nature of business activities combined with recently acquired ability to react rapidly to changes—automatically in some cases.

We may never have the ability to foretell the future accurately, but any improvement in projection will have a beneficial effect on a company's operations. Most companies, in our opinion, have spent too little effort in refining such projections as compared to the effort spent in recognizing and reacting optimally to change. Such projections are an integral part of a management information system, one that must receive increasing attention. They will be most meaningful when based on historical operating and environmental information and when all the tools of management science such as statistics and probability are incorporated.

As a specific example, sales forecasts are usually provided to manufacturing organizations as single value, inviolable numbers without any indications of the probabilities of degrees of deviation above or below the single value. Manufacturing must then optimize based on that number even though experience has proved the original forecast to have transient validity. So we optimize and reoptimize during the ensuing days and months, probably at any time being far removed from the true optimum course of action for the company.

IMPACT ON RESEARCH AND DEVELOPMENT

Many are involved with research and development or closely related technical activities, thus it would be well to reflect upon the impact of management information systems in the areas of plant and process control on manufacturing activities. Some of the areas of impact are these:

1. The ability to optimize rapidly has forced the development and automation of many analytical techniques for stream analysis for incorporation as a part of process units. We can no longer wait several days, or even hours, for the analysis of critical streams, for the determination of catalyst inventory, or for an appraisal of product quality. These must be determined within minutes if we are to use available ability to optimize.

2. Physical measurements of flows, levels, temperatures, pressures, etc., must be much more reliable and rapid than in the past and many more points will be monitored. Fortunately, the new controls aid in this activity by indicating questionable instruments based on conflicts between material balance, heat balances, etc., thus directing attention only to those instruments which need service. Many are engaged in the development of such improved devices.

3. In the past, there has been considerable contention that pilot-plant or semiworks-plant correlations are not applicable to large, commercial units, and the differences have been clouded by poor analysis and physical measurements from the commercial units. With the improved and complete measurements now available on the large process units, meaningful comparisons can now be obtained without special tests, and, surprisingly, true differences in correlations *are* oftentimes apparent. Further, in many instances, the optimization procedures in the plans have directed operations toward uncorrelated regions, and the track indicates that more economic operating conditions are possible. Any time this occurs, the need for an extension of technical knowledge is evident.

4. With the increased number and accuracy of physical measurements and analytical devices becoming an integral part of process units, and with the ability to measure quickly the effects on operations of documented changes in conditions, these large commercial process units are rapidly approaching the equivalent of mammoth pilot plants. They have one major advantage over conventional pilot plants in that their optimum-seeking procedures integrate

technology, economics, and physical restraints. The major advantages of the pilot plant or semiworks are the greater freedom in physical restraints economically possible and the ability to investigate, at low cost, areas which might never be discovered by commercial units because of the cost penalties of experimentation in untried areas. There is a continuing role for experimental units, but the information now available from commercial units will change the need for them. Therefore, this information also should be made available on a routine basis to those in research and development activities.

5. Finally, the development of a new process may now be judged based on its total effect on related company activities. Many have been frustrated by knowing that a newly discovered method for performing a given processing function does so at lower cost, but the feed from other process units or the intermediate products to downstream units are, or must be, somewhat different. The question is whether the savings in the new process are augmented or erased by changes in costs in the adjacent units; and there are usually several other units and various ways in which each can be operated to accommodate the new process. With the information regarding existing processes now available and the ability to answer the questions about the new process on paper and reoptimize the entire complex rapidly, an accurate appraisal of such developments can now be realized—and in time to direct research along profitable channels.

In short, reliable and more meaningful process information is becoming available from commercial process units with an accuracy heretofore considered possible only in technically directed pilot-plant operations. Such information must be included in the total package of data available for research and development planning.

SUMMARY

We have achieved the ability through modern-day computers and associated information systems to recognize and react optimally and rapidly to change—and to do so economically. This demands a tremendous volume of timely and accurate data at the lowest management levels which must be summarized as it flows up the management ladder in such a way that only that part critical to decision making at each level is highlighted. This upward flow is combined with information developed externally to the manufacturing department and reflected through analysis and planning from the upper levels and directed downward so that each management level has the freedom to suboptimize within specified restraints. Meaningful and timely measurements—physical, analytical, and financial—are essential for such a hierarchical information system to function.

AN ACTUAL EXAMPLE—A MANAGEMENT INFORMATION AND CONTROL SYSTEM FOR ABC's REFINERY

The rest of this case study will describe the basic system concepts used in designing and implementing a MICS in a refinery. For propriety reasons, names, illustrations, and reports are disguised although realistic.

OVERVIEW

A significant pattern of control evolving in recent years in the petroleum industry is the gradual step-by-step integration of process control with managerial control. The integrated-systems approach uses a hierarchy of digital computers to relate long-range corporate objectives and a variety of economic factors to the day-by-day control of a plant whose physical and chemical processes have been optimized. Understood in this broad sense, computer control of company operations signifies the endeavor to attain total managerial control of all relationships—economic, physical, and chemical.

A number of petroleum companies have begun to translate this concept into practice, starting at various levels of the control hierarchy—from direct digital control (DDC) of individual process units all the way up to corporate management control. We have started at the middle level—computer control of an entire refinery—to provide operational control, refinery planning, and decision making. An advantage of starting with refinery control is that the system can readily be expanded upward to tie in with a master computer at the corporate level, as well as downward, to include optimal control of individual processes and units; also the high degree of integration at this refinery makes it difficult to control and optimize a single unit irrespective of the effects on units both upstream and downstream. The variability of type and specification of charged crudes and gas oils would require multiple complex models for effective optimization. This variability further compounds the already considerable effort necessary to develop unique models accommodating individuality of the units. As a result of this degree of integration and charge variation, the approach would tend to require a higher initial manpower investment.

This approach does not exclude eventual unit control and optimization but provides a sound basis for learning and developing the technology for unit control, DDC, and other control schemes that prove feasible as implementation progresses. Figure 13.3 graphically illustrates the plant system approach. Control begins at the top, or plant level, and works down through succeeding units.

The steps to implementation are further defined in another fashion in phases:

Phase 1. Present-position reporting

Phase 2. Forward-look reporting

Phase 3. Closed-loop control

Figure 13.4 shows the schematic diagram of typical hardware and communications installed to accomplish phases 1 and 2.

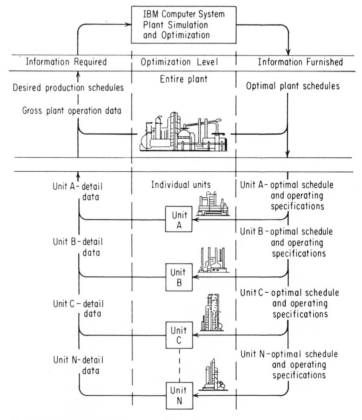

FIG. 13.3 Levels of control.

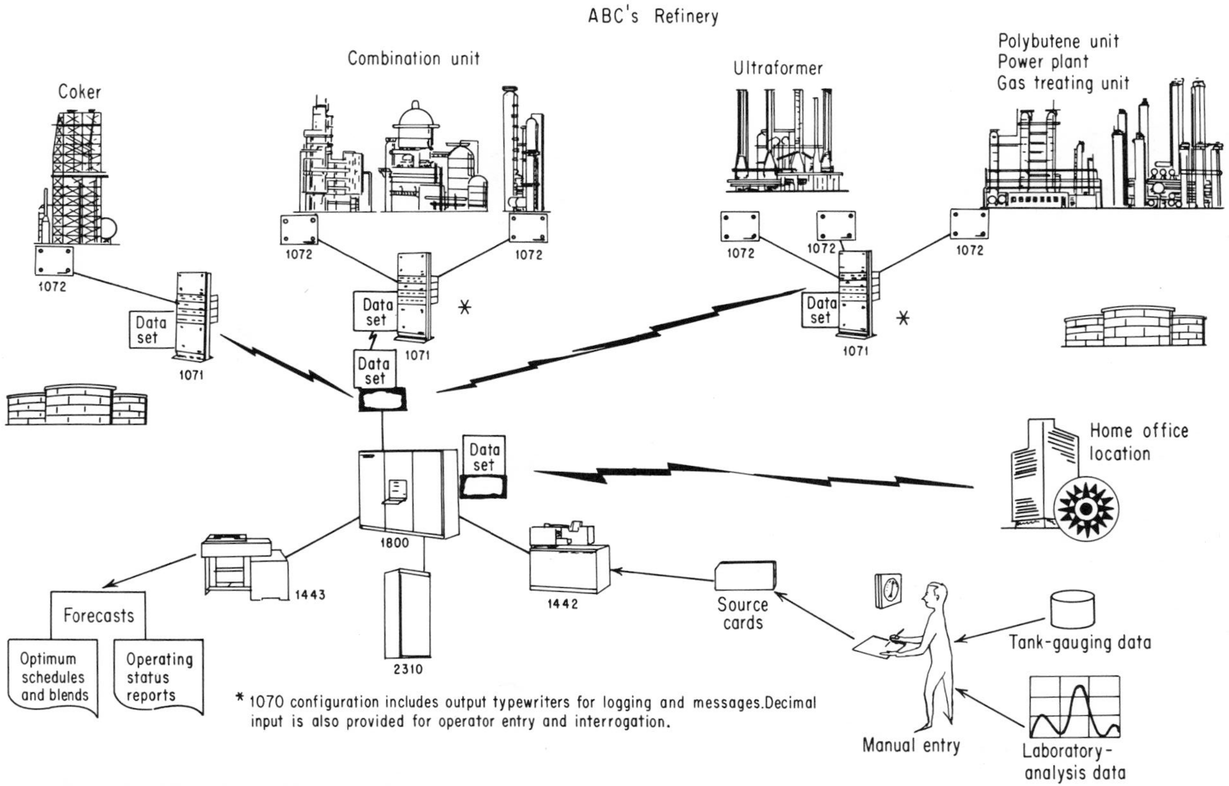

FIG. 13.4 Refinery management information system.

* 1070 configuration includes output typewriters for logging and messages. Decimal input is also provided for operator entry and interrogation.

THE LONG-RANGE OBJECTIVE:
INTEGRATED PLANT COMPUTER CONTROL

We envisage five levels in the corporate structure where computers can be applied for decision making and control: the corporate level, the department level, the refinery level, the process-unit level, and the individual control level. As shown in the diagram (Fig. 13.5), there is a continual flow of control decisions downward from the corporate level to the lower production levels, as well as a reverse flow of information from the lower levels to higher levels. This upward flow of information, in turn, results in improved command decisions, which are transmitted down again.

The flow of information and decisions take place, of course, in any large company, whether it uses computers or not. The intro-

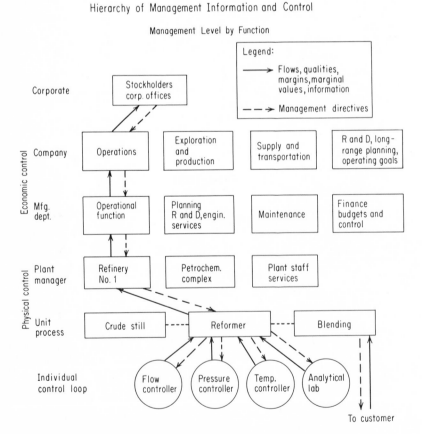

FIG. 13.5   Projected levels of ABC Company's integrated computer control.

duction of computers, however, greatly expedites decision making at all levels by optimizing production operations, automating a great many routine decisions, and transmitting management information to the higher levels in *real time*—while still current and useful.

Thus, we see the function of a master computer at the corporate level in helping to decide what to make, how to make it, and what to charge for it.

At the departmental level, there is presently a planning group that coordinates the requirements and operations of the three major departments—Refineries, Supply and Transportation, and Markets, in terms of their capabilities, operating costs, and other factors. With respect to the refineries, for example, current information on crude availabilities and properties, stock and marketing inventories, product forecasts, plant capabilities, etc., is fed into a linear-programming matrix, which is run on a large executive-level computer. The objective function of this linear program is to minimize refinery operating costs for the next 30 days or so. This, then, provides a monthly operating plan for the refineries. Compared to the day-by-day operation of a refinery, with its not infrequent short-term disturbances, these can be considered relatively constant long-range plans.

At the plant level, the refinery requires its own short-term planning and model programmed on a local computer. This model makes the appropriate short-term adjustments to the long-range plan and endeavors to optimize the day-by-day operation in terms of the financial, material, personnel, and physical operating constraints and capabilities of the plant, as well as in accord with the long-range objectives. Such refinery optimization initially took the form of open-loop data monitoring to alert the operating management to the implications of local disturbances and deviations from plan.

The next step is refinery suboptimization at the process-unit level. Computer control at this level attempts to attain maximum yields at lowest cost for complete process units, such as crude distillation, catalytic reforming, or blending, by using information on cut points, operating temperatures, reformate octane, etc.

Finally, at the lowest "function" level of control, individual process controllers monitor and regulate the various control loops of the process, either singly or in groups. Here, DDC is beginning to replace analog controllers in mutiple-loop applications. The decision loop is closed through the feedback of detailed information from the lower control levels.

NEEDS OF THE REFINERY

Any feasible approach to refinery control has to take into account the following needs and requirements of the refinery:

1. Effective management control of operations in accord with the operating plan

2. Reduction in the cost of disturbances and their effects on refinery operation, by providing a faster reaction time

3. Better understanding of refinery parameters and the interrelationships of important variables

4. More effective use of available manpower

5. Time-engineering analysis of operating data

In brief, a refinery computer would have to meet the basic need for meaningful *real-time* information and analysis upon which timely decisions could be based.

CONCEPT OF THE REFINERY MICS

A management operating system of the type conceived for the refinery performs three overlapping functions: (1) it provides *management* information based on the techniques of management by exception and statistical decision making; (2) it provides *technical* information for analysis and control; (3) it furnishes *optimizing* process control, either by manual or automatic means. To fulfill these functions, the system must (1) automatically collect and reduce data from a great many processing points; (2) represent the operations of the refinery on the basis of an adequate mathematical model; (3) provide the information necessary for refinery operational decision making and control.

As shown in the monitoring and control data flow diagram (Fig. 13.6) the outputs of the system are made available in the following forms:

1. Present position calculation and analysis

2. Future position calculation and analysis

3. Optimization: calculation of minimum cost operation within constraints and manipulation of variables for most effective operation of the refinery

4. Detection and reporting of exceptional conditions

Let us consider these concepts and techniques in a little more detail. The basic need of any refinery is to know its *current* position, not averaged data on yesterday's operations. Present position calculation and analysis satisfies this need by rapid calculation of actual process parameters from time-correlated data and the subsequent economic and engineering evaluation of these parameters. The technique involves (1) the *collection* of required data flows, temperatures, tank inventories, composition analysis, quality determinations, modes of operation, etc.; (2) *the conversion of the data into meaningful forms,* such as refinery material balances and component breakdowns, calculation of theoretical yields, reconstruction of crude true-boiling-point curve, and various special calculations (e.g., catalyst activity decline); (3) the *comparison of actual with planned operations.* These comparisons, in turn, provide information on proper cut points, feed-stock variations, efficient separations, optimal operating modes, and the costs associated with deviations.

When *significant deviations* from plan are detected, requiring possible action, the management is alerted through exception reports, which state the amount of the deviations and the associated costs. The technique of reporting only exceptional conditions re-

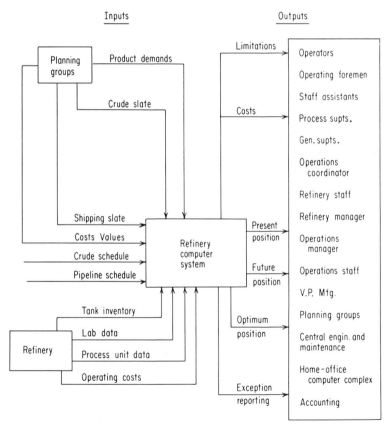

FIG. 13.6 Refinery monitoring and control data flow.

lieves management of many time-wasting routine decisions. In addition to the exception reports, the system must also issue routine historical and accounting reports at scheduled intervals.

Present position analysis and reporting is the core of the refinery operational control. The major objective is to provide refinery management with accurate and timely reports, on an as-needed basis, in sufficient detail for accurate appraisal of the refinery's present position with respect to standards of performance and scheduled pro-

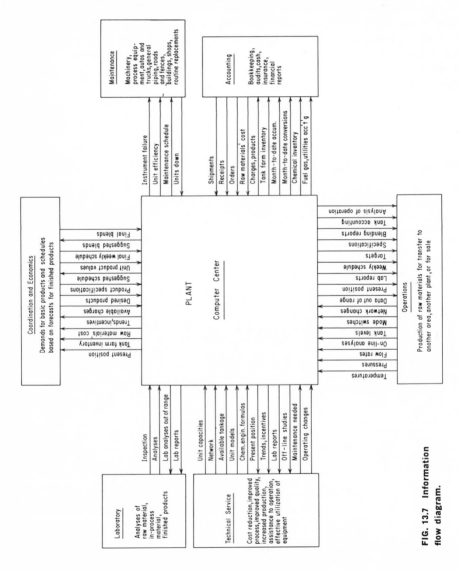

FIG. 13.7 Information flow diagram.

duction. Out-of-tolerance and other unusual conditions are flashed back to the unit operators via message typewriters for corrective action. Information flow is depicted by Fig. 13.7. By supplying to the information system data concerning scheduling, prices, targets, fixed capabilities, orders, receipts, shipments, lab analysis, and tank gauging, in addition to the on-line sensor data of flows, temperatures, pressures, and some quality analysis, the present position of the refinery is determined.

Material-balance calculations form the basis for providing accurate values for determining performance guides and operating schedules. They also allow checks for unexpected material loss and aid in pinpointing faulty instrumentation.

Some of the performance guides upgraded by material balance improvements are:

1. Percentage of recoveries and loss
2. Conversion ratios
3. Yield percentages
4. Thermal efficiencies
5. Catalyst efficiencies
6. Percentage of stream impurities

Considerable work in the area of network simplification calculation and error detection has helped develop algorithms of significant use in the material-balance calculation.

The data collection and material-balance calculations establish the data bank from which management reports are generated routinely or on demand. Typical reports are:

1. *Product Inventory.* (See Fig. 13.8) The uncorrected volume is the volume as measured. The corrected volume is the calculated volume at 60°F. The unavailable volume is a result of the physical arrangement of the process stream outlet nozzle in the tank. The third column, code *S*, is explained at the bottom of the report. The following is a description of certain abbreviations used in the report.

Abbreviation	*Description*
PROD CODE	Product code
TK NO	Tank number
TEMP	Temperature
Q	Quarters of an inch
BS&W	Basic sediment and water
VOL	Volume
BBLS	Barrels
CAP	Capacity

2. *Unit and Plant Operating Summary.* This contains such information as how much charge stock was used, total products, disposition, and operating data. These data can be compared to targets and necessary corrective action initiated. A sample of a unit operating summary (a catalytic cracker) is shown in Fig. 13.9. Plant summaries are derived from unit summaries. These reports summarize for the plant and respective operations target. In addition, they give the gross unit or plant throughput and the gross

```
  6 AM                PRODUCT INVENTORY REPORT                MARCH 23, 196-


 PROD   TK   S TEMP  GAUGE      BS+W    UNCORRECTED CORRECTED   TK  CAP   UNAVAIL
 CODE   NO           FT IN Q   FT IN Q  VOL  BBLS   VOL BBLS    BBLS     VOL BBLS


PREMIUM  GASOLINE
3280   100  T   81  29 06 2   1 04 0    98,855     98,012     99,870     3,940
3281   101  B   85   6 01 3     4 2     10,235     10,147     55,136     1,650
3281   102  K   81  31 07 1     8 3     53,824     53,243     55,255     1,740
                                                   161,402    210,261    7,330


REGULAR GASOLINE
3290   105  P   81  17 04 2   1 02 1    60,915     60,343     101,225    3,610
3292   106  B   84  14 06 1    10 2     24,754     24,428     100,756    3,850
3292   109  K   81  30 10 3    06 3     52,516     52,137     55,206     1,982
3294   110  K   82  31 03 1    08 1     53,105     52,782     55,198     1,865
                                                   189,690    312,385    11,307


KEROSINE
4250   107  K   82  23 10 2     8 2     40,665     39,961     55,175     1,644
4250   108  F   86   6 02 0     6 3     10,453     10,272     54,864     1,780
                                                   50,233     110,039    3,424


DIESEL
4600    98  P   82   8 07 1     7 3     14,763     14,545     55,122     1,745
4600    99  T   81  30 04 0     9 1     51,657     51,096     55,058     1,963
                                                   65,641     110,180    3,708


BUNKER FUEL
4850    75  K   82  12 06 3     6 0      9,603      9,476     10,075       644


SPECIAL NAPHTHA
5240    10  P   80   6 09 3       0      3,390      3,286     10,123       325
5240    12  F   84  13 05 1       0      6,622      6,443     10,078       320
                                                    9,729     20,201       645


BENZENE
5440    14  T   80  20 01 0       0      5,045      4,896      5,144         0
5440    15  F   83   4 06 3       0      1,135      1,077      5,096         0
                                                    5,973     10,240         0


TOLUENE
5640    16  K   79  20 00 3       0      5,023      4,852      5,121         0
5640    17  F   83   9 07 1       0      2,415      2,344      5,130         0
                                                    7,196     10,251         0


S-STATUS CODE, B-BLENDING, F-FILLING, K-OK TO SHIP, P-PUMPING, T-TESTING
```

FIG. 13.8   Product inventory report.

production of key products. For instance, this report indicates that a potential gross revenue of $1,385 per day could be realized for the catalytic cracker unit if it were to operate on target.

3. *Additional Reports.* Figures 13.10 to 13.13 show examples of performance, operations, product distribution, and analytical reports.

Forward-look Calculation and Reporting. These provide the projection of present operations a short time ahead. The analysis of present position, combined with past data, serves as a refinery trend recorder. Known future deviations from planned crude receipts, shipping schedules, shutdowns, and equipment limitations are data added to the information system. This information, along with accurate present position status and performance guides, allows a forecast of a "present position" for some future point in time. Typical time periods are next shift, 24 hours, 48 hours, and 30 days. The forecasting formula is straightforward and is graphically demon-

```
              FLUID CATALYTIC CRACKING UNIT
                  OPERATING SUMMARY
                  DAY ENDING 6 A.M.
                  SEPTEMBER 13,1966
```

CHARGE	OBSERVED	BUDGETED
TOTAL FRESH FEED	26,960	27,300
TOTAL RECYCLE	7,560	7,425

PRODUCTS

	OBSERVED	BUDGETED
BUTANE-BUTYLENE	5,518	5,800
GASOLINE	13,520	13,425
LCCO	4,050	4,000

OPERATIONS

	OBSERVED	BUDGETED
CONVERSION,VOL %	73.5	73.0
GASOLINE FBP (ASTM),F	419	400
LCCO FBP (ASTM),F	543	565
GASOLINE OCT,RES(CLEAR)	93.5	93.9

NOTE	ESTIMATED LOSS,$/D
1.CLOSER APPROACH TO CAPACITY LIMIT POSSIBLE	980
2.ABSORBER IS OFF TARGET	147
3.DEBUTANIZER IS OFF TARGET	55
4.DEPROPANIZER IS OFF TARGET	22
5.GASOLINE ANTIOXIDANT ADDITION RATE NEEDS ADJUSTMENT	61
6.CO BOILER EFFICIENCY IS LOW	120
7.ACCUMULATIVE LOSS IS EXCESSIVE	1,385 ←

FIG. 13.9 Unit operating summary.

FLUID CATALYTIC CRACKING UNIT

PERFORMANCE

DAY ENDING 6 A.M.
SEPTEMBER 13,1966

UNIT CAPACITY LIMITATION APPROACH,%OF MAX.	OBSERVED	MODEL
COKE BURN	97.0	94.2
GAS COMPRESSION	90.3	90.5
MAIN FRACTIONATOR LOADING	98.0	99.6
VALUE OF PRODUCTS,$/D	91,133	91,444
TOTAL FRESH FEED,B/D	26,960	26,960
FRESH FEED VALUE,$/B	3.38	3.40

OPERATIONAL IMPROVEMENT INCENTIVES

MODE OF OPERATION MAXIMUM FEED RATE
CAPACITY AVAILABLE 2.0%(MAIN FRACT LOADING)

INCENTIVE 980 $/D ←

VRU OPERATION (BASED ON OBSERVED OPTIMUM PERFORMANCE)

	BASIS	INCENTIVE
MAIN FRACTIONATOR	MIN. GASO, IN LCCO,MIN. LCCO IN GASO.	0 $/D
ABSORBER	ALL C2 AND LIGHTER IN OFF GAS	147 $/D
DEPROPANIZER	MIN. C4=IN PROPANE-PROPYLENE	22 $/D
DEBUTANIZER	MIN. C4=IN GASOLINE	55 $/D ←

CO BOILER OPERATION
FUEL USED,MSCFH	42,500
BOILER EFFICIENCY,%	78.0
TARGET STEAM MAKE,LB/HR	156,350
ACTUAL STEAM MAKE,LB/HR	153,750

INCENTIVE 120 $/D

ADDITIVE CONSUMPTION
ANTIOXIDANT
GASOLINE TREATED,B/D	11,375
ADDITION RATE	
INCHES/HR	4.0
LBS/1,000 BBL(ACTUAL)	5.5
LBS/1,000 BBL(TARGET)	4.7

INCENTIVE 61 $/D

FIG. 13.10 Unit performance report.

FLUID CATALYTIC CRACKING UNIT

OPERATIONS

DAY ENDING 6 A.M.
SEPTEMBER 13,1966

OPERATING CONDITIONS

→ CONVERSION (CORR)	73.5	VOL%	CAT CIRCULATION RATE	101.0	T/M
→ CONVERSION (UNCORR)	73.5	VOL%	CAT / OIL	15.3	
REACTOR BED HOLDUP	0	TONS	REACTOR CAT CARRYOVER	0.3	T/D
REACTOR BED TEMP	930	F	REGEN CAT LOSSES	2.1	T/D
FRESH FEED RISER TEMP	973	F	COMBUSTION AIR	401,750	LB/HR
RECYCLE RISER TEMP	952	F	REGENERATOR TEMP	1,150	F
FEED PREHEAT TEMP	522	F	CARBON ON SPENT CAT	0.82	WT%
SPACE VELOCITY	12	W/H/W	CARBON ON REGEN CAT	0.38	WT%
THROUGHPUT RATIO	1.7				

CHARGE	METER	MODEL,B/D	ACTUAL,B/D		LB/HR	WT%	VOL%
PIPE STILL GAS OIL	FR-1		22,435		294,062	65.8	65.0
COKER GAS OIL	FR-2		4,525		51,666	11.6	13.1
TOTAL FRESH FEED			26,960	***	345,728	77.4	78.1
HCCO RECYCLE	FRC-1		5,075	*	71,345	16.0	14.7
SLURRY RECYCLE	FRC-2		2,495	*	29,654	6.6	7.2
TOTAL UNIT CHARGE			34,530	*	446,727	100.0	100.0
PRODUCTS							
ABSORBER GAS,MSCH	FR-3		382.6	*	16,830	4.7	---
PROPANE-PROPYLENE	FR-4		3,640	*	27,936	8.1	1.4
BUTANE-BUTYLENE	FR-5		5,517	*	48,557	14.0	20.5
GASOLINE	FR-6		13,520	*	150,508	43.6	50.1
LCCO	FR-7		4,050	*	54,948	15.9	15.0
HCCO	FR-8		0	*	0	0	0
DECANTED OIL	FR-9		975	*	14,117	4.1	5.3
SLURRY	FR-10		0	*	0	0	0
COKE, LB/HR				*	32,737	9.5	----
TOTAL			27,702	***	345,633	99.9	102.3

FIG. 13.11 Unit operating details.

FLUID CATALYTIC CRACKING UNIT

PRODUCT DISTRIBUTION

DAY ENDING 6 A.M.

SEPTEMBER 13,1966

NOTE-PERCENTAGES BASED ON TOTAL FRESH FEED TO THE UNIT

			OBSERVED			MODEL	
	UNITS		VOL%	WT%		VOL%	WT%
C2 AND LTR	MSCFH	334.0		4.66	335.4		4.7
C3	B/D	287	2.91	1.66	743	2.7	1.5
C3 =	B/D	2,590	9.58	5.61	2,540	9.1	5.4
IC4	B/D	1,055	3.90	2.47	1,069	3.9	2.5
NC4	B/D	343	1.27	0.83	308	1.0	0.7
C4 =	B/D	3,490	12.92	8.82	3,500	12.9	8.8
IC5	B/D	963	3.56	2.50	1,013	3.7	2.7
NC5	B/D	171	0.63	0.45	175	0.7	0.5
C5 =	B/D	3,031	11.21	8.14	3,105	11.5	8.4
C6-400F	B/D	9,730	36.00	32.20	9,700	36.0	32.2
LCCO	B/D	4,655	17.22	17.43	4,608	17.0	17.2
HCCO	B/D	0	0	0	0	0	0
DECANTED OIL	B/D	989	3.66	4.12	1,043	3.7	4.2
COKE	LB/HR	39,006		11.11	39,218		11.2
TOTAL	B/D	27,304	102.86	100.00	27,804	102.2	100.0

CONVERSION (CORR)	VOL%	73.5	73.5
CONVERSION (UNCORR)	VOL%	73.5	73.5
SPACE VELOCITY	W/H/W	12	12
THROUGHPUT		1.7	1.7
CATALYST-OIL RATIO			
FRESH FEED RISER		8.6	8.8
RECYCLE RISER		15.3	14.8
REGENERATOR TEMP	F	1,150	1,155
COMBUSTION AIR	LB/HR	402,000	411,060
REACTOR TEMP	F	925	925
RES.OCTANE NO.(CLEAR)		93.5	94.0

FIG. 13.12 Unit product distribution.

FLUID CATALYTIC CRACKING UNIT
ANALYTICAL RESULTS
DAY ENDING 6 A.M.
SEPTEMBER 13,1966

FLUE GAS ANALYSIS

CO2   9.9 WT%   CO   11.1 WT%   02   0.2 WT%   CO2/CO=0.892

LIGHT HYDROCARBON PRODUCT DISTRIBUTION

SCFH	ABSORBER GAS	PROPANE PROPYLENE	BUTANE BUTYLENE	CATALYTIC GASOLINE	TOTAL
INERTS	55,218	0	0	0	55,216
H2	55,818	0	0	0	55,818
C1	163,750	0	0	0	163,750
C2	69,063	41	0	0	69,104
C2 =	38,702	0	0	0	38,702
B/D					
C3	8	925	6	0	939
C3 =	23	2,536	35	0	2,594
IC4	0	97	744	14	855
NC4	0	22	415	27	464
C4 =	0	61	3,257	202	3,520
IC5	0	0	369	605	974
NC5	0	0	34	118	152
C5 =	0	0	659	2,427	3,086
C6 +	0	0	0	10,284	10,284

GAS OIL STREAM ANALYSES

	COMBINED FRESH FEED	SLURRY	DECANT OIL	HCCO	LCCO	CATALYTIC GASOLINE
APIAT 60 F	27.3	6.5	9.7	30.1	38.6	54.8
IBP,F(ASTM)	416			410	416	112
10%	505			502	448	147
30%	618			604	475	184
50%	675			660	486	222
70%	722			690	500	280
90%	760			738	517	369
FBP				760	543	419
OCTANE NUMBER						
RESEARCH,CLEAR						93.5
RESEARCH,3CC/G TEL						98.5
MOTOR,3CC/G TEL						86.5

HYDROCARBON TYPE,VOL %						
PARAFFINS	68.3				27.5	21.6
OLEFINS	4.0				8.2	27.8
AROMATICS	19.5				52.7	36.6
NAPHTHENES	8.2				11.6	14.0
CATALYST CONTENT,LB/100G		2.5	0.5			

FIG. 13.13 Unit product qualities from laboratory.

strated in Fig. 13.14 Eventually, as more data are collected and better models developed, actual plant operation will be simulated to provide more accurate and longer-range forecasts. The establishment of multiple forecast periods allows a request for "present position" at a future date upon demand.

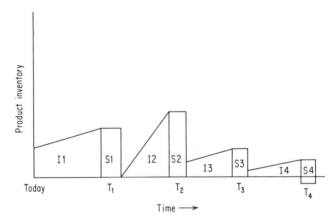

FIG. 13.14   Forecasting inventory and shipments. (Formula to determine new inventory position for each blending stock: beginning inventory plus production according to operating plan minus blended product shipments equals new inventory shipments.)

Forward-look reporting provides early warning of out-of-tolerance conditions and the basis for more optimum production scheduling. By assigning appropriate costs for deviations from schedule, deviations from plans can trigger a refinery reoptimization or indicate to the manufacturing division that a next-level optimization is needed.

Complete closed-loop control of *all* refinery variables is in the future. But the phases discussed above have provided the definition and justification for closed-loop control on *some* key variables. This should be extended in the future as better unit models are developed.

The plant system communicates with a larger corporate computer. Plant physical limitations, product and raw material inventory, and plant performance are routinely and automatically sent to the next higher control level.

In addition to plant and unit operational control, the plant system serves the plant analytical laboratory, routinely controlling the lab quality analyzers.

MAINTENANCE

A natural extension of the operational control system is the implementation of a refinery maintenance management system. Work requests including normal daily needs, forecast needs, preventive-maintenance needs, emergency needs, and uncompleted-job needs will be considered in a *planning* and *scheduling* function in order to make the most efficient use of available manpower and material resources. Algorithms for *work assignments* will then be used for decisions on requirements versus available resources; resource usage will then be reflected in appropriate data bank files during the *work measurement* phase. Current and historical information then will form the basis for *evaluation* and *control*. Both routine and exception reporting will be used to aid maintenance management.

IMPLEMENTATION

Steps leading to the present status were:

1. A management definition of the MICS objectives and requirements, a problem definition of the manager's needs

2. A technical study to establish solution techniques and the data bank and equipment necessary

3. A study of economic feasibility and justification of development costs

4. Acceptance by refinery management as to goals, reports, etc.

5. The application development, system analysis, programming, hardware installation

6. Updating of models, management needs, reports, etc., as more intelligence is gained

CONCLUSION

This particular refinery overall control involved an ambitious scheme for overall computer control. It was well along into phase 2 in 1966 and had some key variables under computer control. One unit was experimenting with DDC. Economic payoff to date has justified the expended effort. All levels of plant management are actively using and enthusiastic about the system. Sample questions asked: "How will shipment of 40,000 barrels of kerosene on April 1, 19—, instead of the 28,000 barrels originally scheduled, affect our gasoline production?" "What effect will this have on kerosene shipments scheduled after this one? How far off target will this put us? Should we replan?" The answers enable the manager to plan for effective action before the fact instead of afterward.

CHAPTER FOURTEEN

A Management Information
and Control System
for Flat-rolled Steel Products

This case study describes a MICS applied to the production of flat-rolled steel. The intent is to provide a general understanding of the various aspects of the system. The depth of material should satisfy the needs of some readers, while forming the basis for more intensive study by others.

An attempt will be made to go into equivalent depth on each of the various aspects of the system. All readers will not have the same depth of knowledge or understanding of steel making and some sections may seem elementary to steelmakers. For example, the section on application base is not intended to enlighten steelmakers on the process of steelmaking but is necessary to establish a common base for all readers.

Readers will also find a degree of repetition in this case study. This is intentional, since integrated systems do not lend themselves to segmented documentation. Instead, each section in the study will tend to be more detailed than the preceding sections to permit a progressively more involved explanation of MICS.

The introduction offers a preliminary acquaintance with the subject and serves as a first pass through the system.

The section on application base is intended to lay the framework for the development of a system, indicating the kind of data which must be gathered relative to materials, facilities, and information requirements. A second pass through the subject will go into more detail regarding how the system works, the services it is designed to provide, and the potential benefits a user may expect to receive (the economics). The later sections will deal in more detail with three specific aspects of control—equipment, supervisory control programs, and some of the more important application programs.

INTRODUCTION

The development of information-handling systems has tended to divide along the lines of (1) business planning and control and (2) operations planning and control. Historically, communications between the business and the operational elements of an enterprise have been maintained by means of a human interface. With the increased complexity of both business and operations, more people have been needed to pick up and manipulate more detailed information from operational functions as inputs to the business office. Conversely, as operations have become more mechanized, there has been a steadily growing need for a greater volume of increasingly detailed information at the operations site. Growth of this complex interface between office and operations has created significant communications problems, such as information delay, inaccuracy, and duplication, in addition to the obvious increase in clerical costs.

Major efforts have been directed to the solution of these problems through the use of electronic computers, and, indeed, many operational improvements can be attributed to data-processing systems. A MICS is an advanced combination of concepts, equipment, and computer logic with new and unique capabilities for helping management and process operators control an enterprise more profitably.

A control system must be based upon the production facilities themselves. The structure of an information-handling system must start with a foundation reflecting the production facilities, materials, and procedures that guide its development. Therefore, the development of such systems must start with a detailed understanding of these production facilities—the units, materials, flows, loads, performance characteristics, operating constraints, and objectives.

Part of the concept is that control must be based upon individual operational events and that the best time to introduce these events into an information-handling system is at their occurrence. The accuracy and timeliness of recording these events has a cumulative effect on all other functions of the system, and the resulting operational control is no more accurate and timely than the data provided to the system. Thus a MICS must provide in-line data and control and a sound basis for extension to higher levels of planning and control. The system must be integrated and employ advanced communication and data-processing equipment. The system must accept data at random from remote manual terminals and receive data automatically from instruments on the process units—in both instances as events occur which originate the data. The system, therefore, has at all times the current, up-to-date status of every function within its scope. These data are examined by the system, and information is generated which is:

1. Sent to remote terminals to be printed as vital information for management or as an advice to an operator, e.g., a foreseeable failure to meet a customer promise commitment.

2. Printed on an on-line printer to form a document desired by management, such as an order status report.

3. Stored for later use or updating when required by the system, e.g, for summary yield records.

4. A combination of the above.

Figure 14.1 illustrates the planning and control concepts of MICS for a relatively simple business and/or operations facility.

Information-handling and communications sytems are worthwhile only to the extent that they help management and operations to accomplish their business objectives. While input (data gathering and collection), filing, and logic (data reduction, calculation, and analysis) are necessary functions of any information system, the true value of such systems lies in the content of their output and in the timely delivery of the output to the persons who most urgently need it. Analysis of what can be accomplished after dynamic, real-time data have been captured by a data-processing system—what applications can be reduced to computer techniques, what outputs can be generated, what operational improvements can result—is the subject of this case study.

A starting point for such an analysis lies with the managers and operators who must make the operational decisions determining whether or not quality products are delivered on time at minimum operating cost. These people represent many departmental functions—operations, production planning, sales, accounting, quality control, engineering, maintenance, and research. MICS, since it has a company-wide effect, requires cooperative effort on the part of all departments.

The classes of data services which such a system is capable of providing are listed in Fig. 14.2. These services are grouped in terms of the past, present, and future information requirements of management and operating personnel to perform their assigned jobs.

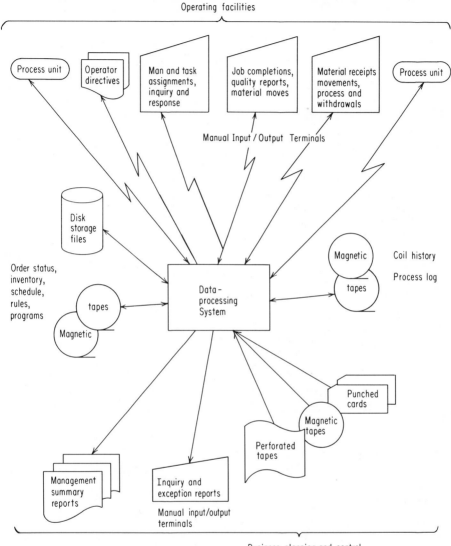

FIG. 14.1 Planning and control concept of a MICS.

Data service			Mill departments				
Group	Class	Examples	Operations	Production planning	Accounting	Quality control	Research
Past	Summary reports	Nonstandard performance	x	x	....	x	
		Product reapplications	x	x			
		Incentive performance	....	....	x		
	Analysis reports	Product text reports	....	....	....	x	x
		Production yield analysis	x	x	....	....	x
		Stores distribution	....	....	x		
Present	Status records and reports	Order backlog	x	x	x		
		Inventory ledgers	x	x	x		
		Customer claim status	....	....	x	x	
	Operating information	Operating conditions log	....	....	....	x	x
		Off-incentive notice	....	....	x		
		Lost/found item advice	x	x			
	Orders and advices	Move orders	x	x			
		Equipment change orders	x	x			
		Expedite orders	x	x	x		
	Exception or trouble notices	Process variable exception notices	x	....	....	x	
		Order or unit yield performance	x	x	x	x	x
		Production schedule deviation notice	x	x			
Future	Estimating services	Product/unit costs	x	....	x	x	
		Operating costs	x	x	x		
		Work order costs	....	x	x		
	Forecasting services	Machine loads	x	x			
		Raw material requirements	x	....	x		
		Labor requirements	x	....	x		
	Planning and scheduling	Operating schedules	x	x			
		Location control	x	x			
		Maintenance schedules	x	x	....	x	

FIG. 14.2 Data services.

Examples of specific data services are associated with the needs of the indicated departments. The examples are for illustration only. Neither do they include many data services which may be provided, nor are they specific recommendations for initial applications.

While accurate and timely information reports are valuable in themselves, it is their effective use by people which will determine the ultimate benefits. For example, up-to-the-minute order status information enables production planning to make early and accurate disposition decisions. Automatic notification of out-of-normal process conditions permits operators to make required changes in operating conditions. Consistent unit sequencing instructions are based on the management-specified balance between promised performance and setup changes. Considerable clerical manpower is required to manually keep track of in-process material. A MICS will perform a large share of these recording functions. Performance records enable management to effectively evaluate individual process units and operators. A process history log forms the basis for significant research studies, serves as a tool for responding to customer inquiries, and acts as a valuable aid in tracing quality problems.

The system goes beyond the definition of application concepts and the provision of equipment to meet the application requirements. It makes a major contribution toward the solution of the application problems themselves.

In a broad sense, computer programs can be divided into two groups: (1) those programs which actually perform the logic and calculations required by the application, and (2) those programs which sequence, optimize, and otherwise control the first. These control programs constitute a large portion (as much as 50 percent in some cases) of any batchlike data-processing application. Real-time, in-line applications add significantly to the control problem as a result of random inputs requiring the selection and processing of different applications programs with varying degrees of priority. The system must automatically handle the requirements of real-time priority processing. It should be capable of monitoring and controlling all applications programs, all the input/output functions, and the data-processing system itself. Necessary reference and operating files must be defined, structured, and detailed. Included in these files are the data needed for order items, unit sequencing, inventories, storage locations, performance records, yields, processing times (including promise dates), and process-unit monitoring. A detailed analysis of the requirements for in-line communications has to be made, and the relationship between input messages, files, and output messages defined. Finally, computer logic is prepared to handle the processing associated with the major, high-traffic communications.

The problem of sequencing individual orders through the various process units to meet promised delivery schedules at minimum costs is common to a broad range of manufacturing industries. It is a complex problem well suited to computer solution. System rules for unit sequencing provide consistent schedules for sequencing material through process units based on promised delivery dates and minimum operating costs.

The installation of an in-line operational system is a major undertaking.

This case study is in the area of flat-rolled steel production. Rules and detailed computer logic were prepared for sequencing coils through the major process units—plate mill, hot-strip mill, pickling, cold reduction, annealing (both batch and continuous), tin-temper mill, electrolytic tinning, galvanizing, and coil warehousing. Studies in depth were conducted, and computer simulation of both flat-rolled production facilities and equipment configurations confirmed the system's capabilities for handling the flow of information. Thus, this case study is written in terms of flat-rolled steel production and is based on the programs, procedures, and data utilized in these studies.

It should be noted, however, that many of the aspects of MICS are independent of specific applications. The problem of supervisory control is common to all in-line information-handling systems, and the structure of in-line communications relates to all manufacturing facilities characterized by the continuous processing of batches of material.

An awareness of the importance and necessity for real-time in-line information-handling systems continues to grow in a wide variety of business and operational areas. Anyone actively concerned with data processing can achieve further insight into the problems of real-time systems and their solutions by translating the following material into the terms of his own environment.

APPLICATION BASE

The foundation for the application of MICS is a comprehensive understanding of both the physical operation under consideration and the information flow needed for effective performance. This section illustrates the type of basic data required and the first steps in the development of a system.

The real starting point is the production facilities themselves. For the purpose of illustration, a simplified schematic of "typical" facilities for the production of flat-rolled steel is described in Fig. 14.3. As shown, steel slabs arrive at the hot-strip mill from either the slab mill or slab yard. Following hot-rolling, steel strip in the form of coils is pickled (cleansed and deoxidized) and cold-reduced to gauge suitable for further processing. Alternate paths show a routing through galvanizing, or annealing, temper rolling, and tinning. A number of end-product points are shown indicating packaging, storage, and shipment of hot-, cold-, and temper-rolled sheets or coils, as well as tinned and galvanized products. A mill, of course, includes many other auxiliary operations such as side trim, shear, and recoil lines. Also omitted from Fig. 14.3 are the many storage lines in the mill—in general, one prior to each major process unit.

In addition to a considerable amount of additional detail regarding the process units (rated capacity, performance specifications, power consumption, etc.), many other plant details must be doc-

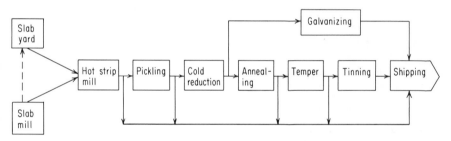

FIG. 14.3 Simplified schematic of material flow and facility layout for flat-rolled steel production.

umented to permit the development of the MICS. For example, data must be collected relative to:

Plant geography: distances, space
Products: types, quantities, qualities
Process instrumentation
Yields: process and product
Performance measurements
Scheduling considerations

The following list of questions exemplifies the kind of information required for each processing unit. It is taken from a more comprehensive listing which provides a systematic approach to the initiation of a project to install MICS.

Preprocessing:
From where are lifts delivered?
What is the capacity of storage locations?
How are lifts transported to the unit?
In what way are lifts identified?
Assuming a continuous line, how are coils
joined together? Are weld detectors used?

Charge:
What is the normal charge frequency?
What is the average charge weight?
What is the procedure when sequenced lift cannot be found?
What is the procedure when sequenced lift is damaged?
Are coils run from a mandrel? From a pit? Other?

Processing:
What are the process steps within the facility?
What are the most critical process variables?
What process variables are monitored? With what equipment?
What process variables are automatically controlled? With
what equipment?
What in-process inspections or other tests are made? By whom?
To whom?
What is time delay between test and results? What action is
taken?

Storage:
What is the next storage location?
Are lifts stacked? If so, how high?
How are storage locations identified?
Is a time delay before the next operation required? Is it per-
mitted? How long?

General:
What people are required to run the unit?
How many? What are their responsibilities?
How many turns does the facility operate?
What performance indexes are used?
How are yields and throughput measured?
What are the reasons for line stops?
What is production recording procedure?

INFORMATION FLOW

The services provided by MICS are based on the communication of information to whoever needs it, when it is needed. Another necessary and early stage in the development of the system is an understanding of the existing flow of information and control decisions in the plant. An evaluation of its effectiveness and a determination of desired improvements lead directly to the formation of a specific system.

Figure 14.4 superimposes a simplified information flow over one of the facilities shown in Fig. 14.3. A similar network can be extrapolated to each plant facility. This figure is both general and incomplete, but it does indicate that considerable information must be sent to a variety of departments. Studies have shown that approximately 50 identifiable types of communications representing several thousand separate messages per peak turn are required in the operation of a "typical" flat-rolled steel facility.

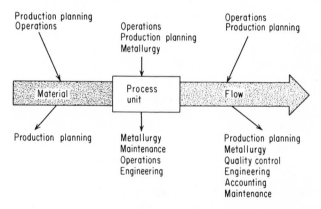

FIG. 14.4   General information flow around a typical steel process.

Consideration of only a portion of the typical present procedures and information load of three departments will indicate the amount of information involved and the kind of data which must be defined for the next steps in the study of the system.

The Production Planning department receives sales orders and produces operating schedules. Initial processing converts a sales order to single line items, commits delivery dates, calculates rough schedules, and determines material loss (yield) allowances for every processing stage in setback fashion. Operating schedules are usually generated weekly. On the basis of promise dates, business levels, operating costs, and other mill constraints, the operating schedule establishes each turn to be worked for each production unit.

Reports of production or shipment of every product "lift" are received from the production floor. These reports are used to update order progress records and to generate unit production schedules and statistical reports. Reports of individual product rejections or suspensions ("dispositions") are received directly from the floor. After Production Planning and Metallurgy decide the disposition of the product, they issue reinstatement, reapplication, and/or retreatment orders, as appropriate.

Production Planning may also put out order items specification information to each production unit foreman, completed order lists to purge the foreman's order item files, detailed production unit work schedules, and statistical summary reports to Operations, e.g., the mill's performance in meeting customer promise dates.

The Accounting department's major inputs are production reports, in-process lift information from Operations, and charges for labor and materials from other departments. The production reports are usually received at the end of each turn, and once a day they are used to calculate crew and individual incentive performances in order to update ledgers showing week-to-date yield performances for each of the operations. In-process lift information may be received every day from product operations just prior to packaging and filed with individual order histories. Miscellaneous inputs include data from the operating units regarding both orders for, and the receipt of materials and services from, outside the area for the purpose of maintaining inventory and accounts payable audit control.

Major outputs of Accounting concern pay incentives, production performance, and cost accounting. Incentive-performance calculations may be made for each of the separate incentive plans for the mill. Further calculations reduce gross pay to net pay. Summary reports of incentive performance may be issued for all the crews in the mill on either a turn or pay-period basis. Accounting may also publish yield and operating performance summaries for groups of cost centers under individual general foremen and for the mill as a whole. Cost accounting reports can include analysis of actual costs by type of product and producing center. The producing cost-center statements may show budgeted (standard) and actual material consumption and yield, operating costs above materials, and the distributed costs of materials and services from departments outside the mill.

The Metallurgical department usually receives reports directly from the production floor and from a testing laboratory. The major kinds of reports from the mill floor include data concerning facilities and product. Most of the data concerning facilities are recorded by metallurgical observers on a sampling basis from indicators and recording devices on the production lines. The main kinds of data concerning product are Rockwell hardness reports, reports of product dispositions, general metallurgy and inspection reports, and automatically generated electrolytic tinning reports. The Rockwell hardness reports are routine tests made on each product lift to determine whether specifications have been met.

Metallurgical reports are recorded by observers of the product at each processing stage. Most routine observations concern the condition of the product's surface and shape. The metallurgical observers are responsible for examination of the dispositioned product to determine the type of product order to which it may be allocated, while Production Planning is responsible for allocating to a specific order within the type approved by Metallurgy. As coil product is processed through an electrolytic tinning line, automatic sensing equipment may be available which can inspect it for a large category of defects. The number of feet with each kind of defect, along with the total defective footage, can be automatically accumulated and read out on a typewriter when the coil is discharged. Automatic sensing equipment may also be used in on-line testing for hardness.

Inputs to Metallurgy from the laboratory again include data on both facilities and product. Certain processing variables, such as solution strength, must be measured in the laboratory, particularly where chemical analysis is required. Different tests are performed on the product, such as analysis of grain structure and the thickness of the alloy layer between the steel and tin. Certain customer orders require extensive testing, most of which is conducted in the laboratory.

Reports received by Metallurgy from outside the mill are almost identical in classification to the reports from within. They are required in order to analyze and predict the effect of process conditions prior to the receipt of materials by mill. Still another output from Metallurgy is product quality analyses, issued at weekly to quarterly intervals.

On the basis of the above examples, MICS may be likened, in one sense, to a switching center for the flow of information. For example, both are concerned with:

Receiving data as events occur
Editing the data for accuracy
Performing any required processing

Providing information to the man who needs it, when he
   needs it
Filing it for future use

THE APPLICATION OF A MICS

MODE OF OPERATION

From an equipment point of view, a MICS is based on two primary capabilities: communications with data-processing equipment
through remote input/output terminals and use of large-scale random-access storage. In an in-plant data communications system,
data-gathering and collection devices are located at the point of
data origination and connected by wire network to the data origination and connected by wire network to the data-processing computer or computers. The computer in turn transmits information
back over the same network to output devices without human intervention. In most cases, the input and output devices are housed
in the same terminals. Large-scale random-access storage is provided
by magnetic disks, which, for all practical purposes, offer an unlimited capacity for the storage of reference files, data, output
reports, and computer programs.

A key technique is the development and storage of short records, each of which describes a single event that occurs in the
plant. Such a single event might be the start-up of a process line,
the processing of a product unit, the results of a quality test, or an
equipment change. Data describing these events are received by
the system from either automatic sensing devices or manual input
terminals. The system adds to these event data the time of their
receipt and whatever additional information is required so that the
event can be uniquely identified when entered into disk storage with
all other records.

The general mode of operations can best be illustrated by relating the material flow in the mill to the information flow in the
system. The "normal" flow of material through a particular facility can be described as follows (see top portion of Fig. 14.5):

1. Given the processing sequence, an operator moves a lift from
the inventory preceding the unit to the facility waiting line.

2. The first lift in the waiting line is charged to the facility.

3. It is processed.

4. It is discharged and weighed.

5. It is moved to an appropriate location in the inventory of the
next facility.

Every event—move, charge, processing, discharge, weighing—is entered in the system as it occurs. Communication of these data is represented in the middle portion of Fig. 14.5, which shows system inputs through manual entry stations or automatic sensing devices on the process.

The corresponding "normal" data flow in the system is best illustrated by reference to the appropriate status files maintained in disk storage (see lower portion of Fig. 14.5). These records

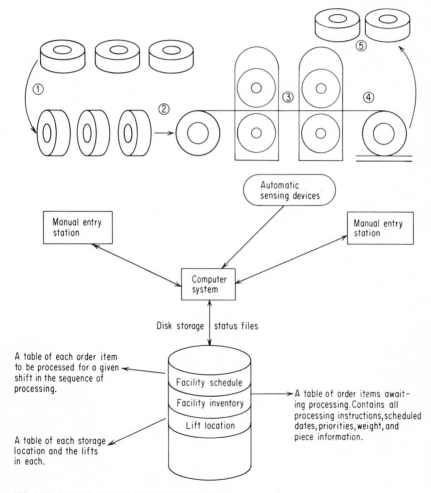

FIG. 14.5 Normal material and information flow.

represent the status of orders (facility inventories), location (lift location), and schedules (facility schedules) for each facility in the mill. As the system receives notification of each event (move, charge, discharge) for any lift in the mill, these files are updated. In this way the system is at all times an accurate, timely reflection of conditions in the mill. Many internal checks must be built in to ensure accuracy. For example, every input message must be checked for general validity of format. The movements of lifts based on schedules should be verified by schedules stored in the system. Discharged coil weight should be verified for reasonableness on the basis of the corresponding charge weight. Many other techniques are available to ensure an accurate status base from which to develop a system to meet the information and control needs of the plant.

Other types of files can also be built as in-line data are received. A processing history for each unit of steel can be maintained. More informatively, this history might contain only process exceptions to operating standards. Discharge weights can be compared with charge weight to yield records by process, product, and order. Equipment performance records can be built for maintenance planning.

The system may accept data from other mill departments as well as Operations. Sales and Accounting can provide customer and order information to build mill order files. These files may be updated with in-line data from the mill. Production Planning records and standards form a basis for maintaining accurate, up-to-the-minute records forecasting initial and final order shipment dates and quantities. Metallurgy can supply results from laboratory tests which are used to develop quality records associated with the work in process.

In-line mill data coupled with information from other departments establish the required base for the MICS. Internal processing of all types of data is performed under a system of automatic priority control. All programs may be assigned relative priorities which the system is capable of recognizing and using in determining the sequence of programs to be executed. In-line inputs always receive immediate validation, verification, or acknowledgment. Further required processing takes place in a queue according to the preassigned priority. In general, those programs required to respond to in-line inputs have a higher priority than those required to update files or prepare scheduled reports. The lowest-priority programs are usually diagnostic routines which check computer and system performance and are automatically processed as time allows.

All the information in the system is available either through in-line inquiries or on predetermined schedules. Most in-line inputs result in a return message; e.g. an input notifying the system that a lift has been discharged from a particular facility triggers a response telling the lift operator where to place the lift in inventory preceding the next process unit. Notification that a facility has shut down gives the system an opportunity to provide a new unit sequencing schedule. A system is also capable of automatically initiating exception reports as a result of processing in-line data relative to operating standards. For example, a comparison between the actual yield (difference in discharge and charge weights) and the standard yields for a particular lift can trigger many significant outputs: (1) to Production Planning for early disposition if poor yields project a failure to meet order quantity, (2) to Accounting for incorporation into incentive wage calculation, (3) to Quality Control or Maintenance for early corrective action. Authorized personnel can request action from the system; e.g., a management decision may be made to expedite the delivery of a particular order which will require the system to produce new sequencing schedules reflecting the change in priority.

Other reports can be generated on a scheduled basis. Accurate, verified data are available within the system to provide a wide range of detail, summary, or exception reports on any desired time interval—turn, day, week, month, etc. Although these reports are partially accumulated before reporting time, the work is done only when no in-line transactions require processing. The system, however, recognizes an approaching deadline and dynamically increases priorities to ensure on-time reports. Examples of scheduled reports include yield performance, backlog status, production records, promise performance, order status, and other user-oriented reports.

The mode of operation of the system may thus be described as immediately acknowledging in-line inputs and giving precedence to in-line responses, but otherwise doing first things first on the basis of established priorities. Outputs will be provided as a result of events, exceptions, inquiries, or clock and/or calendar triggers.

IMPROVED CAPABILITIES

It has been fashionable to use the phrase "total information system" to denote the goal toward which industry, the systems profession, and data-processing equipment manufacturers are striving. The phrase is generally misused, because there is no company, plant, or installation which does not have a working "total" information system, but on the other hand, few have completely mechanized total systems.

Some of the most significant services MICS can offer are described next. Many lend themselves to either exception, on-demand, or scheduled reporting, at the option of operating management.

1. *Unit Scheduling.* The generation of schedules for the unit operations is complex because of high standards of product quality and the diversity of product mix. Procedures, referred to as algorithms, have been constructed which determine the sequence of material to be processed on the operating units. Algorithms are sets of rules which scan continuously changing inventory in front of a unit to determine (1) which orders should become a part of the schedule to be constructed by the system and (2) the proper sequence of material through the unit according to the objectives of satisfying customer promise date requirements and minimizing changeover costs and process disturbances. An algorithm has been designed to assign warehouse space efficiently to the finished product while minimizing the splitting of order locations. Provision is made for generating move orders to increase the amount of accessible space by consolidation when required. These unit schedules can be generated at planned intervals or in response to any one of many events in the shop which require a revised schedule.

2. *In-process Records.* A complete record can be kept on each product as it flows through the plant, including all processing for each lift showing the processing line and date and time of each charge and discharge, together with discharged weight. The record can include all disposition actions and decisions. Exception reports of jeopardized shipping promise dates or weights would be issued automatically at any stage of the process when the need is apparent from reported processing delays or low yields. This record, in effect, contains a coils treatment history which, for example, would permit diversion to another order later in the process. A process conditions log for each process line can be maintained. From this it is possible to reconstruct a full history of the conditions under which each item was processed for later use as needed in troubleshooting, quality analysis, auditing, and process study.

3. *Storage Location Control.* As a lift is charged, the system can determine where it is to be stored for the next process, on the basis of (1) the location of other lifts in the same order item, (2) similarity (significant for scheduling) with other items, and (3) prom-

ise dates. The new storage location would be recorded on the coil at point of discharge. Schedules issued to each department would contain the number and exact location of each lift for each order item. Storage location audits can be maintained by various devices. For example, a tractor operator might find that he could not store a lift where directed because something else was already occupying the space. In addition to his own manual audit of the location area, he might request a report from the system showing the proper arrangement of material in that area. By such means, effective measures can be taken to assure that inventory and location records accurately reflect floor conditions.

4. *Order Status Information.* As each lift passes through each production process, the actual weight discharged is multiplied by a standard yield loss factor to project the number of good pounds which will remain after completion of all further processing. This projection is then evaluated against min/max levels for the item. The anticipated final processing date is also projected against the promise date in much the same manner. These evaluations might then trigger immediate notices to Production Planning, advising of anticipated surplus available, or of anticipated shortages, along with specifications of other orders that are candidates for complementary product reallocation, so that prompt action can be taken to bring the anticipated final results into the proper bounds. The status of every order will also be available upon request at every stage in production for quick, accurate accommodation of customer inquiries.

5. *Schedule Review.* Any of a number of occurrences may affect current work schedules. Temper rolls will require changes. Retreatments, which are seldom if ever anticipated, may be required. Every occurrence reporting contact with a coil or lift will be checked by the system. If the occurrence is not according to plan, the system can determine whether a schedule is involved or may be affected, and, if so, will compute and issue a new schedule.

6. *Performance Analysis.* In-line transactions reporting and processing will now make it possible to develop and evaluate performance by lift, order, product type, process unit, or any combination of parameters. Of particular interest will be an analysis of product yields as related to specific processing units.

7. *Accounting and Reporting.* More conventional accounting and reporting tasks can be performed by the MICS. Of special interest are improvements in cost accounting, production reports, quality control, downtime analysis, and maintenance records based on data introduced into the system in real time.

8. *Services Related to Process Data.* Such a system is capable of automatic acquisition and reduction of data from process instrumentation. In addition to functions directly related to other data services, e.g., automatic input of discharge weights for yield analysis and incentive payrolls computation, this ability significantly broadens the scope to include a vast number of process-oriented services:

Monitoring. The availability of process data enables the system to perform many monitoring functions. Monitoring of process equipment guards against forbidden configurations of valve conditions, motor conditions, etc., thus contributing to personal, equipment, and material safety. Equipment monitoring can also be an effective tool in maintenance programs. Monitoring of the process variables against preset or variable limits alerts operators to danger conditions, either actual or imminent. Monitoring of instruments identifies instrument failures and erratic readings. Calculations on instrument readings can be performed to average or smooth the data in order to obtain more accurate knowledge of the process status. Calibration of instruments is possible with real-time process data and computer capability. Monitoring operator performance in adhering to standard operating practices provides a means for more accurate personnel evaluation and helps assure conformity to those practices.

Logging. A log of directly measured and calculated process variables can be extremely useful. A log for the process operators provides a central report based on all of the most reliable and meaningful data from the process. Supervisory personnel are interested in less detailed log reports showing only exceptions to normal operating practices. Other specialized logs can be prepared for such diverse functions as quality analyses, management reports, and even legal or contractual reports. One type of log is the process history journal.

Operator Guide Calculations. Not all significant process variables are directly measured or measurable; e.g., the amount of tin deposited on a sheet passing through the plating circuit of an electrolytic tinning line cannot be measured directly. As a result, to ensure the minimum coating weight required, extra tin (at extra cost) is used. Coating weight, in turn, is a function of cathode efficiency, which is also not directly measurable. Cathode efficiency can be calculated, however, from line speeds, current density, and solution temperature. Short of actual computer control, a printout to the operator showing cathode efficiency contributes significantly to his ability to minimize tin consumption (cost). Other possibilities of "indirect measurements" would include product hardness throughout the annealing process and extensions of strip in the temper mill.

Another significant operator guide is the logical sequencing of control actions during process start-up or shutdown. A complex sequence of physical actions is required during these operations. This can be reduced to a similarly complex chain of logic which a computer is well suited to implement.

Process Analysis. A system is capable of analyzing the basic nature of production processes. Attempts to understand the fundamental relationships among process variables is a major and continuing effort in industry. Achievements of that kind of understanding have resulted in significant breakthroughs in plant operations, engineering, design, facilities planning, and basic research. It is, of course, a necessary requisite for the application of process computer control.

EXAMPLE OF THE SYSTEM IN ACTION

For a better understanding of how such a system provides some of the more important services for a producer of flat-rolled steel, the following example for one lift of one order item describes the main line of system activity. This example is confined to the operations of a continuous annealing facility. The systems activity for the other process departments is quite similar and can be readily extrapolated from this example. While the example traces the path of one lift, it should be understood that the system will be processing a multitude of transactions on virtually a real-time basis as transactions occur. The following description is not all-inclusive, and many other functions peculiar to a given mill can be built into the system. In the same way, aspects of the described activity which do not apply to a specific mill can be deleted or modified. The attempt is to present those capabilities of the system approach which are generally applicable to any flat-rolled steel mill. The system is assumed to be in operation, with its files containing up-to-date information.

NORMAL MATERIAL AND INFORMATION FLOW

Figure 14.6 represents the flow of material around the process example of a continuous annealing line. The letters shown on the figure are keyed to the following steps:

A. Move from continuous annealing (CA) backlog inventory to waiting line. In accordance with a schedule previously supplied by the system, showing the sequence of coils to be processed, an operator moves a coil from CA backlog inventory to the waiting line ahead of CA. At that time he enters a message into the system via a terminal identifying the CA line and the coil. The system:

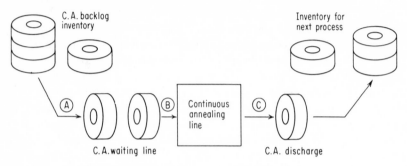

FIG. 14.6   Material flow around a continuous annealing line.

1. Verifies that the coil is included in the CA work schedule. If it is not included, the system requests a review and reentry by the originating location. If a second message still indicates improper identification, a request for disposition will be flashed to production planning, and a follow-up suspense file will be set up awaiting an action response. The system can consider any effect on the work schedule of the next process facility for that coil and issue a new schedule if required.
2. Similarly, verifies that the lift was in the proper scheduled sequence.
3. Updates appropriate files such as inventories, mill orders, and locations to reflect an up-to-the-minute status.
4. Selects a "next process" backlog location for the lift when it is discharged from CA, using logic which places together those lifts on the same order item and which tends to place close together those order items that will be scheduled for processing together.
5. Maintains a copy of the message.
B. Charge to CA waiting line and CA processing. As the coil is charged, an operator again enters information identifying the facility and lift. Steps similar to parts 1 to 3 of step A are executed to ensure an accurate status picture of material in the mill. The system will:

1. Determine whether the lift represents a sufficient change in product type from the last lift charged to require changing the line variable monitoring criteria and, if required, internally select a new table of process limits for comparison with actual process conditions.
2. Check the values of the process instrument signals (representing, for example, line speeds and temperatures) against the table of process limits, record any deviations for further references in evaluating quality against process conditions, and publish deviation values to the line foreman.
3. Have the additional capability of maintaining and publishing all the determinants required for incentive calculations.
4. Maintain a copy of the charge message. Any occurrence while the lift is on the CA that affects the availability of lifts scheduled for downstream process units is evaluated by the system for required rescheduling. Such occurrences could be line stops and starts, missing lifts, and CA work schedule changes.

C. Discharge from CA. As the lift is weighed following discharge, an operator enters lift weight and facility identification into the system. The system recognizes the message as a discharge report and:
1. Verifies the message and updates status files as before. An additional check is made for the reasonableness of the discharge weight versus the corresponding charge weight.
2. Calculates yield for the lift and issues exception reports to Accounting or Production Planning if required. Accumulates discharge weight against charge weight for calculation of order item, turn, and other desired yield figures such as those required for incentive calculations.
3. Responds with a new lift number designating the storage location for the lift in the backlog inventory area for the next process facility.
4. Checks the time discharged against the estimated completion time upon which the "next process" work schedule was based and issues a new schedule if required.
5. Determines whether the lift completes a mill order item. If so, a comparison is made between accumulated final yield estimates and shipping min/max limits. Production Planning is notified accordingly so that timely reallocations can be made if necessary.
6. Maintains a copy of the discharge messages.

It should be noted that each stage has included the storage of the initiating message. These messages are identified so that all transactions relative to each lift of each mill order item can be retrieved from the system to give a complete lift history.

Steps *A* to *C* are typical of the normal flow of material and information through and around the various process units. However, an information-handling system cannot be an effective management tool if it is capable only of responding to the normal or desired flow of material in the mill. It is the random, unplanned, and unexpected events which cause the major operating problems. A MICS must anticipate such events and have an organized plan for responding to them. We shall look at how the system might react to two typical "unexpected" disturbances to normal operations, namely, dispositions and mislocated lifts.

Dispositions. Lifts are frequently damaged while being moved to a new storage location or while in inventory; quality tests or other inspections may reveal that they have failed to meet specification requirements. In such cases, an authorized person enters a message into the system requesting disposition of the lift. The system then updates all appropriate records, e.g., order item records and production schedules, to reflect that the lift is on disposition, assembles the entire lift history, and prints the full body of information for Production Planning's use in making a disposition decision. It then maintains a suspense file, which it reviews periodically and calls to the attention of Production Planning for assurance of a reply.

Production Planning may make one of several decisions. It may restore the lift to full availability for its original order item, reassign the lift to a different order item, direct that the lift be scrapped, or direct treatment to restore the lift to its original order item or to a different order item. Any decision to retreat, reassign, or scrap requires a chain reaction of systems activity. First an audit is made to assure that reassignments are made within the same product group, and a notification is sent back to Production Planning of any improper reassignments. All affected lift, order item, and product records must be updated. The effect of reassignment, retreatment, or scrapping on work schedules must be considered and new schedules issued if required. Move orders to relocate lifts must be issued to operating locations. Final yields for the order items involved must be reassessed and an advice returned to Production Planning for any out-of-tolerance deviations.

Mislocated Lifts. The problem of material identification is a major one in the orderly operation of any production facility. A system offers an organized approach to lift location control as a result of maintaining accurate, up-to-the-minute status records. If floor operations were at all times consistent with the input and output communications, this problem would be solved. However, lifts will be placed in wrong locations in the sense that they do not agree with communications with the system. Emergency conditions in the mill may dictate overriding the system for a period of time. These facts are recognized, and a technique for responding to mislocated lifts is built into the MICS. Two situations will illustrate this approach.

1. The CA tractor operator goes to a storage location to move a lift to the waiting line ahead of CA in accordance with the work schedule and does not find the indicated lift. He then enters a missing-lift notice into the system. After verifying that the indicated lift is in the mill order schedule, the system searches a table which contains records of previously reported found lifts. If a match occurs, all that is required is that the location number of the found lift be substituted for that of the missing lift, and the operator informed accordingly. If a satisfactory match is not found, the system will set up an entry in a missing-lift file, update files to reflect that the lift is missing, delete the lift from the work schedule, reschedule CA if necessary, and determine the effect of the loss of this lift upon the predicted final weight of its mill order item, notifying Production Planning if out of tolerance.

2. The CA tractor operator finds a lift in a wrong location in the sense that it does not agree with its readable identification. The technique employed is essentially the reverse of that for the missing-lift situation: i.e., the attempt is made to match the found lift against the missing-lift file. If successful, lift location numbers are corrected and status files are updated. If no match occurs, an entry is now set up in the found-lift file.

Other combinations of circumstances are also considered. For example, a tractor operator is directed to place a lift in a location which he finds occupied by another lift with the same location number. The important consideration, however, is that a MICS has the capability of responding to the realities of mill operations, and can readily be tailored to meet the requirements of a specific mill.

SOME BENEFITS AND ADVANTAGES

Evaluations of MICS has shown many advantages and benefits. Some of these are:

Throughput Increase. As a result of better planning, scheduling, sequencing, and overall control of material flow, disturbances to the producing lines and to the departments are minimized. The system's programmed logic, all-encompassing memory, and around-the-clock availability smooth steel plant operations.

Yield Improvement. The monitoring of process settings and conditions against standard performance conditions reduces losses caused by error, carelessness, and lack of facility control. Monitoring of product weight by order item throughout the process reduces losses due to overmake and excess primes and permits accurate, economical providing.

Equipment Conservation. This has been achieved through (1) reduced roll changes brought about by better sequencing and scheduling, (2) better location control, and (3) yield improvement.

Fuel and Power Savings. These are realized chiefly because of the reduction in delay time made possible by better scheduling and the smoothing of changes to production lines.

Inventory Reduction. Better scheduling and sequencing permit elimination of the large protection factors carried in many work-in-process inventories. The inventory is adjusted to meet customer demand, mill economics, and management-determined levels of unassigned material.

Clerical Labor Savings. The system assumes the mechanization and improvement of many of the tasks of the mill recorder, mill statistical man, line sequencer, line expediter, and others.

Material-handling Reduction. Improved logical control of the location of work-in-process material effects this reduction.

Fluctuations in Manpower Requirements. These are smoothed as the system smooths operating schedules.

Improved Delivery Performance. This is achieved through the ability of the system to cope with the two most significant aspects of the delivery performance problem: (1) physical problems due to cobbles, off analysis, missed gauge, etc., and (2) clerical problems created by the overwhelming mass, incompleteness, and inaccuracy of required in-plant records.

PART FOUR

Conclusions and
a Look at the Future

CHAPTER FIFTEEN

Conclusions and Forecasts

Knowledge is of two kinds. We know a subject ourselves,
or we know where we can find information upon it.
SAMUEL JOHNSON (1709–1784)

As the reader progresses in knowledge he must begin to reflect on subtle changes that will take place in his plant and firm. The application of computer hardware and management-science tools and techniques are forcing changes in physical facilities and personnel organization. We shall discuss here future changes we believe should, could, and will happen. It is difficult to prevent each of these from coloring the other. A most difficult factor is the time scale.

Technology, automation, and development in information and control theory have changed our basic thinking. We are not yet in an era when everything automatically will get better and better and faster and faster. Some of the most important challenges in the history of man are upon us. Industry as a whole lags far behind present technology. Methods lingering from the last century still abound in some industries, and mechanization of the simplest sort remains to be discovered, let alone applied. The gain in productivity to be obtained from simply upgrading our most backward industries would be fantastic.

But there are some very advanced, highly automatic plants for special products. Some chemical plants are almost automatic factories. The degree of mechanization in some multiple machinery operations, such as automobile assembly, is very high. In many industries, as in steel with continuous process, attempts are being made to automate material handling and storage as well as information handling. There are also projects integrating material and information handling to provide more automatic warehousing.

One of our most serious problems is not the hardware but the people who use it. The accelerated discovery and development of new processes and methods means that production equipment and organizations to produce goods are subject to rapid change. Technology is forcing an increased sophistication in manufacturing machinery. The rise in discretionary income of the consumer is resulting in a continued rise in demand for more and different products. The time cycle between the demand and satisfaction of this consumer demand is getting shorter. Many products grow increasingly complex. Higher quality and lower cost are continually being felt in a more highly competitive world. The obsolescence factor is growing. To meet these demands, the production facilities are trying to approach complete automaticity to give rapid change, increased rate of production, higher quality uniformity, and lower costs. Man is not keeping up with these changes.

Subordinate services to the production facility, such as raw-material sorting, component and product inspection, and packaging, are becoming automated and integrated with the production facility. Similarly, unloading of raw materials, loading of product, transport, and storage are being integrated into the machine organization. The associated informational system, which makes this type of organization possible, also has to be integrated and automatic. Much of the interplant informational flow, not only between plants belonging to a given company but routine purchase orders to vendor companies and routine billings, etc., to customers, is already in computer language.

One of the great problems of automation is the production machine language. A crucial element is how to get the language of the real world cheaply, quickly, accurately, and automatically into a language that the organization of machines can understand. This man-machine communications barrier has attracted much development attention, and some acceptable solutions are already here. Developments in graphic devices, audio input and output, and other communication and display devices promise better solutions tomorrow.

Information, its flow and use, is one of the most important factors in an organization. We are beginning to realize the components of an informational system, the communication of information, and techniques for gaining better intelligence from the facts. The integration of management information and its manipulation is becoming essential to proper administration and supervision.

TOOLS AT HAND

Many firms are not fully aware of the magnitude of changes already taking place and the nature of impending problems of organization of physical facilities and personnel.

Fortunately, an array of impressive analytical and technological tools is available which makes it possible for most firms to face challenges of informational systems with confidence of success. Some of these tools are:

1. The concept of information technology and the marrying of this concept to that of automation.

2. The development of flexible programming paralleled by development of flexible machines.

3. Developments in sensing, transmitting, storing, reducing, and reporting information.

4. The techniques of modern management science with its application of mathematics and computerized techniques of analysis to model building and representation of the management function.

5. The developing technique of management by exception, where the manager can devote more of his time to the crises and let the routine problems solve themselves.

The role of the computer in information systems today is usually described as primarily a means for data storage, processing, reduction, and readout. Another role of the computer for which a number of business applications have already been found is that of decision making. The computer has been used to design transformers, program refineries, schedule production, and locate warehouses. When all variables are specifiable in quantitative terms and clearly stated decision rules can be provided, management-science methods allow computers to make all routine decisions. This routine decision making improves managerial decision making, since the computer is potentially capable of making better routine decisions than a human manager when several variables are interrelated and interacting.

When the routine part of the manager's decision making is automated, he is freed to devote much needed attention to the search for opportunities and to nonroutine decisions—the baffling problems, those for which policy or decision-making rules have not been formulated. It speeds up internal response and increases productive efficiency.

THE FIRM OF TOMORROW

Man-computer decision making is potentially the most powerful competitive tool available to the firm of tomorrow. It will greatly increase the manager's ability to explore rapidly and efficiently numerous entrepreneurial opportunities, a process which is clumsy and slow today. It will also enable the manager to combine thorough quantitative analysis of tangible business factors with such intangibles as risk and social and cultural variables. In the light of this potential, today's decision-making techniques will probably appear to the manager of the future as the Stone Age of entrepreneurial decision making.

The glamor of computers and information technology sometimes tends to obscure the fact that, even without computers, a firm today has a rapidly growing body of analytical tools which will help it meet the challenges of tomorrow. Management science, which is an outgrowth of operations research techniques developed during World War II, has developed many powerful techniques and applications for rational problem solving and decision making within the firm.

However, the use of management science is but one of several symptoms of the rapid acceptance by business of rational, analytic approaches to running the firm. Other symptoms include the grow-ing acceptance of formal planning, the growing emphasis on developing scientifically and technically trained managers, and the widespread interest of firms in providing postgraduate training for managers.

The successful firm of the future will be one structured so that both external and internal problems are given appropriate and continuous attention. The management structure will be conducive to innovations. Planning will be institutionalized, and the accounting, information, and control systems will be oriented toward future prospects, rather than past results (feedfoward control theory).

Managers concerned with the internal efficiency and response of the firm, e.g., the operations manager, manufacturing engineer, quality control manager, accountant, and controller, will be freed by the computer from having to make many of the routine decisions which consume most of their attention today. Their attention will be directed toward the search for better decision rules—policy formulation. In their search, they will have an opportunity, missed by most managers today, for a continuing study of the relationships between their areas of responsibility and the rest of the firm. They will truly manage by exception, i.e., change the rules when appropriate, make decisions when a problem unexpectedly baffles the computer, and monitor computer decisions. These managers will continue to devote their attention to leading, coordinating, and motivating their subordinates.

The firm of the future will see an increasing emphasis on a new type of staff activity which is today in evidence in many firms. This is the activity of technical and managerial decision analysis by planners, management scientists, and computer specialists. The traditional staff activity of data acquisition, compilation, and presentation will be taken over by the computer information and control system.

For the top executive of tomorrow, game theory and the mathematics of making decisions will become his management tools just the same as the balance sheet. Logic, intense discipline, openmindedness, imagination, and a good grasp of the economics of business will be the qualifications for the corporate leader.

IN SUMMARY

American business has lived through "the computer revolution" during the past few years, but what we have seen so far is only the start. The threshold of an information revolution affecting the practice of management in ways which our conventional notions of management techniques of control only hint at is at hand. Some of this evidence is:

■ Capabilities at its disposal are affecting the way management manages. These capabilities are permitting new approaches to management decision making.

■ What management manages is being profoundly affected in terms of organizational structure, makeup of the company work force, and physical facilities. The assembly-line concept as originated in Detroit may not have changed the daily schedule of the chief executive, or even the way in which he made his decisions, but it certainly had an impact on the makeup of his company and the decisions made. Information technology is at least as significant.

■ The external environment in which the manager manages is placing new demands on the enterprise and offers new opportunities for it. The benefits of the information technology are available to government, unions, customers, suppliers, competitors; many are pursuing the gains vigorously.

The change in environment is causing top management interest in information and the cost of securing the correct and necessary information for decision making. The impact of information systems throughout the organization is expanding greatly; there will be more effective performance of existing functions, new functions will be undertaken, and different kinds of processing will be emphasized. Technological and systems advances are changing importantly the makeup of the corporate information and control system.

Several developments in hardware and technology are of interest to policy makers. The communications orientation of systems is evident. A communications central has the ability to direct incoming and outgoing data from a central point or points to the entire organization. Improved technology, together with new services and economic factors, is reducing significantly the cost of long-distance data communications, and the variety of services available is increasing rapidly. In the future, instant transmittal of data from all points in an organization will be economically feasible. Today, for example, a major diversified retail and manufacturing company is currently in the process of centralizing all its nationwide data-processing activities in one location. The basis for the plan is cost, but improved management control of widely dispersed activities is also anticipated.

The increased economy of communications, together with improvements in system speed and reliability, are reducing the cost of data collection. The result is a tendency of making information systems real-time systems; i.e., they reflect important and routine events as they occur. For example, a major paper company in 1966 announced a plan to lease IBM System/360 computers with an estimated value of $10 million to form an information and control system described as the most comprehensive ever undertaken in the paper industry. The integration of nearly a score of computers into the network will provide full information on what is happening—and as it is happening—in the paper company's nationwide manufacturing, financial, scientific, and marketing functions. Conversion to the real-time information system will be completed over a period of years.

A significant aspect of the plan is a gearing to impending developments in data input, throughput, and display. Various computers in the system will be able to communicate with each other while serving numerous locations simultaneously. Credit reports, legal, market, and technical information, and a variety of other special services will be available on call from regional or national centers.

Vastly expanded use of random-access files and memory, along with significant cost reductions for the hardware, permit drawing together on an integrated basis the data needed to manage and operate the company and provide instantaneous and flexible access to them. A common, integrated data base is being substituted for the multiplicity of independent, disparate files now maintained. Data relevant to sales production, labor relations, finance, and other functions can be obtained from the same source on a uniform basis and in proper relationship to other information. In the future the information system will be able to respond on short notice to new, unforeseen questions, rather than only to those that have been preprogrammed into the system. Such a data base, imaginatively used, will be a startling aid to operations and to many kinds of decisions.

Significant strides are being made in the area of indexing and handling of data structure so that the right information will be provided in response to a given question.

All the equipment advances imaginable will not create a MICS; only proper planning and painstaking effort will. The most startling cost performance improvements are not important unless the use of the advances make a meaningful contribution to the practice of management. Management itself must learn to devise the ways for effectively using the new tools. Because of the individual and personal approaches to, and attributes of, management, the utilization of management tools or techniques necessarily must vary from company to company and from administration to administration.

The immutable fact is that the management team of any business or institutional organization has new tools, new problems, and new opportunities as a result of developments in information technology. The task of the management team is to apply the new developments to its company effectively. The success with which this is done will be a significant factor determining the competitive position and growth of the company.

FALSE IMPRESSIONS

Two erroneous impressions have been created in the art. One is that complete mathematical models are widely applicable at present and widely used. A great amount of study and theorizing and some experimentation are taking place. Yet we are not always able to provide accurate mathematical models for real processes and organizations or to provide quantitative data for such models. This is not to disparage the effort which we expect will continue, accelerate, and succeed.

The second is the impression that one cannot advantageously

use data-processing equipment or computers without complete mathematical models. Many functions of well-known processes have required too much time and manpower to be handled manually but now can be advantageously handled by computers. There are many functions not known to us as specifically as the mathematician might like that can be handled by computer techniques.

FOUNDATIONS

Foundations have been laid that are supporting a surprising—even explosive—growth of these hardware and mathematical tools. These foundations are:

1. Capabilities of computers are sufficient for what might be devised; i.e., hardware is no longer a limiting factor.

2. The number of computers in use is considerable and widespread throughout all industries (over 30,000 as of 1966).

3. A knowledgeable cadre of personnel exists and is expanding.

4. An amazing variety of peripheral devices are available (audio, cathode ray, printers, terminals).

5. This country possesses an efficient nationwide computer-compatible communications network. Satellite communications methods promise a computer-compatible worldwide information network in the near future.

6. The time-sharing concept of computer hardware, programming methods, and users has been developed.

7. Management-science concepts and operations research methods and techniques are beginning to be used by personnel at the working management level. Engineers are now using mathematical techniques which only a few years ago were the province of the applied mathematician.

There is no longer any question of economic soundness or of the direct benefits to be gained in applying management science, operations research, and mathematics in "supervision" techniques. The direct benefits are increased output, reduced operating costs, higher and consistently uniform quality, and management efficiency.

This book's approach has been aimed toward total information and control—with interrelated, hierarchical, interacting components—for optimum balance of efficiency and economy. Process or production data interact in a computer system with other operational and decision data (inventory, financial, and marketing, for instance) for centralized guidance or control.

Whether the approach is unilateral (single application) or in terms of totality, the objective is the same: proper balance between economic justification and the job to be tackled. Both approaches are proving successful.

Oil refineries, chemical plants, and power companies are in the forefront of economic optimizing by computer control. Other computer-based processing systems being firmed up for varying degrees of automatic control involve such industries as plastics, rubber, steel, paper, and cement.

Much of the primary control equipment for continuous processes is standard, and the process controllers and instruments are often similar. Where each in its way is distinctive is in the programming: the human masterminding and experience that each company pours into its process operations and wants to implement in its computer controls. In all cases, understanding the process and the organization is the door opener (sometimes an eye opener, as well!). To determine profitable potentials, the production process and organization must be thoroughly analyzed and exact requirements pinpointed. Then, and only then, determination can be made of the equipment that will best and most economically solve the particular problem. Much of the computing needs may already be in an adjoining office!

Economic considerations chiefly dictate the rate of advance in operational control. By their flexibility, through programming and modular substitution or expansion, computer systems can provide optimum solutions in phasing toward any degree of control desired.

AN APPROACH

Developments in systems analysis, in operations research, in mathematics, and in computers and communication systems offer management the tools necessary for effective management control and direction. But before a firm can utilize these tools, at least six things are necessary:

1. A company must first decide whether or not it wishes to try to shape its future. If there is a desire by the company to shape its course, it must stipulate, in meaningful detail, what it wishes to become. A strategic plan must be devised, augmented by supporting and subordinate plans.

2. The firm must forecast in sufficient detail to provide a useful guide, the future environment. This will be a most demanding task. The relevant environment will probably include a large part of the world and its complex affairs.

3. The firm's vision of its future environment must not be colored by its own desires at the sacrifice of reality. The strategic plan and

its subordinate plans are extensions outward from the firm, which must meet and be consistent with extensions inward from the environment forecast.

4. The strategic plan and its subordinate plans must also be compared and blended with the extensions of present activities, the short-term forecasts. The long-range plan and short-range implementation must be considered together.

5. The strategic plan applies to the organization as a whole, and is supported and augmented in a functional sense by a number of subordinate plans. Long-range plans are supported by a corresponding set of short-term plans. The short-term plans are put to work in the form of budgets and similar management control devices. They become the basis for managerial control and provide both the stipulation of goals and the basis for appraising the adequacy of performance at all levels.

6. The process of business planning cuts across all functional and hierarchical levels of the enterprise. It embraces all time periods, from the present to the long-term future. When the whole process is made dynamic by continual review and adjustment, when it flows both up and down in the organization, and when it is set forth in clear detail, it becomes the mechanism by which the firm knows where it is failing as well as where it is going.

We see that the concept of push-button management still remains nearer scientific fiction than fact in United States industry today. But computers are becoming an integral and increasingly important tool of management. The larger and more successful companies are spending more of their sales dollar on computers and people to use computers in more and more management areas.

The end result, we are sure, is leading to a corporate control system with real-time information, utilizing all the latest mathematical techniques, giving each and every manager the intelligence he needs, when he needs it, for the most effective decision making toward furthering the corporation's objectives. The essential element is a sound, long-range strategy (a plan) outlining the roadmap for achieving a total integrated management information and control system.

A Selected Bibliography

ON CONTROL THEORY AND AUTOMATIC CONTROL

"Automatic Control," *Scientific American* reprint, Simon & Schuster, Inc., New York, 1955. (Old but basic and easy to read.)

"IBM Scientific Computing Symposium on Control Theory," IBM, White Plains, N.Y., 1964.

Savas, E. S.: "Computer Control of Industrial Processes," McGraw-Hill Book Company, New York, 1965.

ON PROGRAMMING FOR COMPUTERS

Fisher, F. P., and G. F. Sevindle: "Computer Programming Systems," Holt, Rinehart and Winston, Inc., New York, 1964.

McCracken, D. D.: "A Guide to FORTRAN Programming," John Wiley & Sons, Inc., New York, 1961.

SYSTEM ENGINEERING

Goode, H. H., and R. E. Machol: "System Engineering," McGraw-Hill Book Company, New York, 1957. (A basic text, old but easy to read.)

Leondes, C. T. (ed.): "Computer Control Systems Technology," McGraw-Hill Book Company, New York, 1961.

Tou, J. T.: "Digital and Sampled-data Control Systems," McGraw-Hill Book Company, New York, 1959. (A detailed text on theory with good examples of applications.)

Williams, T. J.: "Systems Engineering for the Process Industries," McGraw-Hill Book Company, New York, 1961.

OPERATIONS RESEARCH AND MATHEMATICAL TOOLS

Chorafas, D. N.: "Systems and Simulation," Academic Press Inc., New York, 1965.

Ehrenfeld, S., and S. B. Littauer: "Introduction to Statistical Method," McGraw-Hill Book Company, New York, 1964.

Hoel, P. G.: "Introduction to Mathematical Statistics," John Wiley & Sons, Inc., New York, 1960.

Meisels, K.: "A Primer of Linear Programming," New York University Press, New York, 1962.

Morgenthaler, G. W.: The Theory and Application of Simulation in Operations Research, chap. 9 in vol. 1 of "Publications in Operations Research," John Wiley & Sons, Inc., New York, 1961.

Raiffa, H., and R. Schlaifer: "Applied Statistical Decision Theory," Harvard Business School, Division of Research, Boston, 1964.

Vajda, S.: "Readings in Linear Programming," John Wiley & Sons, Inc., New York, 1958.

Wine, R. L.: "Statistics for Scientists and Engineers," Prentice-Hall, Inc., Englewood Cliffs, N.J., 1964.

Index

Index